the
Pennsylvania
Sampler

a biography of the
Keystone State and its peopl

narrated and compiled b

the Pennsylvania Sampler

PAUL B. BEERS

STACKPOLE BOOKS

The Pennsylvania Sampler

Copyright © 1970 by
THE STACKPOLE COMPANY

Published by
STACKPOLE BOOKS
Cameron and Kelker Streets
Harrisburg, Pa. 17105

Standard Book Number: 8117-1230-3
Library of Congress Catalog Card Number: 74-100350
Printed in U.S.A.

Contents

PART 1

Colorful People and Places in Pennsylvania

Pennsylvanians of German descent, from
the Plain People to the church people, have
had a massive impact on the state's mores
and politics. Conrad Richter, the noted
novelist and a Pennsylvania German himself,
has memorably captured the unique qualities
of his people.

The Pennsylvania Dutch   31
by Conrad Richter

"...farms and fields look neat as toy yards under Christmas
trees."

The Keystone State has contributed mightily
to the American language.

Pennsylvania: Word Coiner To A Nation   37
by Paul B. Beers

"...the grandmother's attic of wonderful names..."

In the mid-nineteenth century Pennsylvania
had many famous covered bridges and an
ambitious canal system. Charles Dickens
was one of the distinguished foreign visitors
who enjoyed the adventurous mode of
travel they afforded.

Dwight D. Eisenhower had deep family
roots in Pennsylvania, and he thoroughly
enjoyed his farm at Gettysburg. The
General's residence in the town gave its
citizens the feeling of living history.

Drama and human interest aplenty are to
be found in a great reporter's dispatches on
the first spectacular disaster in American
history.

PART II

Pennsylvania Industry: Workers and Entrepreneurs

The great days of Pennsylvania oil lasted
from 1859, when "Colonel" Edwin L. Drake
made the first strike, until 1891. The brief
but colorful career of one oil town typified
the rapidly fluctuating fortunes caused by
the bonanza.

Contents   **9**

PART IV
Pennsylvania in Politics: Past and Present

Contents

Pennsylvania has been a state solidly against slavery but not solidly for the full citizenship rights of its black citizens. In 1969, however, K. Leroy Irvis was the first black man in the nation to become majority leader of a state house of representatives.

by Sanford R. Starobin

"...I think we are well on the way to eliminating the law of the pack....We say by our presence that we are not a pack of wolves led by the wiliest and the strongest wolf."

Here is the answer to Theodore Dreiser's carping query about the Commonwealth, "Why hasn't it produced anything in particular?"

The Keystone State's notables in the fields of business, entertainment, sports, the fine arts, law, national and state politics, the military, religion, science and scholarship.

The Pennsylvania Pageant: People

The Pennsylvania Pageant: Places

Acknowledgments

Special acknowledgment, in addition to the credits given in the introductions and the following acknowledgments, is due my wife, Joan Beers, James R. Doran, John Scotzin, Robert H. Fowler, Dean Gross and the Harrisburg Public Library staff, and A. Hunter Rineer and the Pennsylvania State Library staff, including Louis F. Rauco, Miss B. Elizabeth Ulrich, and Robert B. Wingate. May one silent tribute be paid to the memory of George Draut, from 1954 to 1965 the editorial chief of the Harrisburg *Patriot-News* and in some of his colleagues' thinking the foremost Pennsylvania newspaperman of his era. George Draut, though he admitted to the prejudice of thinking his Pennsylvania the best of all states, used to warn that nothing one heard about her should be swallowed whole.

"The Pennsylvania Dutch" by Conrad Richter, copyright © 1955 by *Holiday* magazine, is reprinted by permission of Paul R. Reynolds, Inc., 599 Fifth Avenue, New York, N.Y. 10017.

"Gettysburg and Ike" by Philip Hamburger is reprinted from *An American Notebook* (Knopf, 1965); originally in *The New Yorker;* © 1964 Philip Hamburger.

"Pithole City, Pa., Oil Town of 1865" is reprinted by permission of Harper & Row, Publishers, from *The Romance of Forgotten Towns* by John T. Faris, copyright 1924 by Harper & Brothers; renewed 1952 by Bethann Faris Van Ness.

Quotations in the introduction to "The American Tragedies" from *A Hoosier Holiday* by Theodore Dreiser, published by John Lane Co. in 1916 and copyright 1916 by John Lane Co., are reprinted by permission of the World Publishing Co.

"Dear John (O'Hara): All Is Forgiven, Love, Gibbsville" by Joseph F. Lowry, which originally appeared in the Philadelphia *Bulletin Magazine* of October 25, 1964, is reprinted by permission of the Philadelphia *Evening and Sunday Bulletin.*

Selections from "The Dogwood Tree" by John Updike are reprinted from *Five Boyhoods,* edited by Martin Levin. Doubleday & Co. Copyright 1962 Martin Levin.

"A Shot Is Heard in Pennsylvania" is abridged and adapted from *Pennsylvania: Birthplace of a Nation* by Sylvester K. Stevens. © Copyright 1964 by Sylvester K. Stevens. Reprinted by permission of Random House, Inc.

"The Mischievous Future President" by Roger Steck is reprinted by permission of Roger Steck and Dickinson College.

"The Boys" is reprinted from *The Art of Government* by A. James Reichley by permission of The Fund for the Republic, Inc. and the Center for the Study of Democratic Institutions.

"Portrait of a Not-So-Dark Horse" by James Welsh, appearing in the *New York Times Magazine* of January 12, 1964, and "Concert at Lincoln Memorial," a review of Marian Anderson's Lincoln Memorial concert of April 9, 1939, appearing in the *New York Times* of April 10, 1939, © 1939-1964 by The New York Times Company. Reprinted by permission.

"Milton Hershey" is reprinted by permission of Harper & Row, Publishers, from *Pennsylvania: Seed of a Nation* by Paul A. W. Wallace. Copyright © 1962 by Paul A. W. Wallace.

"Jim Thorpe, the American Indian" is reprinted by permission of the publisher from *The Tumult and the Shouting, My Life in Sport* by Grantland Rice, published by A. S. Barnes & Company, Inc. in 1954.

"Music Will Out" by Marcia Davenport, appearing in *Collier's* magazine of December 3, 1939, is reprinted by permission of the author.

"K. Leroy Irvis" by Sanford R. Starobin, which originally appeared in the *Philadelphia Inquirer* of February 2, 1969, is reprinted by permission of the *Philadelphia Inquirer.*

Introduction

Even those who know Pennsylvania best, and are fascinated by its variety, interested in its past, and concerned for its future, find it difficult to generalize about the Commonwealth without being instantly, and often unanswerably, challenged.

John Updike, a native son of the Keystone State, once characterized Pennsylvania as "the best, the least eccentric, state in the Union." Yet, typically, he stands corrected, because Pennsylvania often has been the worst, the most eccentric, state in the Union, and willfully so.

Perhaps Henry Adams came closest to plumbing the Pennsylvania psyche when he wrote: "A Pennsylvanian is a wonderful thing; like an anthracite coalbed; dark and dirty in itself but the cause of light."

The state's public personalities, like the Commonwealth itself, are often so full of contradictions or so versatile that they defy pigeonholing in any convenient category. Andrew Carnegie might be stereotyped as just another ruthless baron of industry were it not for his amazingly varied public benefactions. Milton Hershey, whose memorable profile by Paul A. W. Wallace is included in this volume, might be remembered chiefly as a farm boy turned managerial genius who mastered the techniques of mass production before Henry Ford, but it cannot be forgotten that he lived by the creed of his Mennonite heritage and was a great philanthropist.

Gifford Pinchot and William W. Scranton came from wealthy families, in contrast to Carnegie and Hershey. Pinchot became a world-renowned conservationist, Pennsylvania's only two-term governor in the twentieth century, and an accomplished author. Readers may sample Pinchot's skill as a writer and sportsman in "Time like an Ever Rolling Stream," excerpted from his book, *Just Fishing Talk*. Pinchot galloped into politics and thought the White House not beyond his stride. Scranton entered into public affairs gingerly, first to Congress, then to the governorship, and finally into a 31-day Presidential candidacy that had the nation talking about this tall Pennsylvanian with the household name of the place where the "Pennsylvania Polka" started and became "A-number-one." The unusual Scranton personality is investigated in "Portrait of a Not-So-Dark Horse," by James Welsh.

Getting elbow room, either peacefully or by violence, for one's own individuality has always been a Pennsylvania trait. It is, therefore, not surprising that the American Revolution and the march toward independence started in this Commonwealth, as its leading historian, Dr. S. K. Stevens, so ably relates in "A Shot Is Heard in Pennsylvania."

Despite the egalitarian ideals of the Revolution which Pennsylvania did so much to foster, the history of the Commonwealth has been marked by racial and ethnic violence. The Mollie Maguires, whose story is told here, were Irish coal miners organized to terrorize those who discriminated against them. They failed, and twenty Mollies, not all of whom were guilty, were hanged, ten of them on the first day of spring in 1877 in the last mass hanging in the United States.

Discrimination against the black man, even when not characterized by violence, has been persistent and pervasive in the Commonwealth where the Declaration of Independence and the Constitution were written. Today, however, after 300 years (the blacks preceded Penn to Pennsylvania), they have arrived. The heartening story of Majority Leader K. Leroy Irvis is not that of just a black man sitting in the seat occupied by Thaddeus Stevens in 1836, but of a new dignity come to Pennsylvania's public life. Politics, of course, is often the last field to lower its barriers. A galaxy of black stars from Pennsylvania already had brightened the performing arts. The Keystone State's contribution includes Ethel Waters, Pearl Bailey, Billy Eckstine, Bill Cosby, and the incomparable Marian Anderson, whose unprecedented triumphs are chronicled by Marcia Davenport in this volume.

Pennsylvania's ethnic diversity has been a source of strength as well as weakness. When William Penn, at age 36 and one of the most engaging yet irritating of the English nonconformists, was awarded the charter for Pennsylvania in 1681, he was given a land which never had a homogeneous population and never would. Indians already were there in his "Holy Experiment," perhaps 20,000 of them, with a sprinkling of blacks as well, and then came Dutchmen, Welshmen, Africans, Englishmen, Scots, Huguenots, Germans (church and Plain), Swiss, Scotch-Irish, Slavs, Italians, Czechs, and others. They rubbed shoulders to be a rather distinct type of free people, and the list of Pennsylvania's 400 shows they could be talented indeed. Out of this mixture of peoples came a zest for cooperation as well as competition, peaceful rivalry as well as violent conflict. The milieu helped fashion a Pennsylvanian who down through the years has been both refreshing and irksome: in part, an upholder of a long tradition of nonconformity and, in part, an equally strong advocate of acquiescence in a common repressiveness. The late Dr. Wallace, author of the article on Milton Hershey, once commented that Pennsylvania never produced a "supreme revolutionary, no transcendent philosopher, no flaming evangelist." Its people have been pragmatists in the style of their noble Ben Franklin; not overly idealistic, but yet often, the contrary of Franklin, deliberately undaring and cautious, though an ingenious and skeptical people too.

The Commonwealth's melange of nationalities helps to explain the strikingly varied character of its literary output. John Updike, John O'Hara, and Conrad Richter grew up within thirty miles of each other, but their experiences, their attitudes, and their lives have been entirely different. Conrad Richter's Pennsylvania Germans are not the people John O'Hara knew on Mahantongo Street, and O'Hara's background is not that of John Updike's in Shillington and "The Dogwood Tree."

The geography of Pennsylvania presents contrasts as great as those of the cultural backgrounds of its people. Charles Dickens didn't see the same Pennsylvania as he rode the stagecoach to Harrisburg that Stephen Crane saw when he toured a coal mine near Scranton or that Richard Harding Davis saw when he filed his stirring dispatches on the Johnstown Flood.

Pennsylvania has been a hard-working state. Its smoke, soot, and calluses are so noticeable that many Americans are uninformed of its beauty and the forests that cover more than half its acreage. It is a bigtown state, but yet a small-town state. It has 30 cities and 112 boroughs with populations between 7,000 and 25,000, and 31 of its 67 counties remain more than 60 percent rural. The students of national politics categorize it as a "big northeastern industrial urban state," but like all generalizers on Pennsylvania they aren't fully accurate.

The Pennsylvania brand of politics may help to explain why less has been written about the Commonwealth than New England, the South, or the Far West—and correspondingly, why the state has suffered from a lack of national attention. Only one of its native sons, James Buchanan, has become President. Machine politics used to have such a grip on the state that when the national conventions rolled around, Pennsylvania was usually dismissed as either "in the bag" or "impossible to win." Times may be changing. And so too may such Pennsylvania traditions as rotation in office, retiring the elderly, voting with a winner, and not letting political dynasties thrive.

The Pennsylvania Sampler may help to rectify the widespread lack of recognition for the state's considerable accomplishments. It does not attempt to provide a broad, all-encompassing theory, a one-clue and one-answer concept, to explain 300 years of history and a multiplicity of peoples and cultures. Rather, it lets a multitude of voices speak, as they always have, about Pennsylvania and the Pennsylvanians. A battery of men—a reporter like Philip Hamburger, an intellectual like A. James Reichley, and a historian like Paul A. W. Wallace—combine to reveal some of the nuances, shades of uniqueness, gradations of temperament, and twists in events and traditions that make Pennsylvania—even in this age of stifling cultural homogeneity—still worthy to be enjoyed by those who know her as a place apart from all others.

All in Pennsylvania

by Rudyard Kipling

If you're off to Philadelphia this morning,
And wish to prove the truth of what I say
I pledge my word you'll find, the pleasant land behind
Unaltered since Red Jacket rode that way.

Still the pine woods scent the noon, still the catbird sings his tune;
Still autumn sets the maple forest blazing,
Still the grapevine through the dusk flings her soul-compelling musk;
Still the fireflies in the corn make night amazing!

They are there, there, there with Earth immortal
(Citizens, I give you friendly warning).
The things that truly last when man and times have passed
They are all in Pennsylvania this morning.

From the *Delineator* magazine, published in Philadelphia, 1910.

Part I
Colorful People and Places in Pennsylvania

meet
Conrad Richter's
The Pennsylvania Dutch

Pennsylvanians of German descent, from the
Plain People to the church people, have had a
massive impact on the state's mores and politics.
Conrad Richter, the noted novelist and a Pennsylvania German himself, has memorably captured
the unique qualities of his people.

Better than one out of every six Pennsylvanians has some German blood.
Even Princess Grace, Jack Kelly's daughter from Philadelphia, is only half-
Irish.

The Pennsylvania Germans may be divided into two broad categories: the
church people (Lutherans, Reformed, Moravians, Catholics, and the like)
and the Plain People (Mennonites, Amish, and the Brethren groups, such as
the Dunkards or German Baptists and the River Brethren, for whom President Eisenhower's grandfather was a minister). The church people, holding
to worldly ways that are not prohibited in the Bible, quickly blended in with
their fellow Pennsylvanians. They may include small religious sects, such as
the Schwenkfelders, of whom the most famous is now U.S. Senator Richard
Schultz Schweiker, but in their social customs they are almost indistinguish-
able from other Pennsylvanians.

The Plain People are the Pennsylvania Dutch, which is a misnomer origi-
nated by the early English and Scotch-Irish colonists who couldn't, or
wouldn't, pronounce it "Deutsche," or German. These Brethren hold, in various degrees, to a strict interpretation of the Bible and are more interested in
retaining their identity than in total cultural assimilation.

The Amish are the most secluded of Pennsylvania's Plain People, and for
more than 250 years have remained perhaps the most tenacious and un-
homogenized culture in American society. Thaddeus Stevens 150 years ago
admired their principles of humility, simplicity, hard work, and solemnity,

and he called them "those good lumps of earth." There are about 45,000 Amish in 19 states and Canada, most of whom are dead set against television, radios, telephones, automobiles, tractors, store-bought dolls, and other frills of worldly life. Because of intermarriage, large families, and religious principles that have stood the test of time, the Amish culture goes on, but increasingly the outer world is intruding.

Lancaster County has about 9,000 Amishmen. It also has about 3,000 motel units for the almost 4 million tourists a year who want to peer at these Plain People. They learn that the Amish have no engagements nor separation and divorce, that a lively horse with a buggy costs a lad about $1,000, that their cleanliness and farming skills are extraordinary, and that worldly man has made the Amish a bit more quaint than they really are (having a blue-painted gate to announce a marriageable daughter is nothing but a myth, for example).

Though the Pennsylvania Germans, especially the Dutch, refrained from self-ballyhoo and never had a nationalistic movement, the impact of the German culture on Pennsylvania has been immense. Their regard for social decorum, personal courtesy, and occupational skills, as well as their straight-laced attitudes about sex and morals, all influenced Pennsylvania life. The old Germans could be smug, mulish, easily led by political machines, and diverted by Negro and Jewish hate-mongers. But the Pennsylvania German traits of proud citizenship, vigorous community-building, and enterprising self-achievement, coupled with a hidebound philosophy of self-reliance, has made its mark. Republican politics for generations did well in Pennsylvania because it appealed to the middle-class ethnic values of the Germans. Public education did poorly for decades because the low-church Germans thought a little learning a dangerous thing. The Amish to this day permit their children to go only to the eighth grade, with the state-required ninth grade accomplished at home.

Abraham Lincoln in 1860 sent German-speaking Carl Schurz here so that Pennsylvania would go Lincoln-Curtin Republican, and it did. Twelve of Pennsylvania's 38 governors since 1790, including Raymond P. Shafer, had German forefathers. Seventeen of Harrisburg's 29 mayors have been German; 12 of York's 15; 25 of Reading's 38, and 14 of Lancaster's 34. The Midstate today has an all-German Congressional delegation: Edwin D. Eshleman, Herman T. Schneebeli, and George A. Goodling.

Much has been written about the Pennsylvania Germans. A recent book that is highly recommended is *Hex*, by Arthur H. Lewis, a native of Mahanoy City. Lewis writes about a powwow murder case in 1928 in York County, and his study of the Pennsylvania German fascination with hexerei, or witch-craft, shouldn't be missed by anyone interested in the state's cultural history.

Conrad Richter (1890-1968) was almost the exact contemporary of Dwight D. Eisenhower. He was one day older than Ike and died 89 days before him.

Richter was a Pennsylvanian through and through. Perhaps his long article, entitled "Pennsylvania," in the October 1955 issue of *Holiday* magazine, from which this excerpt on the Pennsylvania Dutch is taken, is the most beautifully written essay ever done on this commonwealth and its people. Richter was a superb technician, a gentle philosopher writing in a low key, and one of the most underrated stylists in American literature.

He was born in Pine Grove, lived in Selinsgrove, graduated from high school in Tremont, and knew Donaldson, White Deer Valley, Scalp Level, Reading, Cairnbrook, Milton, and Allentown, where his father, the Rev. John Absalom Richter, served Lutheran parishes. He worked on newspapers in Johnstown, Patton, and Pittsburgh and was a magazine editor in Harrisburg and Reading. Two of his ancestors served in the State Legislature, one of them in Congress, and three uncles, a grandfather, and his father were ministers. Richter and his wife, Harvena Achenbach, both were Pennsylvania Germans. His hometown of Pine Grove in Schuylkill County, 18 miles down the road from John O'Hara's Pottsville and 30 miles up from John Updike's Shillington, is on the border of Dutch and coal country.

Richter lived his middle years in Albuquerque, New Mexico, and when he was forty-seven in 1937 wrote his first and maybe best novel, *The Sea of Grass*. In the thirty-one following years, he wrote thirteen more novels. He won the 1951 Pulitzer Prize for his trilogy—*The Trees, The Fields,* and *The Town*—the story of pioneers in Pennsylvania and Ohio. In 1960 he won the National Book Award for *The Waters of Kronos,* the first of two works he did about a Pennsylvania country minister. *The Light in the Forest,* an Indian story for youth set along the Susquehanna, came out in 1953 and later was made a Walt Disney movie. In 1966 Richter wrote an excellent sequel, *A Country of Strangers.*

Richter was a gentle and kind Pennsylvania German who called himself a Dutchman. He was a superb conversationalist; yet he wouldn't attend autograph parties or testimonials or lecture on the college circuit for $1,000 a night. He admitted to having a "thin skin" for criticism, as did Eisenhower, but he would chat for hours with any critic as he did with his fellow Pine Grove neighbors. He believed in carefully plotted books and rewrote incessantly to get sentences the way he wanted them; yet invariably his end products had a light touch and his comments about civilization came through in an undogmatic and oblique manner.

At one time during the Depression and before his literary career was secure, Richter was earning $7,500 as a Hollywood screen writer, but he said to himself, "This is no life for a Pennsylvania Dutchman," and he went back to his independent and creative ways.

The Pennsylvania Dutch

by Conrad Richter

You will find the Pennsylvania Dutch in the valleys. Like certain species of plants that grow on a particular kind of rock and nowhere else, they flourish in limestone country. If sometimes a Pennsylvania Dutchman is found tilling other soil, it's because there isn't enough limestone to go around. He and his fellows, for the most part, occupy a broad belt running across the state south of the Blue Mountain. Occasional limestone valleys occur in the mountains farther north, where pockets and sometimes an entire county of these people may be found.

Like the French provincials in Canada and the Spanish Americans in the Southwest, the Pennsylvania Dutch keep alive their own language. It's called a dialect but is really more of a German patois, incomprehensible to visitors. And though they settled here 200 years ago, their English still carries a peculiar accent and turn of phrase that can stop an outsider in his tracks. The accent varies in different sections; some of the thickest accents may be found in the Hegins Valley in Dauphin County and between Kutztown and Allentown in Berks and Lehigh counties. Nor can the idiom be imitated easily. *Popa is All* was meant to be a play about the Pennsylvania Dutch, but the title betrays the outlander's heavy hand. Pepper and salt and even vacation may be all, but papa and mamma, never.

Being Pennsylvania Dutch myself, I know how hard it is to get rid of the local (pronounced "logal") speech. Children whose parents have little trace of it, pick it up in school and at play, to be called Dutch the rest of their lives. Native men and women who have lived elsewhere for many years, even college professors of English, find to their dismay that certain inflections cling like birthmarks to betray them, along with telltale phrases such as "come here once," "sprinkle down the clothes," "it will be late till we get home," and referring to one's hair in the plural.

The word "dumb," in the sense of stupid, was in my boyhood purely Pennsylvania Dutch, and our teachers disparaged its use. Similar words used widely in the Pennsylvania Dutch belt by English-speaking people, and which may some day contribute to the American language are: strubbly, used to describe disheveled, unkempt or rumpled hair; to grex, which means to complain or grunt complainingly; doppick for awkward; spritz for splash and spray; wunnerfitzick for inquisitive; and blutz for jolt and bruise. These words undoubtedly persist because they impart a shade of meaning which the nearest English synonym fails to convey, and also, perhaps chiefly, for their comic expressiveness.

The Pennsylvania Dutch like to laugh. Buildings are erected and auto-mobile engines repaired amid frequent sallies and laughter such as I have heard nowhere else in America. An English traveler of nearly 200 years ago left a record of the Pennsylvania Dutch custom of standing outside their churches to joke until it was time for the service to start — then coming out and resuming when it was over. Sometimes they laugh over trifles, out of pure animal spirits. Or they may see another meaning unintelligible to outsiders, as in the classic story about the Pennsylvania Dutch woman who came into a store, the clerk asked what he could do for her, and she said, "Oh, I don't want nothing. I just came in to go out."

There is, of course, one class of Pennsylvania Dutch jokes the outsider can understand and laugh at — those at the expense of the natives. These may be such banal and familiar ones as the sign on the door reading, "If the bell don't make, bump," or the remark of a child watching a freight train go by, "Ain't, Mom, when the little red house comes, then it's all?" For every one of these, however, the observing resident of the southern counties knows a dozen that seldom reach print. The woman who cleans our house said triumphantly after killing a snake, "Well, that's one more copperhead less," a statement that shines with succinctness if not with logic.

Tom Lyter, of Ono, tells the story of the widow who was called on by a man who wanted to see her husband. "You can't see him. He's dead," she said. "Dead?" the man exclaimed. "Why, when did he die?" "Well," she said, "if he'd a lived till Thursday he'd be dead two weeks."

Paul Strickler, of Lebanon, relates how he went with a countryman to look for his lost dog, Wasser. "Now you go up one side of the crick," the man said. "I'll go up the other. You know, he may come back both sides."

If such stories strike you as funny, you have an affinity for Pennsylvania Dutch humor. I have heard these, and many like them, told in my living room until a half score of people, all of them with a dash or more of native blood, shouted with laughter.

On the serious side, the Pennsylvania Dutch have been accused of leaning toward powwowing and hexerei. This is true enough, particularly in the recent past. My grandfather could powwow and was regularly called on to practice his art. He tried to persuade my mother to let me hold a worm in my hand while I was being baptized. This was supposed to give me the power, but my mother, whose maiden name was Henry, declined. As for hex stories, I have heard them all my life, many at first-hand, some told by men and women whose veracity in other matters was unquestioned. I remember as a boy the half-scared sensation of walking past the house of an alleged hex in my hometown, and there were others in the surrounding countryside. Some of these reputed hexes, like their counterparts in New England, had a hard time among their fellows, although the Pennsylvania Dutch, the first to talk against slavery in America, did not hang their witches.

The traveler may think he sees evidence of hexerei in Pennsylvania Dutch barn signs, which an enterprising Yankee by the name of Wallace Nutting told the public were witches' feet. Actually, these are harmless symbols of sun and rain and crop fertility. More than that, they are simply ornaments of which the Pennsylvania Dutch are very fond. Their early baptism and marriage certificates, their furniture and many other articles are decorated with brightly colored designs of tulips, doves, parrots, roosters, vines and like motifs. They love color, especially red, as attested by their big bank barns and by their houses, often of brick and frequently painted over to make the brick redder.

Pennsylvania Dutch houses are "crazy clean." Porches and cellar steps are regularly scrubbed; sidewalks, gutters and sometimes the street are scrupulously swept; even farms and fields look neat as toy yards under Christmas trees. And the food is something to be remembered in Gath.* The tables of the Pennsylvania Dutch groan with good things to eat, particularly when visitors, no matter how humble, are being entertained. The legend that seven sweets and seven sours are served is something of a fantasy, but there are always plenty of both. If there are many guests at dinner, the fare will probably include chicken accompanied by beef or ham, hard-boiled eggs in red-beet juice, as well as vegetables, relishes, fruits and several kinds of pie and cake. Notable Pennsylvania Dutch dishes, for some of which I still grow hungry in far places, are dandelion greens, chowchow, chicken corn soup, pannhaas (a kind of richer scrapple made from country "butchering"), Lebanon bologna, smoked sausage (generally half beef, half pork and cured in an old-fashioned smokehouse), snitz and knepp, fastnachts, pretzels, and shoo-fly pie with deep goo.

---

*Gath. There is no town of Gath in Pennsylvania, though there is a Bath near Bethlehem and Nazareth. The Gath which Richter refers to was the hometown of Goliath the Philistine, a walled city of importance in the Old Testament.

introducing
Paul B. Beers'
Pennsylvania: Word Coiner to a Nation

The Keystone State has contributed mightily to the American language.

The colorful speech patterns of the Pennsylvania Dutch and other groups of Pennsylvanians have attracted national attention. Certainly, Pennsylvania's marvelously descriptive, unpretentious place names deserve more widespread attention than they have received. The following observations are adapted from the "Reporter at Large" columns of the Harrisburg *Evening News,* September 22, 1965, September 6, 1961, and July 7, 1967.

Pennsylvania: Word Coiner to a Nation

by Paul B. Beers

H. L. Mencken, author of the three-volume *The American Language,* found Pennsylvania speech to be utterly fascinating. He noted that we say "spigot" instead of "faucet." Often we use "already" and "yet" in the same sentence to mean the same thing: "I have had algebra already in my freshman year yet." And "yet" is used for "still," such as "When we lived in the country yet."

The coalcrackers' use of "hain't" is marvelous. Mencken comes close to including "hain't." He wrote that he once heard in Scranton, Pa., someone say, "It's a nice day, ain't?" The Pennsylvania Dutch use "ain't" in a similar fashion, just as the French use *"n'est-ce pas"* and the Spanish *"es verdad."* The coalcrackers use "hain't" at the end of an interrogating sentence when they are soliciting approval of what they are talking about. They will say, "Mt. Carmel plays great football, hain't?" If you don't hurriedly agree, a friendly alumnus body-blocks you off your stool.

Mencken says that Pennsylvanians use the word "thinks" as New Englanders use "guesses," Kentuckians use "calculates" and Alabamans use "reckons."

In his book he calls attention to a study done at Hazleton High School in 1942. It was found that the students pronounced their "t's" in "bitter, betting, plotting and sorted," but pronounced a "d" in "bleating, writing, hearty and hurting."

Possibly no other state has had the mixture of nationality groups that Pennsylvania had; yet the old commonwealth is the original source of few words. Mencken said that "stogy" came from here, meaning a cigar shaped like a Conestoga wagon. He writes that "grocery store" was first used in this state, and that William Penn introduced the word "maize."

Some other words, not identified by Mencken, which had their origin here are: "Pennsylvania crude," for our type of oil; "Pennsylvania wagon," for our Conestoga wagon; "Pennsylvania hurricane," for a long, involved lie, and why, I don't know; "Pennsylvania feathers," for coal or coke fuel, and "Pennsylvania mile," for a long mile. The phrase "dollar diplomacy" was used to describe the philosophy of Secretary of State Philander C. Knox, of Pittsburgh. Knox pursued "dollar diplomacy" in Latin America for President Taft.

"Philadelphia lawyer" comes from here. John Peter Zenger in his 1735 trial in New York had Andrew Hamilton, the former solicitor of Philadelphia, defend him. That is one explanation of how "Philadelphia lawyer" came to mean a smart lawyer. "It took a Philadelphia lawyer to get Zenger out," they said. Another explanation is that Europeans used the phrase for brilliance after they had met Ben Franklin, but Franklin was not a lawyer.

The word "punk" probably comes from Pennsylvania. It was used by the Indians to describe rotten wood. But another explanation for the word's being used to describe rotten people is that it was used at the Homestead Riot in 1892. The steel companies brought in Pinkerton agents and they first were called "Pinks." Apparently the steelworkers, many of them new in this country, could not always pronounce "Pinks," and it became "Punks" and stuck.

Pennsylvania, the grandmother's attic of wonderful names, has a conglomeration of perhaps more original and twinkling names than any other 45,000 square miles in the world.

Pennsylvania is the place with "the sharp names that never get fat," as the late Stephen Vincent Benét, the native of Bethlehem who spent his youthful summers in Carlisle, wrote in his famous poem, "American Names," of which this is a poor but kindly spoof:

I have fallen in love with Pennsylvania names,
The sharp names that never get fat,
Simple and crude, no pretentious claims,
Smicksburg, Scalp Level, Grassflat,
Ant Hills, Bug Mountain and Water Gap.

Taste does not demand Forest City,
My choice is common Monessen,
Slickville, Dogtown, Shickshinny,
Whiskerville, Sugar Notch, Calcium,
Virginville, Venturetown and Dauphin.

I will remember Allenvale,
  Sunny Crest, Elkins Park, Duffryn Mawr,
Parkside, Wyebrooke, Oakdale
  And Twickenham Village and Kerrmoor.
I will remember Latta Grove and Bryn Mawr.

But I will fall in love with Mud Pond,
  Moosic, Sober, Wallenpaupack,
Little Oley, Weigh Scale, Shamokin,
  And Lower Gum Stump and Nescopeck.
I am tired of loving Prospect Park.

You may bury my body in Hyde Villa grass,
  You may spend my money at Cottage Hills
And at Oak Knoll or Merwood pay my bills.
  I shall not be there. I shall rise and pass.
Bury my heart at Miners Mills.

Ono, Warrior Run, Blue Ball, Daguscahonda, Coal City, Steelton, Grindstone, Crucible, Catfish, Turtle Creek, Outcrop, Old Forge, Chalkhill, Pansy, Mabel, Bird-in-Hand, Cuddy, Confluence, Defiance, Rough and Ready, Decorum, Catawissa, Nesquehoning, Tamaqua, Hogback Hill, Fryingpan Gap, Grandpap Hollow, Nail Factory Mountain, Pig Hill, Dirtycamp Run, Paw Paw Run, Peach Bottom, Sharon, Tarentum, Young Womans Creek—the names are glorious signposts in the road of time to the poetic wonderment of Pennsylvanians.

Someone said that because of the profusion of these picturesque names—and there must be about 15,000 different geographical names in the state—Pennsylvania is a playground for philologists, professional and amateur.

But is our imagination running dry in these not so glorious latter days? There is strong evidence that it is.

Note the bevy of such names as Pleasant Streams, Bala-Cynwyd, Darlington Corners, Windsor Locks and Cedar Heights—recent additions to the road map. These are names not drawn from earthy curiosity or man's innocent reaction to his environment, but names, instead, that are labels, trademarks, and status symbols.

These names of sweetness and light—though there is not a place in Pennsylvania yet which begins with the name "Happy"—may eventually pass away, however, but a more serious blight could be here to stay. This is the blight of arrogance—and there doesn't seem to be another title for it—of naming places and things after recent or living Pennsylvania politicians, big-time or small-time, beloved or endured politicians.

We have the M. Harvey Taylor Bridge and the George B. Stevenson Dam. The U.S. Senate Public Works Committee renamed the Kettle Creek Dam the "Alvin R. Bush Dam" after that late politician and renamed the Bear Creek Dam after the then living Congressman Francis E. Walter. The Stevenson Dam was to be named the First Fork Sinnemahoning Dam.

If it is arrogance—in the Greek sense of idolatric arrogance—to discard the common-touch names and substitute those of mere men's, perhaps the blame should not be placed on the Taylors, Stevensons, Bushes and Walters, but on the battalion of flatterers who follow political heroes. No politician would dare advance his own name. Or at least one can hope this to be true. (Governor and General Edward Martin died in early 1967, and later that year Governor Raymond P. Shafer went along with the Legislature and renamed Indiantown Gap the "Edward Martin Military Reservation." The new name to date hasn't caught on, however, and isn't likely to.)

The practice of using politicians' surnames is a one-way street to philologic boorishness. These are flat names that go blunt the day after the ceremonial music stops.

And, too, look what we face if we continue to build towns and bridges, dams and by-passes, at every geographical point in the state. Pennsylvania has 49 Laurel Runs, 31 Mill Creeks, 20 Beaver Runs, 14 Beaver Creeks, 18 Bear Runs, 16 Bear Creeks, 16 Dry Runs and 12 Coal Runs. Here are 176 names that could be changed.

Pennsylvania place names have spread across the nation. If you ever get to Hershey, Nebr., stop at the general store or at least make the effort to chat with some of the natives. I got the amusing impression when I was out there that they think Hershey, Pa., is as big as the Ritz. Since the Nebraska Hershey has a population of 504, there is reason enough for its folks to regard Pennsylvania's Chocolate Town with awe.

The late Paul A. W. Wallace entitled his last book, *Pennsylvania, Seed of a Nation.* When you travel across these United States, you can understand that the Commonwealth indeed has served as a seed of a nation—not only for its myriad contributions to political and religious freedom but for its seed of providing Pennsylvania names for countless communities and counties.

Nebraska, for example, has seven counties with names similar to those in Pennsylvania—Adams, Butler, Franklin, Jefferson, Lancaster, Washington and York. In addition to Hershey, it has many towns with Pennsylvania names—Ashland, Harrisburg, Hastings, New Castle, Paxton, Wayne, York and the like.

Dr. William A. Russ Jr., professor of history at Susquehanna University and for three decades one of the most informed men on Pennsylvania lore, in 1948 did a piece for *Pennsylvania History* magazine on Pennsylvania names in the United States. Where he could, Dr. Russ delved beyond just the coincidence of similar names and traced actual connections to the Commonwealth. Wyoming, Nebr., for example, got that name because some pioneers from Wyoming Valley, Pa., settled there. Juniata, Nebr., was named after Pennsylvania's Juniata River, just as Lehigh, Okla., was named after the Lehigh River. Scranton, Iowa, was named after the ancestors of Governor William W. Scranton.

Just as the Pennsylvania pioneers gave Old World names to their communities (such as Carlisle, New Cumberland, Newport, Lebanon and York), the pioneers of the West often enjoyed naming their prairie settlement after a town they fondly remembered in Pennsylvania. There is Gettysburg, S.D.; Tioga, Iowa; Penn Township, Kans., and Ligonier, Ind. There are at least four Eries, in South Dakota, Illinois, Kansas and Michigan. There are Altoonas in Iowa, Kansas and Wisconsin. Plymouth Township, Ohio, was named for the Pennsylvania Plymouth, not the Massachusetts one. There is a New Philadelphia in Ohio, and, though the spelling is different (not really; Pittsburgh, Pa., didn't officially adopt its "h" until this century), there is a Pittsburg, Calif., and a Pittsburg Landing, Ariz.

Lancaster, Pa., at one time was the biggest city in the western United States, so the result is there are Lancasters in Ohio, Kentucky, Oregon and California. Nebraska has both a town and a county named Lancaster.

The nation is dotted with towns and counties named after individual Pennsylvanians. Dallas, Texas, is named for Vice President George M. Dallas, the Philadelphian who served under President Polk. Dallas, S.D., was named for the city in Texas, and thus indirectly for George Dallas.

All Americans loved Benjamin Franklin, and it is difficult to travel 1,000 miles in any direction without going through a Franklin something or other.

There is a Fort Buchanan in Arizona, and counties in Iowa, Missouri and Virginia are named for this President from Pennsylvania. There are two Gallatin counties, in Kentucky and Illinois, for the fiscal genius of western Pennsylvania. Kansas has both a town and a county named for John W. Geary, the Pennsylvania governor who once was territorial governor of Bloody Kansas. San Francisco has a main street named after this politician, buried in Harrisburg, who also was the Bay City's first mayor.

There is a Fulton, Mo., and a Girard, Ill., both named for distinguished Pennsylvanians. Girard, Kans., however, is named for Girardville, Pa., which millionaire Stephen Girard once all but owned. There is a Drexel in North Carolina and Wisconsin, as well as a Carnegie, Okla.

Fort Wayne, Ind., is named for Pennsylvania's Mad Anthony Wayne, and there are Waynes in West Virginia, Illinois, Nebraska and Oklahoma. Arthur St. Clair, a nondescript general in the Indian Wars and a loser for the Pennsylvania governorship, has a town named in his honor in Nebraska. Gen. George Meade, the victor at Gettysburg, is honored with a town in Kansas. Meadville, Pa., is not named for the general, however, but for a Western Pennsylvania pioneer.

No matter what Americans think of the status of politicians, they seem to relish naming communities after them. There is Stevens, Calif., and Stevens County, Kans., both named for irascible old Thaddeus. Harrisburg has Cameron Street, but West Virginia has an entire town named for the devilish Simon, while South Carolinians must have thought Simon's son, Sen. J. Donald Cameron of Middletown, worthy of immortality by naming a town for him. There were many Pennsylvania Democrats in the post-Civil War days who couldn't stand the mention of their own Cong. Sam Randall's name, but Oklahoma named a town for him. And Dillsburg's Matthew Stanley Quay, one of the most oleaginous of the gender of slippery Pennsylvania politicians, is honored in Oklahoma. The people of Illinois thought so highly of Towanda's David Wilmot that they named a town Proviso for his famous anti-slavery document.

Any human would be proud to have a town or county named for him, but I imagine the finest tribute paid a Pennsylvanian is reserved for Governor Gifford Pinchot. In the redwood preserve of Muir Woods, just north of San Francisco, the tallest redwood—a magnificent, inspiring, still-growing tree—is named the "Gifford Pinchot Tree." Old Giff would be cheered to know he has one of the highest memorials in the nation.

travel along on
Charles Dickens'
The Harrisburg Mail

In the mid-nineteenth century Pennsylvania had
many famous covered bridges and an ambitious
canal system. Charles Dickens was one of the
distinguished foreign visitors who enjoyed the
adventurous mode of travel they afforded.

Charles Dickens (1812-1870) was just one of many foreign visitors who
was attracted to Pennsylvania and wrote about his visit.

The "Welcome" sign was hung out by William Penn himself, when in 1681
with a tourist agent's enthusiasm he wrote that his province is "600 miles
nearer the sun than England." William Markham, the deputy governor under
Penn, added that "here people live to be above a hundred years of age."
And so the visitors came: Alexis de Tocqueville, Anthony Trollope, Prince
Albert, Rudyard Kipling, Oscar Wilde, Field Marshal Montgomery, Nikita
Khrushchev, and thousands of others.

Dickens was just thirty when he traveled through Pennsylvania in 1842,
but he already had created Mr. Pickwick and Oliver Twist and was one of the
world's most famous authors. He spent from January to June in the United
States and from his visit came *American Notes,* which went through four
editions in its first year of publication. He stepped ashore as an acknowl-
edged abolitionist, calling slavery a "hideous blot and foul disgrace," and
though he said he wrote "good-humoredly and in a kind spirit," his book
touched off sparks in America. Pennsylvania he found delightful, except for
its prison system with solitary confinement.

Dickens saw Philadelphia as "more provincial than Boston or New York,"
yet it had "an assumption of taste and criticism." Pittsburgh was the Birming-
ham of America. "It certainly has a great quantity of smoke hanging about it,
and is famous for its ironworks," he wrote, adding that "it is very beauti-

fully situated on the Alleghany River, over which there are two bridges, and the villas of the wealthier citizens sprinkled about the high grounds in the neighborhood are pretty enough."

He left Harrisburg by canal boat on a Friday evening and arrived in Pittsburgh on Monday evening. The old canal system lasted in Pennsylvania from 1826 to 1900, and in its heyday had 900 miles of state-owned and 300 miles of privately owned canal. The Pennsylvania Canal through the center of the state, which Dickens rode, lasted only 18 years without competition from the railroads. It cost $101.6 million to build and brought in only $44 million in revenue before the Commonwealth sold it to the Pennsylvania Railroad at bargain prices in 1857. James Buchanan as a state legislator warned it would be an economic loss, but other political leaders, and later Thaddeus Stevens especially, pushed it as a public project. It was built to compete with the Erie Canal, but this New York State waterway had an elevation of only 500 feet in 360 miles, as compared to the Pennsylvania Canal's 2,291 feet in 320 miles. When Dickens rode the Pennsylvania, it was handling a fifth the freight the Erie was. By 1852 the Pennsylvania Railroad had a train between Harrisburg and Pittsburgh, and in 1858 it made a historic Philadelphia-to-Pittsburgh run. The Civil War made the railroads and doomed the canal system.

Canal life was an exciting part of Pennsylvania's past. Immigrant Irish and Slavs hand-dug the ditches, but often it was Dutchmen who operated the boats. Tempers could be short and regulations were ignored. "It was usually the canal boat with the toughest crew that cleared the lock first," writes William H. Shank, a York historian and authority on Pennsylvania transportation.

Dickens was charmed by canal traveling. In *American Notes* he writes of his Pennsylvania experience: "There was much in this mode of traveling which I heartily enjoyed at the time, and look back upon with great pleasure. Even the running up, bare-necked, at 5 o'clock in the morning from the tainted cabin to the dirty deck; scooping up the icy water, plunging one's head into it, and drawing it out, all fresh and glowing with the cold; was a good thing. The fast, brisk walk upon the towing-path, between that time and breakfast, when every vein and artery seemed to tingle with health; the exquisite beauty of the opening day, when light came gleaming off from everything; the lazy motion of the boat, when one lay idly on the deck, looking through, rather than at, the deep blue sky; the gliding on, at night, so noiselessly, past frowning hills, sullen with dark trees, and sometimes angry in one red burning spot high up, where unseen men lay crouching round a fire; the shining out of the bright stars, undisturbed by noise of wheels or steam, or any other sound than the liquid rippling of the water as the boat went on: all these were pure delights."

Before his canal trip, Dickens traveled by stage from York to Harrisburg, an experience in itself. The bridge over which he crossed the Susquehanna was Old Camelback, which stood from 1816 to its collapse in the 1902 Flood where the Harrisburg Market Street Bridge now is. Old Camelback was one of Pennsylvania's greatest covered bridges. The Commonwealth not only had the nation's first covered bridge, the Timothy Palmer bridge over the Schuylkill in 1805, but it once led the nation with more than 1,000 such bridges. Today it still leads the nation, but has only 300 covered bridges left. Old Camelback was built by the great Theodore Burr, whose Burr wooden truss is of historic importance in bridge engineering. Burr himself died in poverty in 1822 and is buried in an unknown grave near Middletown. Prior to the Battle of Gettysburg, Union forces destroyed the Columbia-Wrightsville Bridge, the world's longest covered bridge. Had Robert E. Lee been successful at Gettysburg, Old Camelback undoubtedly would have been burned also by the Yankees to prevent the Confederates from reaching Harrisburg.

Dickens's account of his stagecoach ride to Harrisburg and of meeting state legislators is taken from *American Notes*, as published in 1903 by Macmillan and Co. Ltd.

The

Harrisburg Mail

by Charles Dickens

They packed twelve people inside; and the luggage, including such trifles as a large rocking-chair and a good-size dining table, being at length made fast upon the roof, we started off in great state.

At the door of another hotel, there was another passenger to be taken up.

"Any room, sir?" cries the new passenger to the coachman. "Well, there's room enough," replies the coachman, without getting down or even looking at him. "There ain't no room at all, sir," bawls a gentleman inside. Which another gentleman, also inside, confirms by predicting that the attempt to introduce any more passengers "won't fit nohow."

The new passenger, without any expression of anxiety, looks into the coach and then looks up at the coachman, "Now how do you mean to fix it? For I must go."

The coachman employs himself in twisting the lash of his whip into a knot, and takes no more notice of the question, clearly signifying that it is anybody's business but his, and that the passengers would do well to fix it, among themselves. In this state of things, matters seem to be approximating to a fix of another kind, when another inside passenger in a corner, who is nearly suffocated, cries faintly, "I'll get out."

This is no matter of relief or self-congratulation to the driver, for his immoveable philosophy is perfectly undisturbed by anything that happens in the coach. Of all things in the world, the coach would seem to be the very last upon his mind. The exchange is made, however, and then the passenger who has given up his seat makes a third upon the box, seating himself in what he calls the middle: that is, with half his person on my legs and the other half on the driver's.

"Go ahead, cap'en," cries the colonel who directs. "Go-lang!" cries the cap'en to his company, the horses, and away we go.

We took up at a rural barroom, after we had gone a few miles. An intoxicated gentleman, who climbed upon the roof among the luggage, and subsequently slipping off without hurting himself, was seen in the distant perspective reeling back to the grog-shop where we had found him. We also parted with more of our freight at different times, so that when we came to change horses, I was again alone outside.

The coachmen always change with the horses, and are usually as dirty as the coach. The first was dressed like a very shabby English baker; the second like a Russian peasant, for he wore a loose purple camlet robe with a fur collar, tied round his waist with a parti-colored worsted sash; grey trousers; light blue gloves, and a cap of bearskin. It had by this time come on to rain very heavily, and there was a cold damp mist besides, which penetrated to the skin. I was very glad to take advantage of a stoppage and get down to stretch my legs, shake the water off my great-coat, and swallow the usual anti-temperance recipe for keeping out the cold.

When I mounted to my seat again, I observed a new parcel lying on the coach roof, which I took to be a rather large fiddle in a brown bag. In the course of a few miles, however, I discovered that it had a glazed cap at one end and a pair of muddy shoes at the other; and further observation demonstrated it to be a small boy in a snuff-colored coat, with his arms quite pinioned to his sides by deep forcing into his pockets. He was, I presume, a relative or friend of the coachman's, as he lay atop of the luggage with his face toward the rain; and except when a change of position brought his shoes in contact with my hat, he appeared to be asleep. At last, on some occasion of our stopping, this thing slowly upreared itself to the height of 3 feet 6, and fixing its eyes on me, observed in piping accents, with a complaisant yawn half-quenched in an obliging air of friendly patronage, "Well now, stranger, I guess you find this a'most like an English arternoon, hey?"

The scenery, which had been tame enough at first, was, for the last ten or twelve miles, beautiful. Our road wound through the pleasant valley of the Susquehanna; the river, dotted with innumerable green islands, lay upon our right; and on the left, a steep ascent, craggy with broken rock, and dark with pine trees. The mist, wreathing itself into a hundred fantastic shapes, moved solemnly upon the water; and the gloom of evening gave to all an air of mystery and silence which greatly enhanced its natural interest.

We crossed this river by a wooden bridge, roofed and covered in on all sides, and nearly a mile in length. It was profoundly dark; perplexed, with great beams, crossing and recrossing it at every possible angle; and through the broad chinks and crevices in the floor, the rapid river

gleamed, far down below, like a legion of eyes. We had no lamps; and
as the horses stumbled and floundered through this place, towards the
distant speck of dying light, it seemed interminable. I really could not
at first persuade myself as we rumbled heavily on, filling the bridge
with hollow noises, and I held down my head to save it from the rafters
above, but that I was in a painful dream; for I have often dreamed of
toiling through such places, and as often argued, even at the time, "this
cannot be reality."

At length, however, we emerged upon the streets of Harrisburg, whose
feeble lights, reflected dismally from the wet ground, did not shine out
upon a very cheerful city. We were soon established in a snug hotel,
which, though smaller and far less splendid than many we put up at, is
raised above them all in my remembrance, by having for its landlord
the most obliging, considerate and gentlemanly person I ever had to
deal with.

As we were not to proceed upon our journey until the afternoon, I
walked out, after breakfast the next morning, to look about me: and
was duly shown a model prison on the solitary system, just erected and
as yet without an inmate; the trunk of an old tree to which Harris, the
first settler here (afterwards buried under it), was tied by hostile Indians,
with his funeral pile about him, when he was saved by the timely appearance of a friendly party on the opposite shore of the river; the local
legislature (for there was another of those bodies here, again, in full
debate), and the other curiosities of the town.

Our host announced, before our early dinner, that some members of
the legislative body proposed to do us the honor of calling. He had
kindly yielded up to us his wife's own little parlor, and when I begged
that he would show them in, I saw him look with painful apprehension
at its pretty carpet; though, being otherwise occupied at the time, the
cause of his uneasiness did not occur to me.

It certainly would have been more pleasant to all parties concerned,
and would not, I think, have compromised their independence in any
material degree, if some of these gentlemen had not only yielded to the
prejudice in favor of spittoons, but had abandoned themselves, for the
moment, even to the conventional absurdity of pocket handkerchiefs.

It still continued to rain heavily, and when we went down to the canal
boat after dinner, the weather was as unpromising and obstinately wet
as one would desire to see. Nor was the sight of this canal boat, in which
we were to spend three or four days, by any means a cheerful one; as it
involved some uneasy speculations concerning the disposal of the passengers at night, and opened a wide field of inquiry touching the other
domestic arrangements of the establishment, which was sufficiently
disconcerting.

However, there it was—a barge with a little house in it, viewed from the outside; and a caravan at a fair, viewed from within: the gentlemen being accommodated, as the spectators usually are, in one of those locomotive museums of penny wonders; and the ladies being partitioned off by a red curtain, after the manner of the dwarfs and giants in the same establishments, whose private lives are passed in rather close exclusiveness.

We sat here, looking silently at the row of little tables, which extended down both sides of the cabin, and listening to the rain as it dripped and pattered on the boat, and splashed with a dismal merriment in the water, until the arrival of the railway train, for whose final contribution to our stock of passengers, our departure was alone deferred. It brought a great many boxes, which were bumped and tossed upon the roof, almost as painfully as if they had been deposited on one's own head, without the intervention of a porter's knot; and several damp gentlemen, whose clothes, on their drawing round the stove, began to steam again. No doubt it would have been a thought more comfortable if the driving rain, which now poured down more soakingly than ever, had admitted of a window being opened, or if our number had been something less than 30; but there was scarcely time to think as much, when a train of three horses was attached to the tow-rope, the boy upon the leader smacked his whip, the rudder creaked and groaned complainingly, and we had begun our journey.

relive history with
Philip Hamburger's
Gettysburg and Ike

Dwight D. Eisenhower had deep family roots in
Pennsylvania, and he thoroughly enjoyed his
farm at Gettysburg. The General's residence in
the town gave its citizens the feeling of living
history.

Gettysburg—the site of the bloodiest battle on American soil, the hallowed
ground where the most memorable speech in the English language was
given, and the last home of Dwight David Eisenhower—has almost too much
history. It is no wonder that the 2 million tourists a year who visit it are
overwhelmed.

Gettysburg was an accident. It wasn't specifically arranged that the
Confederates would attack from the north and west and that the Union
forces would hold the high ground on the southeast, and that the great
confrontation would be there in that otherwise somnolent Adams County
village. In the three days of fighting, July 1-3, 1863, there were 50,500
casualties, more than a tenth of whom were killed at the scene. The Battle
of Waterloo had only 4,500 more casualties.

Then came the Gettysburg Address. President Lincoln hadn't been expected to attend the cemetery dedication ceremony on November 19, 1863.
He had to wait a long time to speak his brief message. But what he said has
been read by people who don't even know where Gettysburg is.

The grave site which Lincoln dedicated started the national cemetery
system. One of the slain over whom he spoke was infantryman George
Nixon, the great-grandfather of the thirty-seventh President. By February
of 1968 the original cemetery was filled and an annex was purchased. The
park itself, now 3,200 acres big, became a national shrine in 1885.

And, lastly, there was Ike, who came from Pennsylvania stock and had
his residency at Gettysburg from 1950 and through his Presidency until
his death on March 28, 1969.

The Eisenhowers—or Eisenhauers, meaning ironcutters—left Bavaria and then Switzerland to come to Pennsylvania in 1741. Nicholas Eisenhower, 50, took his family and settled in Bethel Township, then in Dauphin but now in Lebanon County. Nicholas's grandson, Frederick, was killed in the American Revolution. Another grandson, a second Frederick, became the great-grandfather of the President. This Frederick married the grand-daughter of Jacob Miller, one of the original settlers of Lower Paxton Township, now a suburban community in Dauphin County. They lived on fifty-three acres of Miller land just east of Harrisburg. His son, Jacob, was born there, but then the Eisenhowers moved north to Lykens Valley by Berry's Mountain. Jacob, the grandfather of the President, built a sawmill and became a preacher in the Pennsylvania German River Brethren faith. He lived near Elizabethville, where his son David was born in 1864. The house still stands. In 1878 the Rev. Jacob Eisenhower sold his property and moved to Kansas, excited by the promises of cheap land and good wheat. David married a girl from Virginia and they became the parents of six boys, one of whom was Dwight David, born in Abilene, Kansas, on October 14, 1890.

Martin H. Brackbill, once an Associated Press correspondent in Harrisburg and later Budget Secretary for Governor Scranton, did a complete study of the Eisenhower family for *Pennsylvania History* magazine of January 1953.

Dwight Eisenhower as a young officer out of West Point returned to Pennsylvania. From March to November of 1918 he commanded a tank training center at Camp Colt in Gettysburg.

In 1950, two years before winning the Presidency, General Eisenhower bought his 230-acre farm at Gettysburg, the first home that he and Mamie ever owned. The same year his younger brother, Dr. Milton S. Eisenhower, the president of Kansas State College, became the president of the then Pennsylvania State College. During Milton Eisenhower's tenure, Penn State became a university. He resigned in 1956 to assume the presidency of Johns Hopkins University.

General Eisenhower made a typical good Pennsylvania German investment when he paid $44,000 for his farm. In 1967 the Eisenhowers deeded it to the United States as a national historic site. It was valued at $375,000 for federal tax purposes. They got a substantial gift-deduction on their subsequent income taxes and could live there in the 15-room farmhouse-manor—with the well-thumbed Eisenhower Bible bound in soft black morocco in the living room—for the rest of their lives rent and property tax free. "Well, we're back in government housing," Mrs. Eisenhower joked.

Ike enjoyed his Gettysburg farm, though he often left to vacation at Palm Desert, California, or the Augusta National Golf Club in Georgia. He kept close to things, one day going down to Camp David in the Maryland Catoctin Mountains to confer with President Kennedy. It was that meeting, as the two men strolled with their backs to him, that Paul Vathis took the picture that won the 1962 Pulitzer Prize. Vathis, a native of Mauch Chunk, has been the Associated Press photographer out of Harrisburg for fifteen years.

The General was a gentleman farmer, taking an interest in land use, crop growth and rotation, hybrid corn, and the raising of Black Angus. At his death, Eisenhower's estate included 243 choice grade cattle, worth $55,000. The Angus occasionally were entered in the Pennsylvania Farm

Show. Ike was excited about his farm, and one day he grabbed a bull by the tail as a city slicker might do just to move it for a visitor. "I wanted to take a piece of ground like this that had been sort of worn out through improper use and try to restore it," he remarked. "I just said that when I die, I'm going to leave a piece of ground better than I found it."

It was in his office at Gettysburg College that Eisenhower wrote his two-volume *The White House Years* and his last book, in 1967, *At Ease, Stories I Tell My Friends.* He would also hold informal press conferences in the office. In 1967 he made a flub while rattling off the names of potential Republican Presidential candidates. Mrs. Eisenhower leaned over and whispered in his ear. "...and Richard Nixon," Ike added with a smile.

Ike was last in his office in November of 1967, prior to leaving for Palm Desert, where he suffered a heart attack and was transferred to Walter Reed Army Hospital in Washington. His aide, Brigadier General Robert L. Schulz, kept the office a month after Eisenhower's death and then he himself had a heart attack. In September of 1969 the office quarters reverted to Gettysburg College.

A great deal has been written about the Battle of Gettysburg. Three recommended works are *Here Come the Rebels!* by Colonel Wilbur S. Nye, a Civil War historian from Wormleysburg who details the campaign in Pennsylvania prior to the battle; *They Met at Gettysburg* by E. J. Stackpole; and *The Gettysburg Campaign, A Study in Command* by Edwin B. Coddington. Dr. Coddington, once president of the Pennsylvania Historical Association and for years professor of history at Lafayette College, died in 1967, the year before his definitive work on the battle was published.

"Gettysburg and Ike" is from an article entitled "Gettysburg, Pa.," which appeared in the *New Yorker* magazine on April 4, 1964, and later was included in *An American Notebook,* published by Alfred A. Knopf in 1965. Philip Hamburger was born in Wheeling, West Virginia, in 1914, graduated from Johns Hopkins and Columbia Journalism School, and has been a staff writer for the *New Yorker* since 1939.

Gettysburg and Ike

by Philip Hamburger

Alt., 520. Pop., 7,960. No more egregious error can be committed by
the visitor to Gettysburg than to assume that the Battle of Gettysburg
(July 1-3, 1863) is over. In fact, there is reason to believe that hostilities
are only just beginning. Skirmishes take place all over town, and the
most obscure details of the huge, sprawling battle are made available
to strangers, in one form or another, every hour of the day. "I tell you,
I was just an ordinary fellow, with an ordinary fellow's interest in the
Civil War, until I spent two days at Gettysburg," an ordinary fellow who
gave the impression of having been through a protracted siege said not
long ago. "Now I think I could lecture at the War College. It all began
when I took a room in a motel on the edge of the battlefield. This particular motel lay almost directly in the line of Pickett's Charge—athwart
it, you might say. Pickett's Charge, of course, was the unsuccessful
offensive mounted by the Confederate troops on the afternoon of July 3,
when Pickett and his men marched out from the Confederate left flank
on Seminary Ridge and crossed an open field to meet the Union troops
head on on Cemetery Ridge. I would place the start of the charge at
approximately 3 p.m., Eastern Standard Time. I won't go so far as to
say that Pickett's men would have come right *through* my bedroom;
but they might well have bruised themselves on the television set against
my southern wall. Actually, I feel certain that Pettigrew's men—he was
stationed to the left of Pickett—and the men of Archer, Davis, Scales,
and Lane would have come right across my bed, knocking over the telephone and the bed lamp. They ran into Meade's men—Hays, Webb,
Gibbon, and the rest—and at the Angle it was bloody beyond description, and the Confederates were turned back at the Copse of Trees, at
what is known as the High Water Mark of the Confederacy. The Rebels

were said to be incapable of ever again mounting an offensive. Pickett's Charge was all over by ten minutes to four, but I kept going in Gettysburg pretty much around the clock, taking bus rides with built-in sound effects describing every last inch of the battle, watching an electric map with hundreds of little lights blinking and winking to show the position of the troops, looking at a cyclorama of the battle, walking over the battlefield, taking a guided tour in my own car, with a hired guide, and buying toy cannons, old bullets, flags, literature of all sorts, and tons of picture postcards. Now, if I had been Pickett—."

A man can visit Gettysburg, not even stop at a motel, and garner a rich historical background—merely by buying postcards. Postcards abound. They outnumber the people in the town by approximately twenty to one. They have a tendency to jump off the racks and hop into one's pockets. There are pictures of everything and everybody—Devil's Den, General Warren on Little Round Top, Big Round Top, the Valley of Death, Spangler's Spring, General Lee, General Lee's horse, Culp's Hill, the Wheatfield, the Virginia State Monument, the North Carolina State Monument, the Peach Orchard, McPherson Ridge, Barlow Knoll, Oak Hill, the Copse of Trees, the Angle, General Meade, General Meade's horse, General Meade's headquarters, the Jennie Wade House, and so on. The sense of history that pervades the city often produces an anesthetic effect that can take days to shake off. This happens most often to people who hire an official guide to accompany them as they drive around the thirty-odd square miles that constitute the battlefield. Groups of these guides—elderly men, for the most part—sit and sun themselves in front of small stone houses that are scattered about the edge of the field. Many of the guides would make interesting picture postcards. They leave the impression that they are veterans of the battle. They are staggering repositories of information, much of it in the general area of blood and gore. They feel that, seated beside a person who has hired their services for an hour or an hour and a half while he drives along the quiet tree-lined and gun-lined roads, they have a duty to dwell upon the horrors of war. Actually, bodies no longer lie out on the gently rolling, alternately brown and green fields, but the guides are corpse-conscious just the same, and they cannot pass a gully, an open stretch, or a battery of guns without making vivid references to the toll of human life that was taken at Gettysburg. They savor casualty figures, and roll them over and over on their tongues, with special attention to the number of hours or days that "the dead lay out there in the hot sun." Nor is their arithmetical ardor confined to casualty figures. The cost of various monuments titillates them to a frenzy of statistics, and they cite to the penny the amount expended on every monument they pass. "When I got through with one of those guides," a visitor to Gettysburg remarked recently, "I had the feeling that I had been driving around with a man from Price Waterhouse who had come to the field, eagle-eyed, to examine the books." Most of the guides are brigadiers manque, or at least colonels manqué, possessed of a mysterious, superior un-tapped skill in commanding vast armies of men over broad areas under optimum conditions of strategy and tactics. They find it difficult to concede that the generals who fought the battle knew what they were doing, and they make it clear that if they had been consulted, little of what did take place would have taken place. For the most part, they would have everywhere attacked sooner, or later, in a different spot, with different equipment and radically rearranged formations. "By the time I was through with my guided tour, I had no possible way of know-ing which side, if any, won the battle," a man who had visited the battle-field said not long ago. "I decided to go home and read a book about it. The book said the North won."

Gettysburg strongly feels the presence of two former Presidents of the United States—one dead, one living. Lincoln is everywhere: in the National Cemetery, where he delivered the Gettysburg Address; in the tiny maroon-and-gray railroad station, now a tourist center, where he got off the train from Washington the afternoon before he delivered the address; in the Old Wills House, where he spent the night before he delivered the address; and on the old streets down which he rode on horseback on his way to the cemetery and the delivering of the address. The casual visitor poking through the souvenir shops is likely to feel that he is almost entirely surrounded by Lincoln—Lincoln staring at him from picture postcards, miniature busts of Lincoln in imitation bronze and silver, and copies of the address on postcards, silk scrolls, and wooden plaques. Gettysburg's living President is Dwight Eisen-hower. Pictures of Eisenhower, and of his farm and his wife, are not in short supply either. The people of Gettysburg may not catch sight of Eisenhower for weeks at a time—he drives from his farm to his office, on Carlisle Street, swiftly and with military precision and efficiency—but they derive comfort from the fact that he is around. "You can go into a lot of towns that call themselves historical—they are more like historical markers than towns, really—and they leave you with a sense of ancient matters settled long ago," a Gettysburg resident remarked the other day. "It's different here. We don't have much in the way of indus-try—just a shoe factory—and wages are generally low, and the tourists pour through, but we do have this indefinable sense of living history. These two strikingly different men, Lincoln and Eisenhower, have much to do with it. They elevate us and make us feel as though we were actors in some strange pageant that keeps unfolding and is something larger than ourselves."

A recent visitor to Gettysburg, having walked slowly down the main street, past the brooding photographs of Lincoln staring at him from

shopwindows along the way, paid a call on General Eisenhower in his
office, which occupies a modest three-story red brick building on the
campus of Gettysburg College; formerly the house was occupied by the
president of Gettysburg College. The Venetian blinds are always drawn.
Visitors encounter an elaborate but unobtrusive security system at the
front door—an intercom mechanism through which the visitor an-
nounces himself. If he is expected, he is told in metallic tones to enter.
Visitors may also be admitted through the back of the house. Several
secretaries work there, in an enclosed porchlike extension, amid tall
rows of metal filing cabinets with heavy locks. Inside, the house had a
comfortable, easygoing air—warm draperies, many oil paintings, rooms
lined with bookcases containing bound volumes of government reports.
In a large room on the ground floor, the visitor found Colonel John
Eisenhower, the President's son. Colonel Eisenhower has left the Army
and is now working for a publishing house, helping his father put
together his memoirs of the White House years; his desk was covered
with galley proofs of the President's work. "He's deep in Volume Two,"
said Colonel Eisenhower. "Working like fury on it, too, writing all up
and down and along the margins of yellow foolscap. He has many of the
tools to aid his memory right here, on the back porch, in those files you
just passed, and I am cleared to go through them when he needs a fact
to refresh his recollection. There are other files out in Abilene, but not
of the same importance. And there is a great mass of stuff down at the
Library of Congress, in Washington, where my father's assistant on this
project, Dr. William Ewald, has stationed himself. When Father sits
down with pen and paper and relaxes and lets his thoughts spontane-
ously flow forth, we get some pretty vivid, colorful recollections. These
are then typed up and checked over, and then he goes at them again,
rearranging and polishing. He's very fussy about his work." The Colonel,
who is a tall, slim, engaging-looking man with a casual air, then said, "I
have a single-engine Comanche that I keep out at the airport here, and
every chance I get, I go up in her, and fly around the countryside, over
the battlefield—everywhere. I just wheel around and get out of myself
and get off the ground. I feel so free when I am in the air. I am out of
myself. I love it."
   The President works in a corner room on the second floor. He feels
that if he worked downstairs, people would be trying to peer through
the windows. Across the hall from his workroom, a retired brigadier
general acting as an aide handles the large flow of correspondence and
other matters that press into the life of an ex-President. Five stars, form-
ing a circle, are etched in glass on the door leading to the President's
workroom. He sits at a wide desk that is almost totally uncluttered, being
embellished only by a few gadgets and a tiny silver bust of Lincoln.
Behind him are the United States flag and the Presidential flag. The

visitor found him relaxed and cheerful, possessed of a strangely old-fashioned and yet military courtesy, his voice soft but somewhat clipped, his words often tumbling out but giving the impression that at his own command they would instantly cease and he would turn his thoughts to other concerns. His cheeks had a healthy tint, and his eyes were clear blue and quietly scrutinizing. "I sit here and admire that watercolor by Andrew Wyeth," he said suddenly, pointing to a framed picture on the wall across from his desk. "I suppose I admire his work above all others. I have no idea how he does it. Just look at those sycamores! Wyeth did that watercolor on my farm, did it in about 20 minutes—faster than I can conceive of a man turning out such a superior piece of work. I hope you noticed my oil by Churchill on the way up the stairs—a favorite scene of mine, a wadi in North Africa. I love the mountain scenes—the Rockies, the Atlas Mountains. I can look at them for hours. I have most of what I need here to work with. It's great fun to test my memory, see what I can remember from the crowded years."

The President took off his glasses and toyed with them. "Twenty-twenty hindsight is so easy, but I find myself trying to track down the minutiae, the considerations that lay behind a decision," he said. "When the war was over, I wanted time to reflect, to think back, but then SHAPE came along, and the Presidency, and all the years. I had wanted to declare myself a one-term President, and then take a long look, have a breathing spell." The President shifted slightly in his chair. "Now, when I look back, I realize that I was never one for bombast, you know. Persuasion was more in my line. And a great many people still look upon me as a rather unwelcome entry." The President smiled, and put on his glasses. He leaned forward intently. "The Gettysburg roots go deep," he said. "That picture over there on that wall, that's my West Point class of 1915, taken right here in Gettysburg on May 3, 1915. We visited here for three days, pored over every inch of the battlefield. There wasn't much about Gettysburg that we didn't study at the Point, and then we came down to the field itself and studied some more. During the First War, I was stationed here at Camp Colt. Tanks. I went from captain to lieutenant colonel, and I trained my men in discipline and all aspects of this new type of warfare, including machine guns, telegraphy, and the mechanics of tanks. The battlefield fascinated me. I suppose I must have read thirty, forty books on the subject—everything from the Comte de Paris to Haskell. I still read everything I can lay my hands on about the battle. In the old days, during the First War, I would climb into my old Dodge and tour the battlefield and explore every corner of the field and relive the battle. I am still impelled to do it, and from time to time, at dusk, I pack up and look around. Sometimes, I climb one-third of the way up one of those metal lookout towers that are scattered about the field. Don't go all the way up anymore. I had a heart attack, you know."

The President pulled a fresh sheet of paper toward him and swiftly, in a few pen strokes, drew the battle lines of Gettysburg, with the fishhook of the Union lines unmistakable. His eyes were brighter than ever now, and he seemed absorbed in the rapid sketch he had made. "Everybody will argue this battle—everybody," he said. "I think one would be safe in saying that Gettysburg was the highwater mark of the Confederacy, all right, even though you mustn't forget that Grant took Vicksburg the day after the battle ended here. Meade, of course, had his armies lined up and prepared to fall back to Pipe Creek, near Taneytown. Lee didn't have much here, really, and Meade had a great deal. Certainly Lee might have attacked Washington and Baltimore, thrown panic into the North and appealed to much Northern sentiment to end the war. Let me tell you, the sense of history is here. With you all the time. Oh, you just get me started on the Battle of Gettysburg and there's no telling where we'll end up!"

The President pulled another sheet of paper toward him and began to jot down some notes. "Back to work," he said.

The Old Wills House, where Lincoln spent the night before the dedication of the National Cemetery, lies two blocks down from Eisenhower's office and across from the Hotel Gettysburg, on the town's main traffic circle. It is now a museum of sorts, open to the public for a small fee. A room on the second floor is papered in bluish gray with a rose design, and contains a huge four-poster bed and heavy red draperies. A stovepipe hat lies on the bed, an old morning coat beside it. On a wooden table near one window are a white china pitcher and a towel rack, on which a few starched towels hang. In a chair by the bed, with a table before it, is a 6-foot-4, life-size wax image of Lincoln. He is a startling figure, seated at the table in his shirtsleeves, wearing glasses with thin metal frames, and holding a piece of paper. Visitors to the museum are asked to forget themselves for the moment, let reality slip away, and try to believe that the paper he holds is a rough draft of the Gettysburg Address. The 6-foot-4 image and the small, stuffy room produce a strange effect. When the lights dim, the men, women, and children huddled on chairs around the room fall into an uncomfortable silence. Recorded music is heard from somewhere, with the old strains of "The Battle Hymn of the Republic" becoming louder and louder. (Sane men keep telling themselves, "Hokum, hokum," but it is a losing fight, with the battlefield and the cemetery a scant half-mile away in one direction and a living ex-President a scant two blocks away in another.) Suddenly a voice is heard. It is an actor, recorded, impersonating Wills. "There are fresh towels here, Mr. President, and paper on the desk," says the voice. "May the night bring you a pleasant sleep." Then the voice of an actor impersonating Lincoln is heard saying, in measured tones, "Thank you, Wills, thank you. You are most kind." The silence becomes almost unbearable, but then one can hear the scratching of a pen on paper and, once again, the voice of Lincoln, quietly reading the words of the Gettysburg Address. When the lights go up, the wax Lincoln is still there at the table, the paper in his hand, and the people file out with odd looks on their faces.

The lady in charge of the Wills House, who has collected 50 cents from every adult and 25 cents from every child to visit there, refers to the wax figure as "Mr. Lincoln." There appears to be no doubt in her mind that Mr. Lincoln lives in the house. She says she believes that on certain days one can see his shirt front rise and fall as he breathes. Many visitors, she says, swear that Mr. Lincoln stands up several times during the queer séance to move around the room, and that when they reach out to touch him, they feel flesh.

The German Farm

Gettysburg in Adams County is in the heartland of some of the most beautiful farming country in the eastern United States, the southern tier counties of Pennsylvania. Scenic farms dot the counties of Franklin, Adams, York, Lancaster, Berks, and Chester.

"The German farm," wrote Dr. Benjamin Rush almost 200 years ago, "may be distinguished from the farm of the other citizens of the state by the superior size of their barns; the plain, but compact form of their houses; the height of their inclosures; the extent of their orchards; the fertility of their fields; the luxuriance of their meadows, and a general appearance of plenty and neatness in everything that belongs to them."

Dr. Rush (1745-1813) was a Philadelphian, one of the nation's first well-known physicians, a patriot and signer of the Declaration of Independence, and a civic leader in antislavery, penal reform, public health, and education.

introducing
Richard Harding Davis'
The Johnstown Flood

Drama and human interest aplenty are to be found in a great reporter's dispatches on the first spectacular disaster in American history.

The Johnstown Flood of 1889 not only was the first great spectacular disaster in American history, but it also was one of the first natural calamities to receive world attention because of the modern telegraph and newspaper. It was worthy of such attention. No one knows how many persons were killed, but the high count is 2,287 and the low count, 2,205. Only the Galveston, Texas, hurricane of 1900, which killed 5,000 persons, was more severe. A reported 98 Johnstown children lost both parents and 99 families were wiped out. Six of the Johnstown area's 35 physicians and the county sheriff were killed.

What happened is doubly tragic, because as modern engineer-writer William H. Shank of York has stated: "The story of the Johnstown Flood is a tale of carelessness, poor engineering and repeated warnings unheeded. It was a senseless, wasteful catastrophe that should never have happened."

In 1889 the Johnstown area had a population of about 22,000. Fourteen miles east of the borough was the 37-year-old, state-built South Fork Dam on a run which feeds the Little Conemaugh River. The Commonwealth spent $70,000 to build what was then the world's largest earthenwork dam, 931 feet wide and 272 feet thick at its base, to hold back 4.5 billion gallons, or 20 million tons, of water. The dam was 404 feet above Johnstown, and residents called it "our sword of Damocles." The lake behind it, with water as deep as 100 feet, extended for three miles and at some points was more than a mile wide. On the lakeside was the South Fork Fishing and Hunting Club, used by the millionaires of Pittsburgh.

The dam was up only a few years when the railroad replaced the cross-state canal system as the principal means of transportation between Phila-delphia and Pittsburgh. For twenty years the dam was neglected, and at the time it broke was privately owned.

Johnstown on the Little Conemaugh River was used to normal floods, but the spring of 1889 was something else. On April 6 Johnstown had a 14-inch snowfall. In May it had eleven days of rain, and then on Memorial Day between six and eight inches fell. About 4.3 billion tons of water fell on the 52-square-mile Allegheny watershed which fed into the South Fork Dam. At least twenty counties were hit with flooding. Williamsport was three-fourths under water. Clearfield, Lock Haven, Sunbury, and Lewistown were flooded. The Little Conemaugh overflowed, and Johnstown was flooded before the dam broke.

At 3:10 p.m. on May 31 the dam broke. "The dam did not burst. It simply moved away," John Parke, civil engineer at the dam, later wrote. "The water gradually ate into the embankment until there was nothing left but a frail bulwark of wood. This finally split asunder and sent the waters howling down the mountain." In less than an hour's time, a 30-foot wall of rushing, yellow-brown water reached Johnstown. The mass hit like "an armed maniac run-ning amoke," the *New York Sun* reported.

World attention focused on the disaster. The Red Cross, with Clara Barton herself, then 68, rushed to the scene. Governor James Beaver sent his adjutant general, Daniel H. Hastings, later to be governor, to Johnstown with 600 men to maintain order. The press came, including the general manager of the Associated Press, as if this were a civilian Battle of Gettys-burg.

One hoax that came out of the Johnstown Flood bears mention. A New York reporter supposedly wrote as his lead, "God looked down from the hills surrounding Johnstown today on an awesome scene of destruction." His editor, the hoax continues, wired back: "Forget flood. Interview God." In 1904 a similar story came out of the Harwick coal-mine disaster, which killed 179 men near Pittsburgh. Richard J. Beamish, then with the Philadel-phia *North American* but later Secretary of Commonwealth under Governor Pinchot, wrote, "God sits on the mountains of Harwick tonight while below in the valley death and sorrow lurk." The night editor, in this hoax, sup-posedly wired back: "See God. Get interview. Rush picture."

Because of the 1889 incident, the famed Johnstown inclined railway, with a precipitous grade of 71 percent for a distance of 900 feet, was built. The railway carried 4,000 persons to safety during a flood in 1932.

In 1936 Johnstown was flooded again. Twelve persons lost their lives and there was $50 million worth of property damage. About 9,000 persons were made homeless in this the last of the great Johnstown floods. A rumor circulated on that St. Patrick's Day that the Quemahoning Dam, containing 11.5 billion gallons of water and located 18 miles south of the borough, had broken. A famous picture was taken of thousands of persons fleeing the streets of Johnstown as the false alarm spread. It wasn't until 1938 that an $8.5 million project was erected to make Johnstown safe from flooding, but its world reputation endures to this day.

Richard Harding Davis (1864-1916) was one of the many noted reporters who covered the 1889 Flood. He was a native Philadelphian. His father was an editor of the *Public Ledger* and his mother, Rebecca Harding Davis, was a well-known novelist. Davis went to Episcopal Academy, then prep school at Bethlehem. Though he failed to graduate from Lehigh University, he was the handsome star halfback on its football team. When he was discharged from Lehigh in 1885, he told the faculty, "You don't think I am worthy to remain in this school. But in a few years you will find that I have gone farther than you will ever go."

Davis began his newspaper career with the *Philadelphia Record* and then switched to the *Philadelphia Press*. The *Press* had a relatively short history from 1857 to 1920, when it was united with the *Public Ledger,* which in turn was absorbed by the *Philadelphia Inquirer.* In its day the *Press* was famous for many things, including that of twice backing Abraham Lincoln for the Presidency.

Davis was in Philadelphia when the Johnstown disaster occurred, but he talked himself into a delegation of at least five *Press* reporters sent to the scene. He was only twenty-five, but already he had learned the skills of being readable, of interweaving drama and sensation, and of having a sure grasp for news. Before 1889 was over, Davis joined the *New York Sun,* and the following year became managing editor of *Harper's Weekly.* He covered the Spanish-American War, the Greco-Turkish War, the Boer War, the Russo-Japanese War, and World War I. Though he made no lasting impression in fiction, as a playwright he did have *Miss Civilization,* starring Ethel Barrymore, on Broadway in 1906. His talents remained journalistic, and his reports from Johnstown in 1889 offer ample evidence of what he could do.

The Johnstown Flood

by Richard Harding Davis

JOHNSTOWN, June 6—Oklahoma* is not rising more quickly than the temporary buildings of the workmen's city, which includes 5,000 men at least, and who are mingling the sounds of hammers on the buildings they are putting up for their temporary accommodation, with the crash of the buildings they are tearing down. It seemed almost a waste of energy two days ago, but the different gangs are already eating their way towards the heart of the great masses of wreckage that block the streets in every direction.

A dummy engine has already been placed in position on what was the main street, and all the large logs and rafters that the men can not move are fastened with ropes and chains, and drawn out by the engine into a clear space, where they are surrounded by smaller pieces of wood and burned. Carloads of pickaxes, shovels and barrows are arriving from Baltimore for the workmen.

The first store was opened today by a grocer named W. A. Kramer, whose stock, though covered with mud and still wet from the flood, has been preserved intact. So far the greater part of his things have been bought for relics. The other storekeepers are dragging out the debris in their shops and shoveling the mud from the upper stories onto inclined boards that shoot it into the street, but with all this energy it will be weeks before the streets are brought to sight again.

---

*Davis's use of "Oklahoma" has a double meaning. On April 22 a large strip of land was opened for settlement in the Oklahoma Territory and the "Sooners" made their famous dash from Kansas for claims. The name "Oklahoma" also came to mean a type of prefabricated, one-room house used in the territory. Some 1,500 houses in Johnstown were wrecked by the flood and hundreds of "Oklahomas" were erected.

As a proof of this there was found this morning a passenger car fully half a mile from its depot, completely buried beneath the floor and roofs of other houses. All that could be seen of it was one of the end windows over which was painted the impotent warning of "Any person injuring this car will be dealt with according to law."

The workmen find many curious things among the ruins, and are, it should be said to their credit, particularly punctilious about leaving them alone. One man picked up a baseball catcher's mask under a great pile of machinery, and the decorated front of the balcony circle of the Opera House was found with the chairs still immediately about its semi-circle, a quarter of a mile from the theatre's site.

The mahogany bar of Kirby's saloon, with its nickel plated rail, lies under another heap in the city park, and thousands of segars from Murr's manufactory are piled high in Vine street and are used as the only dry part of the roadway. Those of the people who can locate their homes have gathered what furniture and ornaments they can find together, and sit beside them looking like evicted tenants.

Telegraph poles have been reared in the city and another and better temporary bridge than either of the two now up is being erected by the militia....

[*Three remaining paragraphs complete Davis's report.*]

JOHNSTOWN, June 7*—One of the curious finds in the debris yesterday was two proofs from cabinet-size negatives of two persons, a man and a woman. The prints were found within two feet of each other in the ruins near the Merchant's Hotel. They were immediately recognized as portraits of Mamie Patton, formerly a Johnstown girl, and Charles De Knight, once a Pullman palace car conductor. The two were found dying together in a room in a Pittsburgh hotel several months ago, the woman having shot the man and then herself. She claimed that he was her husband. The dress in which the picture showed her was the same that she wore when she killed De Knight.

The Rev. Dr. D. C. Porter, of the Baptist Tabernacle in New York, spent yesterday here getting information on the spot for a sermon next Sunday. He took this course to avoid being misled by the exaggerations of the newspaper reports. After he had looked at the ruins five minutes, he concluded that the difficulty would be in the other direction—to exaggerate the newspaper reports sufficiently to make them equal the truth.

If Pennsylvania Railroad trains ever ran over tougher-looking tracks

---

*This piece appeared in the Philadelphia *Press*, June 8, without a byline, but its style indicates it was a Davis report.

than those used now through Johnstown, it must have been before people began to ride on it. The section from the North end of the bridge to the railroad station has a grade that wabbles between 50 and 500 feet to the mile and jerks back and forth sideways as though laid by a gang of intoxicated men on a dark night. When the first engine went over it, everybody held his breath and watched to see it tumble. These eccentricities are being straightened out, however, as fast as men and broken stone can do it.

The railroad bridge at Johnstown deserves attention beyond that which it is receiving on account of the way it held back the flood. It is one of the most massive pieces of masonry ever set up in this country. In a general way it is solid masonry of cut sandstone blocks of unusual size, the whole nearly 400 feet long, 40 wide and averaging about 40 deep. Seven arches of about 50 feet span are pierced through it, rising to within a few feet of the top and leaving massive piers down to the rock beneath. As the bridge crosses the stream diagonally, the arches pierce the mass in a slanting direction, and this greatly adds to the heavy appearance of the bridge. There has been some disposition to find fault with the bridge for being so strong, the idea being that if it had gone out there would have been no heaping up of buildings behind it, no fire, and fewer deaths. This is probably unfair, as there were hundreds of persons saved when their houses were stopped against the bridge by climbing out or being helped out upon the structure. If the bridge had gone too, the flood would have taken the whole instead of only half of Cambria City.*

The camera fiend has about ceased his wanderings. An order was issued yesterday from headquarters to arrest and put to work the swarms of amateur photographers who are to be found everywhere about the ruins. Those who will not work are to be taken uptown under guard. This order is issued to keep down the number of useless people and thus save the fast diminishing provisions for the workers.

A man who stood on the bluff and saw the first wave of the flood come down the valley tried to describe it. "I looked up," he said, "and saw something that looked like a wall of houses and trees up the valley. The

*Cambria City had been a borough, population 2,223, on the west end of Johnstown and was annexed into what is now the city. It should not be confused with Cambria Township, which still exists and was well away from the flooding. Cambria City suffered terrible damages, as Richard Harding Davis observed. Among those drowned were the grandparents and six aunts of a present-day Johnstown state representative, Joseph J. McAneny. The legislator's father and four uncles survived because they could swim. The grandmother, mother, and aunt of Cong. John P. Saylor were caught in the midst of the flood and couldn't swim, but they were rescued. Saylor has been Johnstown's congressman since 1949. As a young man he knew Gifford Pinchot, and today he is the foremost nationally known conservationist in Congress.

next moment Johnstown seemed coming toward me. It was lifted right up and in a minute was smashing against the bridge and the houses were flying in splinters across the top and into the water beyond."

A 13-year-old girl, pretty and with golden hair, wanders from morgue to morgue looking for ten of a family of eleven, she being the sole survivor.

There were half a dozen bulldogs in one house that was heaped up in the wreck some distance above the bridge. They were loose amid the debris, and it is said by those who claim to have seen it that after fighting among themselves, they turned upon the people near them and were tearing and biting them until the flames swept over the place.

[*In the next three paragraphs, Davis describes the railroad situation in Johnstown, and then he concludes his piece.*]

Zill Gruber, of Kernville, on Friday morning last, had jet black hair, moustache and beard. That night he had a battle with the waters. On Saturday morning his hair and beard began to turn gray, and they are now well streaked with white. Gruber attributes the change to his awful Friday night's experience.

JOHNSTOWN, June 10—In telling of the daily resurrection of the dead here and of the experiences of those who survived, little time has been found to say a word for the less striking acts of kindness and charity with which the people of the place are helping to make life more bearable for themselves and for those who have come to assist them. The spirit of the disaster seems to have left a chastening touch on every man, woman and child who has fallen under its shadow. You hear no quarreling, you see few acts of selfishness, the children—what children remain—go unscolded, and the busiest of men find time to answer questions politely, if briefly. Too much can not be said in praise of these men in authority, who have worked unceasingly, without pay and without rest, at their self-imposed tasks. In their hardest working minutes they keep a pleasant word or a kind look for everyone. Even the railroad employees seem to have fallen under the spell. One man, an operator in the Baltimore and Ohio depot, has been on duty for the last three consecutive days, and he is as quiet and patient in his answers as though he were a gentleman of leisure and not doing the work of three men.

One family, a widow, Mrs. William Watkins, and her three daughters, who live on Adams Street, have turned their home into a free hotel where everyone is welcome. The food is furnished them by the committee of distribution and they cook and serve it from seven in the morning until late at night. They welcomed the doctors of the Philadelphia relief party, who had not had a meal for thirty hours, as though they were blood relatives. Every housekeeper can appreciate what labor cooking meals all day for half-famished men entails, and yet these people refuse every offer of money and serve as many of the workmen, militia and relief workers as come to their doors.

One of the Philadelphia relief party stopped in front of a cottage the other day and asked for a couple of crackers, a box of which stood in a window. The woman who owned the house went inside and was gone so long that the Philadelphian started off on his way. As he did so, the woman ran to the door and called after him, "Don't go, your dinner is almost ready."

Without a word she had set to work and prepared the best dinner her larder allowed and was quite indignant when the stranger offered to pay for it. "I'd be a queer woman," she said, "if I took money for the food that people are sending us for nothing. It's little enough any of us can do, Heaven knows."

These instances give one an idea of the sentiment of the place.

[*Davis concludes the article by describing how food and clothing are distributed to the victims of the flood. He comments, "The act of feeding 12,000 a day lacks the easy grace of an afternoon tea, and the way canned meats, sardine boxes, loaves of bread and bundles of tea fly through the air and are shoved into the baskets of the refugees would make a delicately organized nature lose its appetite for a week."*]

Part II
Pennsylvania Industry: Workers and Entrepreneurs

feel the excitement of
John T. Faris'
Pithole City, Pa., Oil Town of 1865

The great days of Pennsylvania oil lasted from 1859, when "Colonel" Edwin L. Drake made the first strike, until 1891. The brief but colorful career of one oil town typified the rapidly fluctuating fortunes caused by the bonanza.

Edwin Laurentine Drake was a most unlikely character to launch the great American oil industry in northwestern Pennsylvania. He was, first of all, a bogus colonel. His background consisted of being a steamboat clerk, a hotel employee, a dry goods salesman, and a railroad express agent and conductor.

At age 40 and in ill health, Drake had one thing going for him—he had free passes on the railroad. Because of this, some speculators titled him "colonel" and sent him to Titusville, Pennsylvania, to drill for oil. Drake was lucky enough to hire an old salt-well driller, William A. Smith of Salina. "Uncle Billy," as he was known, made his own drill tools, supplied the labor of his 15-year-old son free, and was willing to drill for $2.50 a day. On August 27, 1859, Uncle Billy reached 69.5 feet and hit oil. The strike set off so much excitement that no one measured the production of the well, but it was probably eight to ten barrels daily. A few feet to the left or right and Drake might have missed the oil, and the Titusville area would have lain dormant for years.

It was known in 1755 that there was oil in Pennsylvania. In the 1840s petroleum from the salt wells was bottled for medicine and also used for illumination. What Drake proved was that a dependable suppl' of this vital natural resource could be obtained by drilling.

Drake neglected to obtain patents on his ideas, and thus didn't profit from his luck. He served as a justice of the peace and an oil buyer in Titusville, but left there in 1863. Just fourteen years after he struck oil, he was so crippled by neuralgia and destitute living in Bethlehem that the Legislature voted him a $1,500 annual pension. Drake died in 1880, and in 1901 his body was removed for burial in Titusville. During the centennial of the great strike, Governor Lawrence officially appointed Drake a "colonel" in the Pennsylvania National Guard.

Oil opened up northwestern Pennsylvania. By 1864 the area was producing 6,000 barrels a day. One striker made about $1.7 million, another close to $5 million. Fortunes were lusty, for land was valuable and oil sold for about $4 a barrel. Today's prices, inflation and all, are only $4.49 for Pennsylvania Crude, which is a lighter, finer oil than most other American petroleum, which sells for $2.94 a barrel. Among the early speculators were Andrew Carnegie, John Wilkes Booth, John D. Rockefeller, J. N. Pew, and Milton Hershey's father. Ida M. Tarbell was born in Erie County two years before Drake hit oil. She graduated from Allegheny College, and in 1904 published her famous two-volume *History of the Standard Oil Company.*

The great days of Pennsylvania oil, when as much as 31.4 million barrels annually was produced, lasted until 1891. By then Texas, Oklahoma, California, and Louisiana had taken over the bulk of the industry. From 1859 through 1968, however, the 30 western Pennsylvania counties, with 287,000 oil wells, produced 1.3 billion barrels. There is an estimated 59.2 million barrels of Pennsylvania Crude yet in the ground that could be tapped. In 1968 Pennsylvania produced 4.1 million barrels, or what it did 100 years previously.

Striking oil still is an adventure in Pennsylvania. Some 700 wells a year are dug, going down an average of 2,200 feet, or more than 30 times the depth of Drake's lucky strike. The big business today, however, is oil refining. The state, ranking fifth in the nation, has 13 refineries, with a capacity of 620,000 barrels a day. Underneath the ground it has almost 60,000 miles of oil and gas pipeline, and on the surface there are 12,000 gasoline stations to fill the motorist's tank and check the oil.

The human drama of the oil excitement is best told in stories like this about Pithole, which was written by John T. Faris in his 1924 Harper and Brothers' book, *The Romance of Forgotten Towns.* Faris (1871-1949) was an ordained Presbyterian minister from Missouri who lived much of his life in Philadelphia and became well known as a Sunday School magazine editor, lecturer, and free-lance writer. He wrote more than sixty books, including many about his adopted state such as *Seeing Pennsylvania,* 1919.

Pithole, Pennsylvania, population 15,000 in 1865, lasted barely 500 days, or as long as the Frazier and Homestead wells flowed. Enthusiasm among the speculators, many of whom were returning Civil War veterans, was so high that the first oil pipeline of its kind was laid from Pithole to the closest railroad 5.5 miles away. By January of 1866, however, the boom was over, though it wasn't until 1935 that the last remnant building, the Methodist

Church, was torn down. Pithole literally reverted to being just an open field on a hillside.

In 1969 Governor Raymond P. Shafer dedicated the $1 million Drake Well Museum at Titusville. Meanwhile, the Pithole property, twelve miles from Titusville, has been donated to the Commonwealth for a historical site by James B. Stevenson, publisher of the *Titusville Herald*. Stevenson, past president of the Pennsylvania Newspaper Publishers Association, was named to the Pennsylvania Historical and Museum Commission in 1952 and has been its able chairman since 1962.

Pennsylvania Horseless Carriages

The oil industry ushered in the automobile era in Pennsylvania. In 1900 Pennsylvania ranked third in the nation with a production of 74 automobiles. In the heyday of garage manufacturing, the Pullman auto was made in York, the Bantam in Butler, the Autocar in Ardmore, and the Wright in New Cumberland.

Pennsylvania lost its predominance in auto manufacturing, thanks to the genius of Henry Ford, Walter Chrysler, and others in Michigan. Today only parts are made in the Commonwealth, at least until Chrysler sets up its plant at Stanton in western Pennsylvania in the mid-1970s.

The automobile united the farflung Commonwealth as much as any invention has, but it also led to troubles. The modern problems are crowded highways and traffic accidents. In 1968 Pennsylvania had 6.6 million drivers, or 1.4 million more than it had in 1962; it had 4.9 million cars, or almost a million more than in 1962.

The death rate on the highways has been enormous, and many more Pennsylvanians have lost their lives in collisions than in battle in the nation's wars. From 1951 through 1969, there were 36,521 known traffic fatalities. The death mark for 1969 was 2,401. Amazingly enough, the worst year was 1930, when the low number of motor vehicles was offset by few policemen and fewer traffic regulations. That year, 2,566 Pennsylvanians died on the highways.

Complete accident statistics are of recent origin. In 1969, Insurance Commissioner George F. Reed did note the turmoil that existed on Pennsylvania highways in 1968. There were 2,410 persons killed in 2,122 fatal accidents; 138,389 injured in 88,041 accidents; $171.9 million worth of property damage in 189,500 other accidents, and, in total, an insurance cost of just under a half-billion dollars.

Pithole City, Pa., Oil Town of 1865

by John T. Faris

In the days of the oil excitement in Pennsylvania, when fortunes were being made—and lost—overnight, and towns were undergoing tremendous booms, the attention of prospectors was drawn to every watercourse in Crawford, Warren and Venango Counties. Then towns like Oil City and Titusville had booms which proved to be permanent. But there were other towns whose booms came to nothing, in spite of wonderful promise.

The most spectacular boom—followed by the most awful, thumping fall—was experienced by Pithole City, on Pithole Creek, a few miles from its junction with the Allegheny River.

In spite of the fact that Pithole Creek was not far from the rich lands of Oil Creek, and from Oil City, which was located at the mouth of the creek, prospectors were so long in learning of oil there that maps and circulars of the oil country, prepared not only for proper commercial purposes, but also to lure the dollars of the unwary, either gave the creek without a name, or assigned no importance to the name.

But all this was changed by the discovery of a gushing well in May, 1865. Then began a rapid development that led to the growth of Pithole City, the marvelous oil town, the beginning of whose meteoric career was told in a little book printed in Pithole City itself. The writer was enthusiastic, though he was giving his message when the town was on the downgrade:

"Two years ago the traveler passing through the township of Cornplanter would have found it a barren and almost uninhabited district. The few backwoodsmen it sustained depended more on their rifles and the products of the forest for a living than their farms. Money existed as a general thing, only in the imagination; greenbacks were unknown, and less than two years since we feel safe in saying that not more than $100,000 was in circulation in the county contiguous to Oil Creek. The settlers who then inhabited this region little dreamed of the vast treasure lying beneath their farms, but in their peaceful homes cared not for the outside world, and the idea of thriving and populous cities springing up on their farms never entered their heads.

"But upon the discovery of oil by the United States Petroleum Company on the Thomas Holmden farm, an immense business sprang up as if by magic along the entire Pithole Valley. The necessity of a business center soon became apparent. The Holmden farm naturally became the center of trade. Thither thousands daily rushed, bearing with them capital from every state. It was not an uncommon thing, at this time, for $1 million to change hands in a single day. Fortune seekers from all parts of America and Europe were attracted. On every train they came rushing to 'the land of derricks.' From the railway terminus they scattered on rickety horses or rickety coaches over rickety roads, in search of some spot where the 'grease' should shower upon them untold millions.

"Buildings were erected rapidly. Solidity and elegance were sacrificed to rapidity of construction. But a people who displayed such 'go-ahead-ativeness' in the beginning of an enterprise might safely be trusted with its completion, and the Pithole City of today is not the offspring of speculative excitement, but the result of Anglo-Saxon energy."

Here is a contemporary description of the city—which soon contained from 12,000 to 15,000 inhabitants:

"It is a wooden town; not a brick or stone house in it. The streets are narrow, with but a single plank for a sidewalk, and in many instances the plank is so far beneath the surface that more than ordinary length of limb is required to reach it. The buildings on either side are of every size and shape imaginable, from a four-story hotel to the diminutive stand of gingerbread or peanut merchant. The smell of new lumber, fresh paint, and the 'crude' is everywhere discernible. Here may be seen a building which is neither sided, floored, nor finished, but the roof is up. From the peak swings a sign, informing the public that Oil Leases will there be bought and sold, if the building gets finished and the owner gets time."

Pithole was not on a railroad. It was necessary to transport oil by wagon over roads that, after a rain, were all but bottomless. A pipe line was built down Pithole Creek to the Allegheny River; its fall of 360 feet in seven miles made the movement of oil satisfactory. But the people were not content until they had a railroad of their own—the Oil City and Pithole Branch Railroad, 16 miles long, built at a cost of $800,000. The line was built and operation of trains was begun within six months—rapid work for those days. Another road—the Reno, Oil Creek and Pithole Railroad—was begun, the bed was graded, and ties were laid, but it was abandoned after a time.

Until the Pithole City Water Company began operations, water was retailed on the streets for $1 a barrel, or 10 cents a pail. At times $1 was paid for a pailful, while 10 cents was the price of a cup of the necessary fluid. But when 11,000 feet of three-inch pipe took water to all parts of Pithole, from the reservoir above the town, prices fell.

Three or four hotels, which cost from $40,000 to $100,000, were opened. There was talk of building an expensive structure for the use of the post office, but this was one of the plans destined never to be carried out.

The post office was not opened until there were 10,000 people in town. The first mail sent out contained more than 1,000 letters, while there were five times as many in the fourth mail. In 10 days the office force handled 10,000 letters a day. It was recorded that, when business was at the height in 1865, it was found necessary to throw open every window to accommodate the crowd. Evidently doors were not sufficient as exits. At times a late comer, who entered through a window, noting the length of the line before the general delivery window, would buy himself a place near the front, and so save himself what he thought was valuable time. Official records show that for many months the Pithole post office was third in size in Pennsylvania; only Philadelphia and Pittsburgh did more business.

A visitor to such an oil town left on record his breezy impressions of the life there:

"Whew! What smells so? Nothing but the gaseous wealth of the oily region. But pigs, mud, no sidewalks! Ah, but you are on the riverbank yet. Business cannot afford to wash the ways down which oil vessels run nor to scrub their leaky sides. Wait until you reach the main thoroughfare, the grand promenade, the fashionable streets of the place. I waited. That is, I walked between wells and oil yards, barns and farms, along the shipping ways, keeping my bearings as I could. I found the main street, the promenade, the leading thoroughfare. It was bare of trotting buggies. It was bare of handsome carriages. It was not at all dusty. Upon one side rose a ledge of shale rocks, crowded on top with the primeval forest. At the immediate foot ran the street. No, it didn't run. It couldn't run; neither could it stand still. It was just too thick for water, and wholly too thin for land. Horses dragging heavy teams with a few barrels of oil sank below the scum and tugged on. Horsemen, booted to the middle, floundered this way and that. The narrowest plank walk, filled with hurrying men, muddy and eager, pushed by. A slip of a team horse, and his effort at recovery, sent the liquid, oily, earthy mixture of the street in showers among the walkers. Everybody was used to it."

The story of speculation has been repeated hundreds of times since, often with far less reason. Oil leases were bought at large prices and were sold for prices much larger. Farmers found themselves looking at more money than they had ever dreamed of. Bank accounts grew miraculously, and losses and failures came just as suddenly.

Many wells once thought promising proved failures, some which had been bonanza producers soon gave out. The farm on which the original discovery was made sold, at one time, for $1.6 million; then it became worthless. Word came of prospects elsewhere that were more encouraging, and the inhabitants of Pithole City began to steal away. Within a few months the city was all but deserted. It did not even have opportunity to figure in the census of 1870. In fact, the very year that witnessed the birth of Pithole also saw its rapid decline.

In 1891, when Pennsylvania's oil production reached its height, Pithole was but a shadow. And today the city that was once famous not only in America but in other lands, is only a memory of millions earned, of perhaps more millions lost.

introducing
Paul B. Beers'
The Mollie Maguires

In an era when the barons of industry ruled
supreme, wages were a pittance, and ethnic
animosities ran high, desperate Irish coal miners
resorted to terrorism.

"On no account should anyone in old age come to this state, because the
work here is difficult and different from that in the Old Country," an immigrant Wilkes-Barre miner named Lawrence wrote to a friend in Wales in
1869. "Eight cars a day are filled here, and there are two tons in each car
making up sixteen tons a day. It is stone coal here, eighteen inches thick and
sharp as a knife."

Stanley Covelski, the spitball ace from Shamokin, recalled in 1969 when
he was elected to baseball's Hall of Fame that the laborer's lot was grim
even as late as 1902. "When I was twelve," he said, "I started working in
the mines eleven hours a day, six days a week, for $3.75 a week." He would
have spent the rest of his life in the mines if he hadn't had a strong right arm.

Pennsylvania was the American capital of the Industrial Revolution, because nature had been lavish to her. "In point of fact, it may be doubted if
there is on the earth's surface another area of 43,000 square miles, which,
considering all things, is better fitted by nature to yield large returns to
labor," wrote Henry George, a native Philadelphian, in 1886. But to develop
and reap the rewards from coal, iron, steel, coke, tin, slate, glass, oil, timber,
railroading, and many of the other necessities, labor was pushed to the extreme. Clever, and often just rash, entrepreneurs risked all they had; and
those who succeeded, seldom without exploitation, gained fortunes.

Pennsylvania became the land of the asthmatic, crippled workman and the
philosophizing, philanthropic millionaire. Mountains of culm banks, 10,000

miles of railroad track, 1,200 miles of hand-dug canal, untold tons of steel, and denuded forests—Pennsylvanians took 28 million acres of woodland and chopped it down to just 25,000 acres of original forest within three generations' time—attest to the back-breaking day's work that was done. It is unlikely that the slaves of the Pharaohs labored more diligently and longer than did the free citizens of Pennsylvania.

Work came first, and all the institutions of man—politics, the church, education, family life—bowed to it, and occasionally twisted their principles to keep it first.

Pennsylvania in the 1880s burst with riches, but Henry George observed such a neighborhood: "The employees were lodged in dreary, monotonous rows of company houses, divided by thin partitions into from two to four tenements of from two to four small rooms. These houses are of wood, built in a cheap and flimsy manner, usually unfinished inside and unpainted outside. The only evidence that there is such a thing as paint in the world—as for whitewash, that seems to be unknown—is generally the company number painted in bold figures; but in some rare cases the doors, and in still rarer cases the whole exterior, has at some time or other been treated to a coat of dull-colored mixture which serves as an apology for paint." The rent for such slum housing averaged $5 a month for a workman earning $20 to $35 a month.

Management need not bargain or compromise with labor because it had the upper hand, controlling government with the complacent support of the farmers and the emerging middle class. The North's triumph in the Civil War ensured the domination of the Republican Party, and the Democratic Party all too often was either the captive of the GOP or in even more reactionary hands than the majority party. The state's leading Democrat in 1875, Senator William Wallace, thought it his duty to prosecute 56 strikers in Clearfield and send 36 of them to jail for doing what today would be no crime.

There was a political, religious, educational, economic, and ethnic establishment clamping down upon Pennsylvania Irish, Italian, Slavic, Czech, Hungarian, and Polish workingmen, making physical violence often the only protest possible. George F. Baer, the Reading coal boss, in 1901 expressed the sentiments: "The rights and interests of the laboring man will be protected and cared for, not by the labor agitators, but by the Christian men to whom God in his infinite wisdom has given the control of the property interests of this country." Finley Peter Dunne spoofed that incredible remark by having Mr. Hennessy ask, "What d'ye think iv th' man down in Pennsylvania who says th' Lord an' him is partners in a coal mine?" And Mr. Dooley answers, "Has he divided th' profits?"

It was incredibly fortunate that the American ideal of the open society—of the melting pot and upward mobility—withstood sixty-five years of labor-management and ethnic polarization. Perhaps more credit should be given to life's diversions, like sports and drinking, two pastimes in which Pennsylvanians achieved a national reputation. Maybe it was just the promise of American democracy that prevented all the energies of the haves and have-nots from totally destroying one another, a dream that cut off the turbulence and rancor before permanent bitterness set in.

The record of legislation is deceptive. In 1848 Pennsylvania passed the nation's first child labor law and was the first state to ban garnishment, or the attachment of wages. The ten-hour work day became law in 1848; the eight-hour day in 1868. Unions in 1872 were given the right to strike without charges of criminal conspiracy leveled against their members, but the proviso was carefully drawn that strikers couldn't prohibit others, even scabs, from working. Women coal miners were banned in 1885, and finally compulsory education was adopted in 1895, though it took another twenty years to get effective child labor legislation.

What actually happened is different. The coal industry didn't get an eight-hour day until the 1920s; the steel industry until the 1930s. Injunctions against strikes were commonplace until the 1930s. Blacklisting and "yellow dog" contracts, or those prohibiting workers from joining a union, weren't outlawed until the 1930s.

Because of the civil violence, ethnic bigotry, and political repression, sides were quickly drawn. The Noble Order of the Knights of Labor, the United Mine Workers, the American Federation of Labor (with its Pennsylvania affiliation in 1902), and the Congress of Industrial Organizations either were founded or were given much of their early support in Pennsylvania.

Organized business had industrial cabals of all sorts, the National Association of Manufacturers in 1895 and then Joe Grundy's Pennsylvania Manufacturers Association in 1911. Unfair voting laws were maintained for decades. Lawmakers were bought off for special-interest legislation. The hated Coal and Iron Police, with its deputized and armed industry policemen, lasted until 1935. The State Police, the first in the nation in 1905 and now of high repute, was formed essentially as a force to keep order on the labor scene, and workmen called troopers "the Cossacks." The politics of reactionism was at times almost unbelievable. Pennsylvania to this day hasn't ratified the Sixteenth Amendment for the national income tax. At a time when a sixth of all Pennsylvanians were foreign-born, the 1893 Legislature nevertheless could pass a resolution: "Resolve, that we recognize in the constant influx of an ignorant and vicious class of immigrants a great and growing evil and highly injurious to American workingmen and dangerous to American institutions."

The Know-Nothings in the mid-1800s, the Ku Klux Klan in the 1920s and 1930s, and the extreme right wing in the 1950s and 1960s all received substantial support in Pennsylvania. At the other end of the political spectrum, minority ethnic movements, the Communist and Socialist parties, and the far left never attained much leverage.

With a frustrated, often half-illiterate working class confronting a stalwart establishment, Pennsylvania had repeated strife. In intensity and loss of life, the violence far exceeded that experienced in the 1960s from racial and urban disturbances.

In the 1844 anti-Catholic riots in Philadelphia, 13 persons were slain and 50 wounded, 30 homes damaged and two churches burned. In the 1877 railroad riots, at least 32 Pennsylvanians were killed, and in Pittsburgh 1,600 railroad cars and 126 locomotives destroyed. Unofficially, 16 persons were killed and 60 injured in the Homestead Riot of 1892. In the Lattimer Massacre of 1897, sheriff's men killed 19 Polish, Slovak, and Lithuanian miners and wounded 40. In 1902 at least 14 were killed in the anthracite strike, and a steel strike at McKees Rocks in 1909 took 13 lives.

Religious bias was coupled with antilabor and ethnic opposition. It can be argued that Pennsylvania has been a melting pot, but a slow one. The first Catholic to make high state office was Lieutenant Governor Tom Kennedy in 1934, but the first Catholic governor, David L. Lawrence, wasn't elected until 1958. No Pole, Slovak, Hungarian, or Italian yet has run for governor. There has been only one Pennsylvania U.S. Senator of the Catholic faith, Francis J. Myers of Philadelphia, 1945-1951. And there were only a handful of Catholic mayors of major Pennsylvania cities until after World War II.

Today's Pennsylvania labor scene is a far cry from the bloodied past. The tory dinosaurs of business are gone, while many contemporary labor leaders were schooled in the enlightened statesmanship of such great Pennsylvanians as William B. Wilson and Philip Murray. Employment is high, and wages are competitive; the memories of the destructive brawls of the past contribute to the relative labor peace of today. In 1880 alone Pennsylvania had 304 strikes; in 1967 and 1968 it had a total of but 131. A Federal Reserve Bank study revealed that from 1956 to 1966 Pennsylvania ranked tenth as a high-strike state, not first as it once did.

The Mollie Maguire story is an integral part of Pennsylvania's labor, ethnic, and religious heritage. This article appeared in the August 1966 issue of *American History Illustrated.*

The
Mollie Maguires

by Paul B. Beers

In the spring of 1877 about three dozen Mollie Maguires languished in the Pottsville and Mauch Chunk jails in the anthracite coal region of Pennsylvania. The terrorism of the Mollies was over. The hangings were to come and the legend of Mollie Maguireism was to be further embellished, but the days of violence were gone.

The Mollie Maguires were unlike any other ruffians in American history. For fifteen years these Irish workmen flourished, denying their villainy but killing and burning, plotting and mutilating, in an attempt to protest the dismal life of the unskilled, immigrant laborer in the coal fields.

No one knows how many Mollies and Mollie supporters there were. Estimates range from 300 to 3,000. The *New York Times* described the organization that spring of 1877 as being "yet powerful," and until this century many have taken the word of the prosecutors that the Mollies subdued the Pennsylvania hard-coal towns with their violence, and even exercised much political influence.

Under the guise of the legitimate, fraternal Ancient Order of Hibernians, the secret society of Mollies was formed in the late 1850's and early 1860's in the Pottsville and Mauch Chunk region. Few Hibernians were Mollies, but all the Mollies, to the embarrassment of the national Order of Hibernians, were Hibernians at one time or another. Many of the Mollies were labor agitators and had belonged to the short-lived Workingmen's Benevolent Association, a primitive miners' union, but the WBA was never controlled by the Mollies.

The Mollies were an Irish gang, not an Irish Mafia. They took their name presumably from a legendary Irish widow who pitted herself against English landlords back on the old sod. In irregular and clandestine units, they met at taverns in the coal towns to drink and swap stories. Each unit was headed by a bodymaster, or chairman, and there was a $3 initiation fee. The code of recognition was the right hand to the right hip and, as a reply, the forefinger and thumb of the left hand on the left ear. Most Mollies were simple workmen, some illiterate and none well-educated. They knew nothing of the great issues and forces of their time and they did not associate themselves, politically or ideologically, with anyone else. They plotted, not to make social change, but to settle personal vendettas, to punish unpopular mine bosses, and to war upon rival cliques of Welsh, English, and German workers and barroom toughs. Their violence was clumsy and senseless.

Mollie Maguire country was centered in Schuylkill and Carbon counties, about sixty-five miles northwest of Philadelphia. The area includes Northumberland, Columbia and Luzerne counties and is bounded today by the Susquehanna River, Route 22, and the Northeast Extension of the Pennsylvania Turnpike.

In the 1860's and 1870's all the worst effects of the Industrial Revolution showed up in the coal fields. Men, women, and children were exploited to bring the black diamond to the surface and get it to the markets in Philadelphia and New York, and the beautiful Appalachian mountains and streams were ripped and blackened in the process. The coal and railroad companies never hesitated to add to their monopolization and suzerainty of the industry, the people, and the land, and they usually got helpful bills through the state legislature without much difficulty. Life in the coal towns was dismal. The greed of the absentee landowners and managers triumphed over the simple pieties of the entrapped laborers. Economic oppression was coupled with religious and ethnic discrimination, and out of this hopeless condition arose the inarticulate protest of the Mollies.

From Pine Grove north to Scranton and from Lehighton west to Shamokin, impoverished miners' families lived in dilapidated company houses, a muddy block away from the coal breaker. With wage coupon books, the wives bartered in the "pluck-me" company stores for overpriced food and merchandise. Until the 1900's few miners' children received any formal education, and it is not surprising that among the least educated Mollies were the ones who grew up in the Pennsylvania mine patches, not in Ireland.

Children were expected to work. A lad started in picking coal as a "breaker boy" and before he was old enough to have a beard he was in the pits from dawn to dusk. The minimum working age in Pennsylvania in the 1870's was twelve, and there was no prohibition against using women in the mines. (One of the Mollies, Mike Doyle, was injured severely when he was a boy in the mines.) In 1870 there were 9,051 boys employed in the hard-coal fields. For a minimum 10-hour day, they earned an average annual wage of $132.21, according to a government study at the time.

Wages were low in the mines and layoffs frequent. "There must be more than 100 cents in a dollar, as there has been more than that amount of percentage taken off already," a miner groaned to a reporter in February of 1877 when the mines announced another pay cutback. The average year's wage was about $400, and the pay scale fell steadily during the 1870's.

Law and order was maintained by the Coal and Iron Police, who were private employees of companies but also were commissioned by the state after 1865. These officers earned the hatred of all laborers, but especially those at the bottom, the Irish.

Most of the clergy, the press, and the political leadership in the coal region were subservient to the coal and railroad barons. They saw the depravity but preached rectitude, not reform. For decades even the initial steps needed for improving the lot of the lower class were effectively thwarted. Store-order paychecks were not outlawed until 1881 — fifty years after Great Britain banned them — and the "pluck-me" stores were not abolished in Pennsylvania until 1891. Pennsylvania was one of the last major states to pass a compulsory education bill in 1895, and children still worked in the mines until World War I. The Coal and Iron Police lasted until 1935.

Mollie Maguireism sprang from this social and economic background. The brutality of the Mollies came from the brutality of their lives. During the 1870's alone 2,248 miners were killed and crippled in the anthracite pits.

While the Mollies were in jail that May of 1877, seven men were killed and seven injured in an explosion at the nearby Wadesville shaft. Eight children were left fatherless, and some of the remains of newly wed Thomas Connors of Summit Hill were taken home to his bride in his dinner can. Back in 1869 in Plymouth, ninety-two men and nineteen children under age 14 were killed in the Avondale disaster, the worst in American anthracite history. The mine was poorly ventilated and had only one exit. The Legislature hurriedly passed a law to ban such outrageous mining practices, but the law went unenforced. The coroner's jury for the Wadesville tragedy reported that the ventilation was faulty and that lives could have been saved if there had been the required number of escapes. The coal company was censured and a mine inspector was charged with gross neglect of duty. The day before the hanging, the Harleigh Mine near Hazleton had a cave-in. Joseph Pearsons, father of seven, and James Murrish, a bachelor, were killed.

Death was common in the coal regions in the 1870's. The Mollies added only arson and terrorism. To some intended victims, they sent crude "coffin notices." Others they struck down without warning. Their plans often went awry, for the Mollies were never more than a disorganized gang, not a syndicate of criminals. Some of the men slain had offended members of the Mollies. Others died because they represented the coal and railroad companies and the public authorities that were making life miserable, often purposely, for Irish laborers and their families.

Many well-known figures were cut down. Alexander W. Rea, a former newspaperman and superintendent of the Locust Mountain Coal and Iron Company, was slain at Centralia. David Muhr, a colliery superintendent in Foster Township, was ambushed within 200 yards of his mine. Henry H. Dunne, a Pottsville mine superintendent and highly respected Episcopal vestryman, was shot to death while riding in his rig. William H. Littleshales, a mine superintendent, was one of the few robbed before he was killed. Tamaqua Policeman Benjamin F. Yost was shot as he lighted a street lamp. Burgess George Major of Mahanoy City was killed in a street fight. Mine foreman Frank W. Langdon was stoned to death at Audenried, near Hazleton, and a year later near that same place George K. Smith, a mine owner, was murdered in his home before his family. Bartender William Williams was slain presumably because his brother, a mill foreman in Tamaqua, had sacked three Mollies. Thomas Sanger, son of a Methodist minister, was murdered because he was a mine boss at Raven Run. William Uren, a 22-year-old laborer and Sunday school teacher, was slain simply because he happened to be with Sanger when the assailants struck. Henry Yiengst, a boss carpenter in Mahanoy City, refused to hire Irishmen, and he had his skull fractured and his tongue pulled out. Charles Green, a school teacher in Centralia, made some disparaging remarks about the Mollies and had his ears cut off.

The crackdown on the Mollies began in 1874 and was initiated chiefly by Franklin B. Gowen, the boss of the Reading coal and railroad interests. Gowen was a dynamic figure in his forties, a second-generation Irishman himself, a prominent state Democrat and even past district attorney of Schuylkill County. As the D.A. in the Pottsville area in 1863 and 1864, Gowen prosecuted few Mollies, but in the 1870's, after he had become one of Pennsylvania's most aggressive business leaders, he developed a fanatical hatred of the Mollies. He schemed to link the outlaws with the miners' union movement and thus deal organized labor a severe blow.

Gowen hired the Pinkerton National Detective Agency, which assigned James McParlan, alias James McKenna, to infiltrate the Mollie organization. McParlan, a 29-year-old native of County Armagh and an engaging 5-foot-8 brawler with a gift for blarney, was just the man for undercover work. Without much difficulty he moved into the coal regions, had himself initiated into the Mollies, and took a room in the very household of ringleader Muff Lawler. McParlan spent thirty months in the Shenandoah area, sent intelligence back to the Pinkertons and Gowen, and may have helped to perpetrate some of the Mollie crimes just to get additional data. Just when the Mollies began to suspect the double-dealing of McParlan, he escaped. That was in March 1876, but the first Mollie arrests had been made the prior September and the trials began in January 1876.

With the first verdicts of guilty, Mollie Maguireism was dead, though few suspected it at the time. The trials were held in the county seats of Schuylkill and Carbon counties, Pottsville and Mauch Chunk (now known as Jim Thorpe). Admittedly the trials were stacked against the Mollies, though some distinguished attorneys, such as Congressman John B. Reilly and Lin Bartholomew, represented the defendants. Gowen the spellbinder—it is said spectators crowded the Philadelphia Academy of Music just to hear him read the Reading's annual stockholders' report—joined the battery of prosecuting attorneys and brilliantly, if not always accurately, drew the most damning portraits of the accused. McParlan returned to testify, and the antagonistic Pennsylvania Dutchmen on the juries readily accepted much insufficient and suspected evidence to condemn the Irishmen.

One of the oddities of the entire Mollie episode is that the prosecution had little difficulty getting captured Irishmen to turn informer. It is just as puzzling that the Mollies at large only grumbled and let the songbirds get away with it. Frank McHugh, of Mahanoy City, turned state's evidence and did ask to be jailed for his own safety at the time of the hanging. Manus "Kelly the Bum" Cull, former Mollie leader Muff Lawler, Dennis Canning, and Patrick Butler all told on their colleagues and lived to see another day.

The key turncoat was an improbable character named James Aloysius Xavier Kerrigan, a 4-foot-11-inch roughneck who participated in at least two murders and then provided enough details to doom five Mollies. Kerrigan had been a hero in his day. He fought at Shiloh, Antietam, and Gettysburg during the Civil War, and he earned the nickname of "Powderkeg" for allegedly placing a keg of dynamite on some hot coals in a mine slope after his fellow miners would not move over to give him a seat. Kerrigan survived that incident, survived raising a family of fourteen children, and even survived a wife who publicly called him a "little rat" for turning state's evidence. He lived until 1901. The Mollies, a sentimental lot in many respects, should have made a special effort to silence "Powderkeg" for a poem he wrote in jail four months before the mass hanging. Kerrigan insulted not only Irish unity but also Irish lyricism. He began his fifteen-stanza rhyme:

Gentlemen, I'm that squealer they talk so much about,
You all know the reason of that I have no doubt;
If not, I will tell you as near I can,
For I'm a bold American, and my name is Kerrigan.

He then went on to tell how ringleaders Jim Carroll and Aleck Campbell, plus Edward Kelly and Mike Doyle, invited him to join the murder
party to do in mine boss John P. Jones at Summit Hill in 1875. Kerrigan
said he had just stopped by at Carroll's saloon "to take my beer, as usual,
but not to get a fill," and then he was led astray. He concluded his poem
by offering infuriating advice:

I think I will lay down my pen when I say a word to ye,
That's to quit drinking liquor and keeping company,
For if you don't you will rue it until the day you die,
So Kerrigan, now, with a glad heart, says to you all good-bye.

It is amazing that old Mollies or relatives of the doomed Mollies never
sought out Gowen or McParlan for revenge. Gowen lived until 1889.
His business career crumbled, and then in a Washington hotel room he
put a bullet in his head. McParlan went on to be a professional antilabor spy and was involved in a sensational legal case in the West. He
lived until 1919.

In all, twenty Mollies were condemned to death by hanging. On
May 1, 1877, Governor John F. Hartranft set the first day of summer,
June 21, as the day of execution of six Mollies in Pottsville and four in
Mauch Chunk. In upholding the county courts' death sentences the
Pennsylvania Supreme Court said that the Mollies had "traded in blood,
taking life for life by compact, burning houses, mills, breakers, and other
valuable structures at the instance of each other, and (were) banded
together by means of concealment, money, and perjury, to shield each
other from punishment."

Pottsville and Mauch Chunk, forty miles apart, both had dark,
massive stone jails. The Pottsville jail, opened in 1852 and still in use, is
on the hill behind the Schuylkill County Courthouse. The Mauch Chunk
jail was opened in 1869 and had never had an execution. This jail, also
still in use, is built into the side of a mountain right off the town's main
street. While the Pottsville jail appeared to be impregnable, the Mauch
Chunk jail was especially susceptible to attack because of the ridiculous
ease with which its walls could be scaled by outsiders coming down the
mountain.

Up until the hour of the hanging, there were fears in both towns that
the Mollies would be sprung. One rumor was that Mollie conspirators

would launch a night attack on the Mauch Chunk jail from nearby Nesquehoning or Summit Hill, hotbeds of Mollie Maguireism. The night before the execution the telegraph offices in the region were ordered to remain open so that assistance could be summoned at any hour to any place. Another fear was that the Mollies would try to blow up the jails in the daytime during visiting hours, when proud officials conducted hundreds of sightseers down the corridors to view the condemned.

The extent of the Mollies' efforts to break from prison was unspectacular. Jimmy Boyle was caught trying to cut through the Pottsville jail floor; he was removed to a dank dungeon and placed in chains. The 25-year-old bachelor from Summit Hill, once noted for his nonchalance, was in despair. While he was in prison, his brother Jack died in a fall from a coal train near Hazleton and his cousin Kate Boyle was sent to the same jail for perjury. Pottsville jailers also found a knife in Tom Munley's cell. Munley, 32, was a native of County Mayo and had a large family living in nearby Gilberton. Boyle and Munley both denied they had intentions of escaping.

A few of the most colorful Mollies, and naturally ones rumored to be the most vicious, escaped arrest. Rumors were rife that some of these would mobilize all the desperadoes in the coal region and attempt a take-over in Pottsville or Mauch Chunk before their old friends could be hanged. Tom Hurley, of Shenandoah, was at large. He was said to have been the Mollie wearing the top hat who attended the Rescue Hook and Ladder picnic at Glover's Grove and brazenly walked up to the bartender Gomer James, a Welsh tough, and shot him dead. Another fugitive Mollie was William Love, who, people said, was the Mollie who murdered Squire Thomas Gwyther, justice of the peace in Girardville. James "Friday" O'Donnell, of the notorious O'Donnell clan, probably had been in on a double slaying with Hurley, and he also was not in jail. John "Humpty" Flynn, "Pugnose Pat" Gallagher, and Jimmy McAllister were others at large. Mike Doyle, of Shenandoah, escaped arrest, but he is thought to have hurried back to Ireland for safety.

Only about a dozen important Mollies were able to avoid imprisonment, however, and it remains a mystery why more of the Mollies did not flee the coal region before it was too late. Those who prosecuted the Mollies, in print as well as in the courtroom, maintained that the ruffians were so arrogant that they thought the law would be afraid to arrest them, let alone any jury convict them. That deduction is far too simple. Captain Robert J. Linden, who played a major role in rounding up Mollies as both a Pinkerton agent and an officer in the Coal and Iron Police, told a reporter, "I often wondered why the damned fools stayed until they couldn't get away." Of course, many of the harmless rank-and-file Mollies did flee.

Ten months after the mass hanging, William W. Scranton, general superintendent of the Lackawanna Coal and Iron Company, told a legislative commission that large numbers of Mollies were driven out of Schuylkill County in the fall and winter of 1876 and went north to Wilkes-Barre and Scranton. Scranton, grandfather of the later governor of Pennsylvania, said that it was these Mollies who fomented the summer railroad riots. His assumption that the riots could be traced to the Mollies unquestionably was groundless. Nevertheless he instructed his private Coal and Iron Police to shoot to kill if the laborers made trouble.

The execution of the ten Mollies in Pottsville and Mauch Chunk on "Black Thursday," June 21, was the last mass hanging in Pennsylvania. As the hour approached, the entire coal region grew excited and the ferment was increased by the awareness that the hanging of the Mollies was not only a national event but the top news story of the day.

The saloons in both towns were ordered closed from the night before the hanging to the day afterward. Gowen's company issued an order that any worker not on his job the day of the hanging would be fired.

The Mauch Chunk scaffold for four was erected in the jail corridor on Monday. On Tuesday the men were measured for their $16 stained-wood coffins. At Pottsville three double scaffolds of the best oak were built in the courtyard. All the gallows for the Mollies were designed with a fall of four feet, six inches—just a little more drop than usual.

From Tuesday on, a squad of Coal and Iron Policemen ate their meals in the Mauch Chunk jail. The Easton Grays, a cavalry troop, arrived in town as a last-minute security measure.

The doomed Mollies were provided with candles the last night to light their cells, and most of them did not retire until after midnight. All were awakened at 4:30 a.m. for coffee, and at 6 a.m. their wives and friends were admitted for the last farewells. An hour later the priests came to celebrate the last mass. All the men were Catholic and all attended services. "Yellow Jack" Donohue, a native-born Irishman and the most fluent and plucky of the Mollies, tried to maintain his sense of humor. Prison barber William Schwank gave him his last shave, and "Yellow Jack" asked, "What would you charge to draw that blade across my throat?"

The widow of mine boss John P. Jones requested that she be allowed to spring the Mauch Chunk trapdoor. She was refused, as Warden Raudenbush planned to perform that task. The identity of the executioners at Pottsville was kept secret for fear of Mollie reprisals.

The Mauch Chunk execution got underway first. The four men were each given an opportunity to say last words and all did but "Yellow Jack" Donohue, who preserved his stoicism to the end and told the sheriff that he could not express what he wished to say. After the condemned were handcuffed and had their thighs bound with leather straps, white caps were drawn over their heads. The trapdoor was sprung at 10:54 a.m. Donohue, Aleck Campbell, 22-year-old Edward Kelly, and Mike Doyle of Mt. Laffee hung for twenty minutes before being cut down. Their bodies were placed in coffins and delivered by the Coal and Iron Policemen to the relatives. Detachments of deputized officers attended each burial. The funerals attracted hundreds. For the wake of her husband, Mrs. Campbell is said to have ordered sixteen pounds of tobacco, a gross of pipes, and $30 worth of whiskey.

At Pottsville the Mollies went to their deaths in pairs, each wearing or carrying red roses. First came Jimmy Boyle and the tall, strapping, native-Irishman Hugh McGehan. Boyle stood on the platform, looked the crowd over, spat unconcernedly, and said, "I ain't a bit sorry to die." The trap was sprung at 11:04 a.m. Next came the illiterate Jimmy Roarity and Jimmy Carroll. Both protested that they were innocent. The trap was sprung at 12:17 p.m. Tom Munley and Tom Duffy were last. Munley amazed the *New York Times* reporter, because he "appeared to be utterly unconcerned about his fate, his nerve was the most astonishing of all." Duffy, a handsome young man of 25, was tense. He had been kept until last because there was a chance that a reprieve would come. He had been convicted of participating in the Yost murder, though the most the prosecution presented as evidence was that he offered $10 for the slaying of the policeman and that he stayed at Carroll's saloon the night the crime was committed. Munley and Duffy plunged to death at 1:13 p.m.

Meanwhile on that "Black Thursday" an eleventh man, Andrew Lenahan, was hanged in Wilkes-Barre. Lenahan was convicted of killing a Captain John Reilly in 1874 following a drinking spree after a political meeting. Lenahan denied that he was a Mollie, and it is unlikely that he was.

Other Mollie hangings followed those of June 21, 1877. Patrick Hester, Patrick Tully, and Peter McHugh were hanged March 25, 1878, in Bloomsburg, Columbia County. Three days later Thomas Fisher was hanged in Mauch Chunk. Dennis Donnelly was hanged June 11 in Pottsville. James McDonnell and Charles Sharpe were hanged in Mauch Chunk on January 14, 1879, just minutes before a five-day stay of execution arrived by telegraph from Harrisburg. Martin Bergen was hanged January 16 in Pottsville, and two days later Jack Kehoe, reputed to be "the king of the Mollies," was hanged, also in Pottsville. Kehoe, a native of County Wicklow, ran the Hibernian House in Girardville and only three years earlier had been elected the Democratic constable. The governor delayed signing the death warrant for Kehoe until after the gubernatorial election. Kehoe may have been a participant in some murders, but it is questionable if he was fairly convicted for the 14-year-old Langdon murder. The twentieth and last Mollie, Peter McManus, was hanged October 9, 1879, in Sunbury, Northumberland County. The life of John O'Neill, who was regarded as a moron, was saved by a last-minute reprieve.

Mollie Maguireism ended, but not the legends. For years following the hangings, ballads were sung in the coal regions about the Mollies. "Powderkeg" Kerrigan's poem became a song, and three ballads believed to have been written by Mike Doyle and another by Hugh McGehan made the rounds. Among other popular folksongs were "Muff Lawler the Squealer" and a dirge simply entitled "Tom Duffy."

But the most enduring legend is that of the handprint on the Mauch Chunk cell wall. Before he literally ran up the scaffold steps, Aleck Campbell angrily placed his hand over his head on the east wall of his cell and said, "My mark will stay here as long as this prison remains" or, as another version has it, "That mark of mine will never be wiped out. There it will remain forever to shame the county that is hangin' an innocent man." Campbell, in his mid-forties and one of the oldest Mollies, was a ringleader, but he probably hadn't even been at the scene of the murder for which he was convicted.

Cell 17 has been repainted many times since Campbell protested his innocence. Fifty years after the hanging, the jail warden even tried to chip the mark out, but a handprint can be seen today. The cell hasn't been used for years, and when the current warden, Charles Neist, turns on the dangling electric bulb in the cell, the smudged print is revealed. "You don't believe it? I don't believe it. Nobody believes it, but there it is," Neist said. "We've visitors all the time to see it. Just the other day a fellow from New York City wanted a look."

introducing
Stephen Crane's
In the Depths of a Coal Mine

The brilliant writer Stephen Crane toured a coal
mine near Scranton in 1894 and vividly re-created
his impressions of the miners' underground way
of life.

Stephen Crane (1871-1900) was born in Newark, New Jersey, the four-
teenth child of a Methodist minister, but grew up in Port Jervis, New York,
across the Delaware from Pennsylvania's Pike County, where he often
camped. Though only 5-foot-6, weighing 125 pounds, Crane as a youngster
wanted to be a professional baseball player, but in September of 1890
enrolled in Lafayette College to study mine engineering. He spent most of
his time playing baseball, boxing, smoking, and reading, received a zero in
theme writing, and was asked to leave Lafayette; he dropped out the following January. He went on to Syracuse University and dropped out of it also.

Crane was a novelist, short story writer, a strikingly good poet, and a
correspondent for newspapers and magazines, covering the Greco-Turkish
and Spanish-American wars. At the end of his life, he moved to England,
where he was friends with Henry James, H. G. Wells, and Joseph Conrad,
the latter of whom exclaimed, "Your temperament makes old things new
and new things amazing." Biographer John Berryman said Crane "was a
writer and nothing else: a man alone in a room with the English language,
trying to get human feelings right."

Before he was twenty-two, Crane had written *Maggie: A Girl of the
Streets,* and by twenty-four, without ever having been to war, he wrote the
masterful *The Red Badge of Courage,* which H. L. Mencken said began modern American literature. The short novel was first serialized in the Philadelphia *Press* in December of 1894. When young Crane visited the

newspaper, the editors, reporters, proofreaders, and compositors left their work to shake his hand.

On June 5, 1900, not yet twenty-nine but with writings enough to fill twelve volumes, Crane died of tuberculosis in a German sanatorium. His funeral was held in New York and Wallace Stevens, a native of Reading and later the great poet, attended it as a reporter for the New York *Tribune.* Crane, he wrote, "lived a brave, aspiring, hard-working life. Certainly he deserved something better than this absolutely commonplace, bare, silly service I have just come from." But Crane was more than something of a rebel. He once told his friend Willa Cather, the Pittsburgh schoolteacher who became a great novelist, "I haven't time to dress. It takes an awful slice out of a fellow's life."

The definitive biography of Crane is by R. W. Stallman and was published in 1968.

Crane in the spring of 1894, when he was twenty-two and completing *The Red Badge of Courage,* toured a coal mine near Scranton. His story was published in *McClure's Magazine* of August 1894.

In 1894, Pennsylvania's 140,000 hard-coal miners produced 51 million tons of coal, and 446 men were killed. For 40 million tons of soft coal, 123 miners out of 86,000 were killed. But this was by no means the worst year. In 1907, there were 806 soft-coal miners and 708 hard-coal miners killed. From 1870 to 1968, Pennsylvania had 31,047 known fatalities in the anthracite mines; from 1877 to 1968, 20,071 known fatalities in the bituminous mines.

The coal industry, like Stephen Crane's life, has been a glory and a tragedy. In the Geologic Time Scale, the "Pennsylvania Period" is the name used to designate that era 280 million to 310 million years ago when most of the world's coal was formed. Pennsylvania itself was given one of the world's largest deposits, and until 1950 ranked first in the nation in coal production (West Virginia does now). In 150 years an estimated 9 billion tons of coal has come out of Pennsylvania. It brought employment to millions, death to thousands, riches to a few, poverty to many, blight to hundreds of acres of once lush landscape, acid-polluted rivers and streams which will take billions of dollars to purify, and a mining culture to Pennsylvania that is especially its own.

Today the coal industry is in a prolonged decline, anthracite mining worse than bituminous mining. Production reached a peak of more than 176 million tons in 1918. The last time Pennsylvania had a total of 100 million tons of both soft and hard coal was in 1957, and it last had as many as 50,000 miners employed in 1960. There are two prominent indications that Old King Coal isn't what he used to be. The growth of the atomic industry is a fact of the postwar years. The first full-scale civilian nuclear power station to produce electricity for commercial uses in the United States began operation at Shippingport, 30 miles west of Pittsburgh, on December 18, 1957, and Pennsylvania-based industries have taken a leading role in the development of nuclear energy. The once powerful political leverage the coal industry had is dissipating, as evidenced by the aggressive campaigns in the Lawrence and Scranton administrations for tough mining and pollution controls, especially against strip mining, which since World War II replaced deep-pit mining in importance.

It is unlikely that ever again will Pennsylvania coal, the fuel of the industrial revolution, be as much in demand as it was when Stephen Crane descended into the ink-black labyrinth he described. It is just as unlikely, too, that there will ever be a time when Pennsylvania coal is not mined or that there will be as brilliant account of this occupation as the one set forth by Stephen Crane.

In the Depths
of a Coal Mine

by Stephen Crane

The breakers squatted upon the hillsides and in the valley like enormous preying monsters, eating of the sunshine, the grass, the green leaves. The smoke from their nostrils had ravaged the air of coolness and fragrance. All that remained of vegetation looked dark, miserable, half-strangled. Along the summit line of the mountain a few unhappy trees were etched upon the imperial blue, incredibly far away from the sombre land.

We approached the colliery over paths of coal dust that wound among the switches. A breaker loomed above us, a huge and towering frame of blackened wood. It ended in a little curious peak, and upon its sides there was a profusion of windows appearing at strange and unexpected points. Through occasional doors one could see the flash of whirring machinery. Men with wondrously blackened faces and garments came forth from it. The sole glitter upon their persons was at their hats, where the little tin lamps were carried. They went stolidly along, some swinging lunchpails carelessly; but the marks upon them of their forbidding and mystic calling fascinated our new eyes until they passed from sight. They were symbols of a grim, strange war that was being waged in the sunless depths of the earth.

At the top of the breaker, laborers were dumping the coal into chutes. The huge lumps slid slowly on their journey down through the building, from which they were to emerge in classified fragments. Great teeth on revolving cylinders caught them and chewed them. At places there were grates that bid each size go into its proper chute. The dust lay inches deep on every motionless thing, and clouds of it made the air dark as from a violent tempest. A mighty gnashing sound filled the ears. With terrible appetite this huge and hideous monster sat imperturbably munching coal, grinding its mammoth jaws with unearthly and monotonous uproar.

In a large room sat the little slatepickers. The floor slanted at an angle of 45 degrees, and the coal, having been masticated by the great teeth, was streaming sluggishly in long iron troughs. The boys sat straddling these troughs, and as the mass moved slowly, they grabbed deftly at the pieces of slate therein. There were five or six of them, one above another, over each trough. The coal is expected to be fairly pure after it passes the final boy. The howling machinery was above them. High up, dim figures moved about in the dust clouds.

These little men were a terrifically dirty band. They resembled the New York gamins in some ways, but they laughed more, and when they laughed their faces were a wonder and a terror. They had an air of supreme independence, and seemed proud of their kind of villainy. They swore long oaths with skill.

Through their ragged shirts we could get occasional glimpses of shoulders black as stoves. They looked precisely like imps as they scrambled to get a view of us. Work ceased while they tried to ascertain if we were willing to give away any tobacco. The man who perhaps believes that he controls them came and harangued the crowd. He talked to the air.

The slatepickers all through this region are yet at the spanking period. One continually wonders about their mothers, and if there are any schoolhouses. But as for them, they are not concerned. When they get time off, they go out on the culm heap and play baseball, or fight with boys from other breakers or among themselves, according to the opportunities. And before them always is the hope of one day getting to be door-boys down in the mines; and, later, mule-boys; and yet later, laborers and helpers. Finally, when they have grown to be great big men, they may become miners, real miners, and go down and get squeezed, or perhaps escape to a shattered old man's estate with a mere miner's asthma. They are very ambitious.

Meanwhile they live in a place of infernal dins. The crash and thunder of the machinery is like the roar of an immense cataract. The room shrieks and blares and bellows. Clouds of dust blur the air until the windows shine pallidly afar off. All the structure is a-tremble from the heavy sweep and circle of the ponderous mechanism. Down in the midst of it sit these tiny urchins, where they earn 55 cents a day each. They breathe this atmosphere until their lungs grow heavy and sick with it. They have this clamor in their ears until it is a wonder that they have any hoodlum valor remaining. But they are uncowed; they continue to swagger. And at the top of the breaker, laborers can always be seen dumping the roaring coal down the wide, voracious maw of the creature.

Over in front of a little tool house a man smoking a pipe sat on a bench. "Yes," he said, "I'll take yeh down if yeh like." He led us by little cinder paths to the shed over the shaft of the mine. A gigantic fanwheel near by was twirling swiftly. It created cool air for the miners, who on the lowest vein of this mine were some 1,150 feet below the surface. As we stood silently waiting for the elevator we had opportunity to gaze at the mouth of the shaft. The walls were of granite blocks, slimy, moss-grown, dripping with water. Below was a curtain of ink-like blackness. It was like the opening of an old well, sinister from tales of crime.

The black, greasy cables began to run swiftly. We stood staring at them and wondering. Then all of a sudden the elevator appeared and stopped with a crash. It was a plain wooden platform. Upon two sides iron bars ran up to support a stout metal roof. The men upon it, as it came into view, were like apparitions from the center of the earth.

A moment later we marched aboard, armed with little lights, feeble and gasping in the daylight. There was an instant's creak of machinery, and then the landscape, that had been framed for us by the door-posts of the shed, disappeared in a flash. We were dropping with extraordinary swiftness straight into the earth. It was a plunge, a fall. The flames of the little lamps fluttered and flew and struggled like tied birds to release themselves from the wicks. "Hang on," bawled our guide above the tumult.

It was a journey that held a threat of endlessness.

Then suddenly the dropping platform slackened its speed. It began to descend slowly and with caution. At last, with a crash and a jar, it stopped. Before us stretched an inscrutable darkness, a soundless place of tangible loneliness. Into the nostrils came a subtly strong odor of powder-smoke, oil, wet earth. The alarmed lungs began to lengthen their respirations.

Our guide strode abruptly into the gloom. His lamp flared shades of yellow and orange upon the walls of a tunnel that led away from the foot of the shaft. Little points of coal caught the light and shone like diamonds. Before us there was always the curtain of an impenetrable night. We walked on with no sound save the crunch of our feet upon the coal-dust of the floor. The sense of an abiding danger in the roof was always upon our foreheads. It expressed to us all the unmeasured, deadly tons above us, as if the roof were a superlative might that regarded with the supreme calmness of almighty power the little men at its mercy. Sometimes we were obliged to bend low to avoid it. Always our hands rebelled vaguely from touching it, refusing to affront this gigantic mass.

After a time we came upon two men crouching where the roof of the passage came near to meeting the floor. If the picture could have been brought to where it would have had the opposition and the contrast of the glorious summer-time earth, it would have been a grim and ghastly thing. The garments of the men were no more sable than their faces, and when they turned their heads to regard our tramping party, their eyeballs and teeth shone white as bleached bones. It was like the grinning of two skulls there in the shadows. The tiny lamps in their hats made a trembling light that left weirdly shrouded the movements of their limbs and bodies. We might have been confronting terrible spectres.

But they said, "Hello, Jim," to our conductor. Their mouths expanded in smiles—wide and startling smiles.

In a moment they turned again to their work. When the lights of our party reinforced their two lamps, we could see that one was busily drilling into the coal with a long thin bar. The low roof ominously pressed his shoulders as he bent at his toil. The other knelt behind him on the loose lumps of coal.

He who worked at the drill engaged in conversation with our guide. He looked back over his shoulder, continuing to poke away. "When are yeh goin' t' measure this up, Jim?" he demanded. "Do yeh wanta git me killed?"

"Well, I'd measure it up today, on'y I ain't got me tape," replied the other.

"Well, when will yeh? Yeh wanta hurry up," said the miner. "I don't wanta git killed."

"Oh, I'll be down on Monday."

"Humph!"

They engaged in a sort of an altercation in which they made jests. "You'll be carried out o' there feet first before long." "Will I?"

Yet one had to look closely to understand that they were not about to spring at each other's throats. The vague illumination created all the effect of the snarling of two wolves.

Sometimes the scenes in their weird strength were absolutely infernal. Once, when we were traversing a silent tunnel in another mine, we came suddenly upon a wide place where some miners were lying down in a group. As they upreared to gaze at us, it resembled a resurrection. They slowly uprose with ghoul-like movements, mysterious figures robed in enormous shadows. The swift flashes of the steel-gleaming eyes were upon our faces.

From this tunnel of our first mine we went with our guide to the foot of the main shaft. Here we were in the most important passage of a mine, the main gangway. The wonder of these avenues is the noise—the crash and clatter of machinery as the elevator speeds upward with the loaded cars and drops thunderingly with the empty ones. The place resounds with the shouts of mule-boys, and there can always be heard the noise of approaching coal-cars, beginning in mild rumbles and then swelling down upon one in a tempest of sound. In the air is the slow painful throb of the pumps working at the water which collects in the depths. There is booming and banging and crashing, until one wonders why the tremendous walls are not wrenched by the force of this uproar. And up and down the tunnel there is a riot of lights, little orange points flickering and flashing. Miners stride in swift and sombre procession. But the meaning of it all is in the deep bass rattle of a blast in some hidden part of the mine. It is war. It is the most savage part of all in the endless battle between man and nature. These miners are grimly in the van. They have carried the war into places where nature has the strength of a million giants. Sometimes their enemy becomes exasperated and snuffs out ten, twenty, thirty lives. Usually she remains calm, and takes one at a time with method and precision. She need not hurry. She possesses eternity. After a blast, the smoke, faintly luminous, silvery, floats silently through the adjacent tunnels.

In our first mine we speedily lost all ideas of time, direction, distance. The whole thing was an extraordinary black puzzle. We were impelled to admire the guide because he knew all the tangled passages. He led us through little tunnels three and four feet wide and with roofs that sometimes made us crawl. At other times we were in avenues twenty feet wide, where double rows of tracks extended. There were stretches of great darkness, majestic silences. The 300 miners were distributed into all sorts of crevices and corners of the labyrinth, toiling in this city of endless night.

We were made aware of distances later by our guide, who would occasionally stop to tell us our position by naming a point of the familiar geography of the surface. "Do you remember that rolling-mill yeh passed coming up? Well, you're right under it." "You're under th' depot now." The length of these distances struck us with amazement when we reached the surface. Near Scranton one can really proceed for miles, in the black streets of the mines.

Over in a wide and lightless room we found the mule stables. There we discovered a number of these animals standing with an air of calmness and self-possession that was somehow amazing to find in a mine. A little dark urchin came and belabored his mule "China" until he stood broadside to us that we might admire his innumerable fine qualities. The stable was like a dungeon. The mules were arranged in solemn rows. They turned their heads toward our lamps. The glare made their eyes shine wondrously like lenses. They resembled enormous rats.

About the room stood bales of hay and straw. The commonplace air worn by the long-eared slaves made it all infinitely usual. One had to wait to see the tragedy of it. It was not until we had grown familiar with the life and the traditions of the mines that we were capable of under-standing the story told by these beasts standing in calm array, with spread legs.

It is a common affair for mules to be imprisoned for years in the limit-less night of the mines. Our acquaintance, "China," had been four years buried. Upon the surface there had been the march of the seasons; the white splendor of snows had changed again and again to the glories of green springs. Four times had the earth been ablaze with the decorations of brilliant autumns. But "China" and his friends had remained in these dungeons from which daylight, if one could get a view up a shaft, would appear a tiny circle, a silver star aglow in a sable sky.

Usually when brought to the surface, the mules tremble at the earth radiant in the sunshine. Later, they go almost mad with fantastic joy. The full splendor of the heavens, the grass, the trees, the breezes, breaks upon them suddenly. They caper and career with extravagant mulish glee. A miner told me of a mule that had spent some delirious months upon the surface after years of labor in the mines. Finally the time came when he was to be taken back. But the memory of a black existence was upon him; he knew that gaping mouth that threatened to swallow him. No cudgellings could induce him. The men held conventions and dis-cussed plans to budge that mule. The celebrated quality of obstinacy in him won him liberty to gambol clumsily about on the surface.

After being long in the mines, the mules are apt to duck and dodge at the close glare of lamps, but some of them have been known to have piteous fears of being left in the dead darkness. We met a boy who said that sometimes the only way he could get his team to move was to run ahead of them with the light. Afraid of the darkness, they would follow.

In wet mines, gruesome fungi grow upon the wooden props that sup-port the uncertain-looking ceiling. The walls are dripping and dank. Upon them, too, frequently grows a moss-like fungus, white as a druid's beard, that thrives in these deep dens, but shrivels and dies at contact with the sunlight.

Great and mystically dreadful is the earth from a mine's depth. Man is in the implacable grasp of nature. It has only to tighten slightly, and he is crushed like a bug. His loudest shriek of agony would be as impo-tent as his final moan to bring help from that fair land that lies, like Heaven, over his head. There is an insidious, silent enemy in the gas. If the huge fanwheel on the top of the earth should stop for a brief period, there is certain death. If a man escape the gas, the floods, the squeezes of falling rock, the cars shooting through little tunnels, the precarious elevators, the hundred perils, there usually comes to him an attack of miner's asthma that slowly racks and shakes him into the grave. Meanwhile, he gets $3 per day, and his laborer $1.25.

In the chamber at the foot of the shaft, as we were departing, a group of the men were resting. They lay about in careless poses. When we climbed aboard the elevator, we had a moment in which to turn and regard them. Then suddenly the study in black faces and crimson and orange lights vanished. We were on our swift way to the surface. The fleeting walls became flecked with light. It increased to a downpour of sunbeams. The high sun was afloat in a splendor of spotless blue. The distant hills were arrayed in purple and stood like monarchs. A glory of gold was upon the near-by earth. The cool fresh air was wine.

Of that sinister struggle far below there came no sound, no suggestion save the loaded cars that emerged one after another in eternal procession and went creaking up the incline that their contents might be fed into the mouth of the breaker, imperturbably cruel and insatiate, black emblem of greed, and of the gods of this labor.

Sheppton's Inscrutable Darkness

One of the most vivid mining stories in the annals of Pennsylvania is the dramatic rescue of two miners entombed 300 feet underground at Sheppton in 1963.

David Fellin, Henry Throne, and Louis Bova were working a "dog-hole" mine, or a one-exit slope, near Hazleton when there was a cave-in on August 13, 1963. Fellin and Throne were discovered alive on August 18 and were finally pulled to safety nine days later through a carefully drilled escape hole. Bova was never found. For nine days the fate of Fellin and Throne, trapped in darkness, was the concern of the nation. Their rescue cost $500,000, including $60,000 of state-appropriated money.

The Sheppton mine was one of 189 of 459 small mines in the anthracite area without a second access shaft. It was owned by Fellin, and had been inspected a month earlier and a report issued stating, "An attempt is being made to provide a second outlet."

Part III
Pennsylvania in Literature

life duplicates fiction in
Paul B. Beers'
The American Tragedies

Theodore Dreiser's A Hoosier Holiday, **which records a 1915 motor trip through Pennsylvania, reveals his strong reactions to the cities of the state. Wilkes-Barre charmed him, but Scranton repelled him; the reasons make fascinating reading.**

Theodore Dreiser (1871-1945) was a native of Indiana, but often wrote a-bout Pennsylvania. His 1912 novel, *The Financier*, was set in Philadelphia, a city in which he lived in 1902 for seven months. When Dreiser was twenty-three, he was a reporter for a brief period for the Pittsburgh *Dispatch*. In his spare hours, he read Balzac, Thomas Huxley, and Herbert Spencer at the Carnegie Library, developing his personal philosophy of a struggle for exis-tence which six years later flowered in his first novel, *Sister Carrie*, 1900.

Dreiser once wrote of Pittsburgh: "Of all the cities in which I ever worked or lived, Pittsburgh was the most agreeable....What a city for a realist to work and dream in! The wonder to me is that it has not produced a score of writers, poets, painters and sculptors, instead of—well, how many? And who are they?" Always fascinated by mountains, he jotted down a description of "the brown-blue mountains of Western Pennsylvania," with a "sun-gray, almost cloudy, at best a filtered dull gold haze" over them.

The best writing Dreiser ever did about Pennsylvania is found in *A Hoosier Holiday*, published by the John Lane Company of New York in 1916. Dreiser in the summer of 1915 decided to take a motor trip back to his home in Indiana, which he hadn't seen in years. Franklin Booth, a friend and adver-tising illustrator, as well as a native of Indiana too, had a Pathfinder touring car, plus a chauffeur named Speed. Dreiser at the time had a fair reputation as the author of five novels.

The three chapters, "The Pennsylvanians," "Beautiful Wilkes-Barre," and

"In and Out of Scranton" are in the typical Dreiser style. They are long-winded, yet have a powerful and awkward beauty. Much is almost thrown together, but had the work been carefully rewritten and edited undoubtedly the genuine Dreiser flavor would be lost. Dreiser is a sensitive reporter, but often an inaccurate one. He confuses Senator Simon Cameron with Governor Andrew G. Curtin, though both were living when he was young, and he never bothered to check his facts. He is totally subjective. Swiftwater he loved because of a woods nearby. Wilkes-Barre charmed him, especially the initial view of it that he got as he came down off the mountain. "There are city scapes that seem some to mourn and some to sing," he wrote. "This was one that sang. It reminded me of the pen and ink work of Rops or Vierge or Whistler, the paintings of Turner and Moran. Low hanging clouds, yellowish or black, or silvery like a fish, mingled with a splendid filigree of smoke and chimneys and odd sky lines."

Dreiser found himself exclaiming for joy once inside Wilkes-Barre, for it "gave evidences of a real charm." He was especially pleased with the care Wilkes-Barre had taken in preserving its riverfront. Scranton, on the contrary, displeased him. "Once down in the heart of Scranton, I did not care for it at all," he writes. "It is so customary—an American city like Utica or Syracuse or Rochester or Buffalo—and American cities of the 100,000 class are so much alike....They never think of doing an original thing....It's the rarest exception when, as at Wilkes-Barre for instance, a city will take the slightest aesthetic advantage of any natural configuration of land or water."

Dreiser did stroll through Scranton, and the heart of this lumbering, rather ugly man comes out in his writing: "It was a warm night and as we descended into commonplace streets we could look through the open windows of homes or apartments or flats and see the usual humdrum type of furniture and hangings, the inevitable lace curtains, the centre tables, the huge, junky lamps, the upright pianos or victrolas. Whenever I see long, artless streets like these in the hot, breathless summertime, I feel a wave of commiseration sweep over me, and yet I am drawn to them by something which makes me want to live among these people."

Though hardly a profound thinker, Dreiser was a compulsive philosopher. He was forever taking on the American middle-class idea that immigration threatens the well-being of the nation. In northeastern Pennsylvania he, of course, saw many foreigners, and in his narrative in *A Hoosier Holiday* he had to digress for typical Dreiser opinionizing;

"I could see no evidence of that transformation of the American by the foreigner into something different from what he has ever been—the peril which has been so much discussed by our college-going sociologists. On the contrary, America seemed to me to be making over the foreigner into its own image and likeness. I learned here that there were thousands of Poles, Czechs, Croatians, Silesians, Hungarians, etc., working here in the coal mines and at Wilkes-Barre, but the young men on the streets and in the stores were Americans. Here were the American electric signs in great profusion, the American bookstores and newsstands crowded with all that mushy adventure fiction of which our lady critics are so fond. Five hundred magazines and weekly publications blazed the faces of alleged pretty girls. 'The automat,' the 'dairy kitchen,' the 'Boston,' 'Milwaukee' or 'Chicago' lunch, and all the smart haberdasheries so beloved of the ambitious American youth, were in full bloom. I saw at least a half dozen moving-picture theatres in as many blocks—and business and correspondence schools in ample array.

"What becomes of all the young Poles, Czechs, Croatians, Serbians, etc., who are going to destroy us? I'll tell you. They gather on the street corners when their parents will permit them, arrayed in yellow or red ties, yellow shoes, dinky fedoras or beribboned straw hats and 'style-plus' clothes, and talk about 'when I was out to Dreamland the other night,' or make some such observation as 'Say, you should have seen the beaut that cut across here just now. Oh, mamma, some baby!' That's all the menace there is to the foreign invasion. Whatever their original intentions may be, they can't resist the American yellow shoes, the American moving picture, 'Stein-Koop' clothes, 'Dreamland,' the popular song, the automobile, the jitney. They are completely undone by our perfections. Instead of throwing bombs or lowering our social level, all bogies of the sociologists, they would rather stand on our street corners, go to the nearest moving pictures, smoke cigarettes, wear high white collars and braided yellow vests and yearn over the girls who know exactly how to handle them, or work to someday own an automobile and break the speed laws. They are really not so bad as we seem to want them to be. They are simple, gauche, de jeune, 'the limit.' In other words, they are fast becoming Americans."

Dreiser's long day ends with a rented room in a farmhouse in Factoryville. The place had a porch with a wooden swing, the katydids sang lustily, and "the perfume of country woods and fields" drifted into his room, which had a large porcelain bath bowl and "pictures of all the proprietor's relatives done in crayon."

The next day he, Franklin, and Speed took their Pathfinder north. "We were making our way up a wide valley as I could see, the same green Susquehanna Valley, between high hills and through a region given over entirely to dairy farming. The hills looked as though they were bedded knee-deep in rich, succulent grass. Groups of black and white Holstein cattle were everywhere to be seen. Some of the hills were laid out in checkerboard fashion by fields of grain or hay or buckwheat or great thick groves of trees. Before many a farm dooryard was a platform on which stood a milk can, or two or three: now and then a neighborhood creamery would come into view, where the local milk was churned wholesale and butter prepared and shipped. The towns for the most part were rarely factory towns, looking more as if they

harbored summer boarders or were but now starting on a manufacturing
career. Girls or women were reading or sewing on porches. The region of
the mines was far behind."

In 1934 Dreiser returned to Pennsylvania as a distinguished newspaper
correspondent to cover a famous murder trial. The circumstances of the
crime closely paralleled those of the murder described by Dreiser in his
classic novel *The American Tragedy,* as is shown by the following article,
reprinted from the "Reporter at Large" column, Harrisburg *Evening News,*
September 8, 1967.

The American Tragedies

by Paul B. Beers

It is sometimes said that Theodore Dreiser patterned his novel, *An American Tragedy*, on a murder that took place at Harvey's Lake, between Wilkes-Barre and Tunkhannock. This is not so. What actually happened is that Dreiser used another murder for his plot and then the Harvey's Lake murder came along to duplicate the one described in his classic.

The second half of 1934 was the heyday of great American murder cases. From August to October there was this one, the Edwards-McKechnie case in Luzerne County. Then, to the grisly delight of newspaper readers, came the "Kelayres Massacre" up in Schuylkill County on election eve, and the Babes in the Woods slaying at Pine Grove Furnace in Cumberland County.

In Kelayres, population 700, Democrats on election eve staged a political parade. As they marched by the home of the Republican town leader, shots rang out. Five persons were killed and fourteen wounded. The Republican candidate for Governor, William A. Schnader, just happened to be State Attorney General. He immediately issued word that he would do all he could to prosecute, but the incident helped lead to his defeat to George H. Earle III.

Three weeks later, on November 24, 1934, three young girls were found murdered at Pine Grove Furnace. The murder touched off a national search. "We'll find out what killed these little girls even if the tax rate in this county has to be raised," the Cumberland County District Attorney announced. A week later the case was resolved when the names of murder-suicide victims in Duncansville, near Altoona, were determined. Elmo J. Noakes, 32, a widower from Roseville, Calif., murdered his daughters, Norma, 12, Dewella, 10, and Cordelia, 8, drove on to Duncansville and there killed his niece, Winifred Pierce, 18, and then himself. No motive was ever determined for the spree. After the national reporters got the story, they hurried back to Flemington, N.J., where the Lindbergh baby murder trial was taking place.

The origin of the 875-page Dreiser novel happened on July 11, 1906, at Big Moose Lake in the Adirondacks, 60 miles north of Utica, N.Y. Chester E. Gillette, 23, had spent two years at Oberlin College and while working in his uncle's shirt factory in Cortland, N.Y., met Grace Brown, 20. Chester wanted to marry a girl he thought more respectable, so when Grace was four months pregnant he took her out on a rowboat on Big Moose Lake, hit her with a tennis racket and caused her to drown. Governor Charles Evans Hughes refused clemency, and Chester was electrocuted on March 31, 1908.

Dreiser followed the Gillette incident in the newspapers, and then wrote *An American Tragedy,* published in 1925. In the novel, Clyde Griffiths on a July 8 takes his former sweetheart and pregnant Roberta Alden out in a rowboat on the fictional Bit Bittern Lake somewhere north of Utica. Clyde has a tennis racket in the boat, but he uses a camera to belt Roberta and cause her to drown. Dreiser explains that Clyde wanted to marry a richer girl named Sondra, but because of society's narrow moral prohibitions he is unable to break his relationship with Roberta other than by slaying her. To Dreiser, the "American Tragedy" is that society in its self-righteous fashion continues the absurd cycle by then taking the life of the boy. It is from the Dreiser novel that the movie, starring Elizabeth Taylor and Montgomery Clift, was taken.

Thousands of readers around the world were familiar with the true Gillette case and the fictional Griffiths one, and then came the Edwards murder case at Harvey's Lake.

Robert Allen Edwards, 22, had a jutting chin, deep-set eyes and "hair as black as the anthracite his family has mined for generations," according to the *New York Times,* which frontpaged his trial. Bobby was a young coal surveyor from Edwardsville, his father was superintendent of his church Sunday School, and he himself had once thought of becoming a minister.

Bobby off and on was in love with a neighborhood girl, Freda Mc-Kechnie, 27, a 5-foot-1 telephone operator with whom he once worked. When Bobby went to Mansfield State College, he fell in love with a girl named Margaret from East Aurora, N.Y. He dropped out of Mansfield— probably without ever reading Dreiser's *An American Tragedy*—and Margaret graduated to be a music teacher in Endicott, N.Y. Bobby resumed his friendship with Freda, and when she was five months pregnant, he panicked because he wanted to marry Margaret, who he thought had more social standing.

On the rainy night of July 30, 1934, Bobby took Freda to a beach at Harvey's Lake. They swam out to a floating dock and then swam back and got in a boat. Bobby clubbed Freda with a blackjack, pushed her off the boat and she sank in four feet of water. On the way home, he stopped and bought some chocolate bars for his mother as he promised he would do. The next day three young girl canoeists saw Freda's body and lifeguard George Jones, for years a prominent Pennsylvania sports figure, helped pull her from the lake.

The Edwards case quickly made the national headlines, and when handsome young Edwards on October 1 came to trial, the nation's press was there. The *New York Times* sent F. Raymond Daniell, one of its best. Jimmy Kilgallen was there for the Hearst newspapers. Al Clark covered for the *Harrisburg Telegraph,* and seated next to him was the mighty Theodore Dreiser, on assignment from the *New York Post* and *Mystery Magazine.*

Bobby's father, a coal company paymaster, took a $2,000 mortgage on his house to finance the defense of his boy. The jury heard how Bobby and Freda often went to church together and how he thought of eloping to West Virginia instead of killing her.

Newspapermen eagerly tried to learn if Margaret, 24, would attend the trial. She sent Bobby a Bible, but remained in New York State and said she decided never to marry him even if he were judged innocent.

District Attorney Thomas M. Lewis headed the prosecution. His assistant, J. Harold Flannery, a brilliant young lawyer and amateur actor, read portions of 172 letters Bobby wrote to Margaret, and these letters played a major part in convincing the all-male jury to convict Edwards. Judge W. Alfred Valentine sentenced him to death. Flannery went on to be a congressman and a judge, and Lewis became a judge too.

At least 1,000 letters asking for clemency, including ones by Dreiser and Harvey's Lake Chief of Police Ira C. Stevenson, were sent to Governor George H. Earle, who took office in January of 1935. Edwards' father went to the Governor's Office just hours before the execution, but to no avail.

Edwards, "poker-faced, silent and sombre," refused a special last meal. News stories reported that "fully 3,800 persons were on the streets and the highways were clogged with cars; thousands stood along the roads looking at the death house."

Among the six official witnesses at Rockview Penitentiary were Al Clark and Edward J. Donohoe, now editor of the *Scranton Times.* Donohoe's account of how Edwards' body was pumped with 2,000 volts and 13 amperes of electricity is still one of the gems of Pennsylvania journalism.

Edwards died at 1:30 a.m. on May 6, 1935, after a chilling rainy night —just the sort of night he had killed Freda McKechnie.

introducing
Joseph F. Lowry's
Dear John (O'Hara):
All Is Forgiven,
Love, Gibbsville

John O'Hara's prolific literary output has given
the critics, pro and con, plenty of ammunition.

There is the John O'Hara who is the handsome, 6-foot, 195-pound grandson
of a Civil War Irish-immigrant militia captain, the cocky kid who made it up
out of the Pennsylvania coal regions to comfortable fame. And there is also
the John O'Hara of international literary note who delights millions of readers
but stumps many of the critics.

The first O'Hara, the Pottsville emigré, is as colorful a character as any of
the fictional ones he has ever drawn in his almost forty books over a career
of four decades.

This is the O'Hara who started off on Mahantongo Street and was the talk
of the Fountain Springs Country Club even before he immortalized it in his
fiction; when it burned to the ground in 1969, the Associated Press said it
was famous because it was "used as the setting in stories by famed author
John O'Hara." Today O'Hara lives outside Princeton, New Jersey, in a nine-
room French manor house at Pretty Brook Road and Province Line Road,
and he has a summer beach house at Quogue, Long Island. This is the O'Hara
whom Governor Richard Hughes of New Jersey sent as a birthday present a
license plate, "JOH 1," for his Rolls Royce, and then O'Hara got ticketed for
going 64 miles an hour in a 50-mile zone. He did get his license lifted for
30 days, but he was fined only $1, presumably because the Jersey magis-
trate was another of his readers.

O'Hara was, as were so many others from his fictional Gibbsville, quite a
boy. He had what he called his "drinking days," when he'd go on 48-hour

cycles of working, drinking, and ripping Manhattan telephone books in half. He married into society, danced and golfed at the best clubs, did the circuit with the established rich, and was pals with Ernest Hemingway, F. Scott Fitzgerald, Dorothy Parker, James Thurber, and Robert Benchley. He was so busy being John O'Hara that he seldom got back to Pottsville, though geographically and creatively it was never far away.

The older O'Hara is more sedate. A hemorrhaging ulcer in 1953 almost killed him. He is off liquor and on milk. He admits to being much more conservative, and it shows in his rejection even of many of the top younger writers of the country. He talks of writing so that a book will be read ten years in the future, forgetting that that goal was never his during those seven months in 1933-1934 in a dingy, midtown Manhattan hotel room when he was unknown and broke. Out of it came *Appointment in Samarra,* his first and still his greatest novel and one that has been read for far longer than ten years by Americans, Albanians, and everybody else.

The senior-citizen O'Hara, like the coal miners and railroaders he knew as a boy, has never retired nor rested on his laurels or invested income. He types on, adding to a record as the most productive major American writer in history. He has a small study, with a Remington Noiseless, and from midnight to 3 a.m. or 4 a.m. he pounds out his stories. His first draft on yellow-sheeted paper seldom needs rewriting or editing. His talent—his sense of character flaws and his feeling for the pressures of circumstances and fate—is so expert and durable that he can refer to creative writing and story-telling as a "business" and a "craft" for which there are basics to be mastered.

Some critics claim that O'Hara is only a skillful hack, not a novelist at all but a rare breed of advanced journalist. Judging by O'Hara's rules and assessing his body of work as he mass-produces it to be consumed, even the most stubborn critics don't deny that he is remarkable. The record is phenomenal: 15 novels, more than 400 short stories, and 20 million sales. In the face of this very real John O'Hara market, the more careful critics have been impelled to hedge their judgments and withstand the scorn of academes as to just how much of a hack O'Hara really is.

Future generations will be the final arbiters of the lasting value of O'Hara's prose. It is more than a bit presumptuous for anyone to attempt definitive commentary now on the man and his literary place.

What can be seen at this date is that O'Hara is a genuine artist with the commitments of one. "I feel I owe something to my talent, which is damned close to a religion with me, close because maybe it is God-given," he has said. There is no question of his talent, for it has been ample enough to be a source of continuing fascination, regardless of the era, for the book-buying and movie-going public. Now even the scholars are beginning to recognize the O'Hara talent. Yet there are those who would dispute that O'Hara puts any more purpose into his work than just telling, often vividly, a good story.

O'Hara says his theme is "men and women, that's what it all comes down to," and that there is "no greater theme than men and women." He divides the sexes by having his men think morally about what should be and his women about what they want. The men invariably deteriorate and disintegrate—and O'Hara takes 897 pages of *From the Terrace*, 1958, to show how Alfred Eaton, of Port Johnson, Pennsylvania, over a span of fifty years first makes it big and then crumbles apart. The women are tougher and shrewder about life, often nastier. "He does create beautiful women," said fellow Pennsylvanian John Updike. "His women are really there; you get a feeling of their fatigue."

In *John O'Hara*, published in 1966 in Twayne's U.S. Authors series, scholar Sheldon N. Grebstein of Harpur College analyzes O'Hara's strengths: his ability to create intensely visualized scenes, his understanding of tension and conflict, his sense of timing, his dialogue, his concern with character interaction and class differences, his professional deftness in making a story, his directness of language, and his ability to create characters whose behavior is always credible and usually not predictable. "His best stories," Updike said, "have the flowing ease and surprisingness of poems."

Grebstein also describes what he sees as O'Hara's weaknesses: his cast of not-profound though vivid characters, his tedious detailing, his repetitiveness, his settling for just surface reality, his character and plot manipulations, and often his lack of a solid philosophical standpoint so that his work sometimes is but terse, precise hollowness. O'Hara, says Grebstein, views man as a social animal who needs love, communications, and company. He sees society—without defining it—as forcing upon man duties and roles that he cannot fulfill, and thus the tragedy of man.

Money, liquor, sex, family, and the accouterments of success preoccupy O'Hara, and it is the reader's option to delve into the unconscious of Julian English, Alfred Eaton, Joe Chapin, John Appleton, and the other O'Hara people if he so wishes.

Though O'Hara has written about localities other than eastern Pennsylvania, he is at his best in this environment and he knows it. Often he has a character travel beyond Pennsylvania, New York City, Washington, or Hollywood—his limits of familiarity—but when he does, he usually deliberately ceases to be specific on details. Alfred Eaton's visit to Louisiana, for example, is not elaborated upon.

O'Hara's Pennsylvania facts invariably are correct, or close to it. He has fictional governors from Erie and Allentown, because only he and a few others know that these are the biggest Pennsylvania cities that haven't yet elected a native son governor. In *Ten North Frederick*, the winner of the 1964 National Book Award, O'Hara mentions the 1882 Pennsylvania gubernatorial election and, with the exception of one detail, is factually accurate as always. Dr. Mac E. Barrick, of Dickinson and now Shippensburg State College, has traced O'Hara's use of upper middle-class, eastern Pennsyl-

vania proverbs and sayings. He found that for the scholarly folklorist, O'Hara
has much to contribute.

Joseph F. Lowry visited Pottsville and wrote "Dear John (O'Hara): All Is
Forgiven, Love, Gibbsville," for the Philadelphia *Bulletin Magazine*, October 25, 1964. Lowry, a long-time O'Hara reader, was born in Philadelphia in
1917 and has been a feature writer and political correspondent for the
Bulletin since 1934.

Dear John (O'Hara): All Is Forgiven, Love, Gibbsville

by Joseph F. Lowry

Pottsville, Pa., is one of the best-known small towns in the United States. It enjoys that fame—although not everyone in town has always strictly enjoyed it—because of a native son, John O'Hara.

O'Hara, of course, is one of America's great and most prolific authors. He created his fictional "Gibbsville," the locale of much of his writing, out of the Pottsville mold. He painted it a rowdy red and stripped some very important people there of their dignity.

He lambasted the seat of Schuylkill County with a barrage of naughty words, causing some persons to remark, "He seems to have remembered everything about his early life," and others to say, "As a social historian, he's a flop; he saw little and imagined a lot." Regardless, O'Hara's roots extend back to Pottsville from the very top of the literary world, from his permanent home in Princeton, N.J., and his summer place at Quogue, Long Island.

On January 31, 1905, about 101 years after Pottsville was founded by mill owner John Pott, a 6-foot-2 physician threw out his broad chest and announced: "It's a boy!" He was Dr. Patrick Henry O'Hara. His wife was the former Katherine Delaney of Lykens. The son was John, with middle name Henry.

The boy was nothing out of the ordinary, except that he liked to read. And that wasn't really extraordinary for Mahantongo Street, where the family lived over Dr. O'Hara's offices. Mahantongo Street—Lantenengo Street in O'Hara's stories—was coal operator's row. People who built there had money or brains. The Indian name fits this street well. Mahantongo means "plenty of meat."

Dr. and Mrs. O'Hara were certainly not out of place on Mahantongo. She was valedictorian of her class at Eden Hall, the fashionable girls' school in Torresdale; spoke French and played bridge. Dr. O'Hara was the busiest physician for miles around.

As John waltzed into his teens, his wishes ran to horses and his father provided the money for him to ride. In fact, the grand young man of Mahantongo Street had the best of everything. While he played golf and tennis and rolled an eye at the girls, he was holding a firm finger on the pulse of society, as befits a physician's son.

Dr. O'Hara owned five cars at one time. His stock investments were hefty. But he worked too hard, and died in 1925 at age 57. As soon as he was laid to rest, it became clear he had invested unwisely. The bad state of the family's finances smashed John's fondest dream: a Yale education. He never got to college.

John had gone to St. Patrick's Parochial School, without being expelled even once, and then on to Keystone State Normal in Kutztown and Fordham Prep in New York, leaving both rather abruptly. He wound up at Niagara Prep at Niagara Falls, as valedictorian, no less. Because this celebrated graduate loved to celebrate—and did, riotously, after commencement in 1924—his angered father made him put off plans to enter Yale. Dr. O'Hara said he should work a year, grow up a little.

John went to the now-defunct Pottsville *Journal* as reporter and writer at $6 a week. His father died before the year had ended. The story goes that O'Hara was later fired by the *Journal,* because, of all things, he couldn't write. Walter S. Farquhar, a writer with the Pottsville *Republican,* refused to confirm this, yet wouldn't deny it. He said, "I worked with John on the *Journal.* A nice guy. Not much of a reporter. Too artistic. We used a lot of names in our stories. He rebelled at this. Oh, and another thing, he didn't like to fish for news over the phone. He hated it. But John was a swell fellow."*

*Walter Farquhar commented to Professor Sheldon N. Grebstein: "John liked to write but he didn't like to report. He didn't have the news sense. He was too impatient to do routine drudgery, too much of an artist. He missed routine assignments because he didn't think they were worth covering."

In 1949 O'Hara told the late critic Harvey Breit: "The newspaper influence is good for the writer. It teaches economy of words. It makes you write faster. When you're on rewrite as I was, you can't fool around at half-past nine trying to write beautiful lacy prose."

O'Hara in his collection of short stories, *Assembly,* added: "A young newspaper reporter sees so much in the first few years that he begins to think he's seen it all. That makes for a very unattractive wise-guy attitude, what I call unearned cynicism. After you've lived a good many years I don't see how you can be anything but cynical, since all any of us have a right to expect is an even break, and not many get that. But I thought I knew it all, and I didn't. It took me many more years to realize that a reporter covering general news lives an abnormal life, in that he sees people every day at the highest or lowest point of their lives. Day after day after day, people in trouble with the law, having accidents, losing control of themselves—or experiencing great successes. In one month's time a district man would see enough crime and horror and selfishness to last most people the rest of their lives."

After leaving the *Journal,* O'Hara worked a while on a Tamaqua paper and reportedly was fired there for not being punctual. A few months later, he set out for the bright lights of New York.

Eugene A. O'Hara, the youngest of the eight O'Hara children, remembers well the day John left home. "I can see him now: raccoon coat, the gold watch dad left him, the banjo he loved so much to play, his Buick roadster. Oh, how I hated to see him go. We were very close. I idolized him. What a terrific sense of humor! I can recall John pulling out a notebook, jotting down witty thoughts the second they came to him, anywhere, anything."

Eugene, who still lives on Mahantongo Street, said the Pottsville dandy's departure was a sad moment for the entire family. He said his mother and the others—Mary, Joseph I., Mart E., Thomas P., James E. and Kathleen—were either in tears or mightily close to them. Mart, once the chauffeur for David L. Lawrence, who later became governor, and James both still live in Pottsville. Tom became a political reporter for the New York *Herald Tribune.*

John was virtually unknown when he reached New York. It wasn't long, however, before he knew the bartenders in the swank speakeasies, show people and a few editors. They say he spent more time in bars than the average man did in bed.

He sold his first short story to the *New Yorker* in 1928. This was by no means the top of the ladder, only the first rung, and he didn't have a tight grip. But jobs seemed easy to find. He was a soda jerk, ship's steward, amusement park guard, gas meter reader, day laborer, railroad freight clerk, switchboard operator, once turned down a job as a bootlegger. He went three days without food on an excursion to Chicago when he failed as a panhandler. At various times, he also worked for *Newsweek,* the *Herald Tribune,* the *Mirror, Time, Editor and Publisher,* as editor-in-chief of the *Pittsburgh Bulletin-Index* and as secretary to Heywood Broun.

After selling a few more stories to the *New Yorker,* he became a staff reporter there—until one day his editor, the late Harold Ross, with a glaring lack of prescience, decided he didn't like O'Hara and ordered him fired.

So John, now down to his last suit, got to thinking again of Pottsville, or rather "Gibbsville," the name he gave the town in a salute to his best friend, the late Wolcott Gibbs, then a *New Yorker* editor, later its drama critic, and playwright. It wasn't that he wanted to go home. He simply felt compelled to put all those things he knew so much about into a manuscript.

He went to work, and in 1934 *Appointment in Samarra* hit the bookshelves. O'Hara's realistic dialogue was an immediate success. Critics hailed this "master of the vernacular," this "social historian," the "voice of the hang-over generation."

O'Hara was made. And Pottsville was mad. The reaction was almost as vigorous as the writing, almost as earthy. "Old Doc O'Hara would put a switch to that boy were he alive today," was one comment. Another was, "Let that fresh kid stay in New York."

This didn't stop O'Hara. He used other Pennsylvania towns in his novels and short stories. These places included Harrisburg, Lykens, Pottstown, Minersville, Schuylkill Haven—all under different names. A temporary relief, but it didn't soothe tempers in Pottsville, the seat of O'Hara's fictional world.

Along came *The Doctor's Son, Butterfield 8, Hope of Heaven, Pipe Night, A Rage to Live, The Farmer's Hotel, Ten North Frederick, Ourselves to Know, The Cape Cod Lighter, The Big Laugh, Elizabeth Appleton,* and right in the middle of all this *Pal Joey,* a series of short stories he wrapped up into a Broadway musical in 1940, which won honors as the best musical of 1951-52 when it was brought back in a revival.

Time, as it usually does, cured "Gibbsville's" wounds. I spent a few days in Pottsville and learned that O'Hara's former neighbors no longer react to his name with a sneer. Now, all is forgiven. At least, almost all.

"I'm not holier-than-thou," said Miss Edith Patterson. "Like others in Pottsville, I was shocked. I didn't like the things O'Hara wrote, nor the way he wrote them. He brought a foreign vocabulary to our people, one they were not used to. Of course, the reaction was strong. Now, however, there is a lot of smut in the book world. It makes O'Hara look mild. And I must admit, like the present generation, I have come to accept John."

Miss Patterson was Pottsville's librarian from 1918 to until she retired in 1950. She remembers O'Hara as a boy. "He came in once in a while. I can see him today over at the poetry shelves, in a snappy suit." She once bought *A Rage to Live,* read it and sent it back to the publisher. "Too trashy for our shelves" was her verdict. She also recalled that the Pottsville Library Board, objecting to O'Hara's portrayal of the town, once banned his books. "However, it wasn't long before we bought all his works," she said. "We kept them under lock and key for a long time. You couldn't lend them out to just anyone."

There is no special O'Hara section. In fact, his books find their place in an obscure corner. Nothing intentional. The O's just happen to stack up there. Nevertheless, the public manages to find them. The day I was in the library, there wasn't an O'Hara book to be borrowed.

Daniel Purcell, who has been around Pottsville most of his seventy-seven years, remembers the entire O'Hara family. "Old Doc treated me several times," he said. "He was a big, strong, handsome man. I'm not much of a reader, so I can't say I ever read any of John's books, but I hear they were pretty raw. They sure created a lot of excitement around here years ago."

Leonard Weiner, who sells custom kitchens on the first floor of the three-story wood and brick building where O'Hara was born, said he knew O'Hara well. "John poked a lot of fun at a lot of neighbors," Weiner said. "If I lived next door to him, I could write some pretty nasty things too and leave out all the good, but he did write some fine stuff."

Herrwood E. Hobbs, postmaster of Pottsville, who used to work on the *Journal* with O'Hara, recalled some sharp criticism of *Appointment*. "But, frankly," he said, "I no longer hear anyone talking about O'Hara. He's remote, comes here only once in a blue moon. The people he wrote about on Mahantongo Street weren't disreputable. Those who live there today aren't. They're the people who did the most for Pottsville."

Eugene O'Hara said, "Talk about the better people in town not liking him is nonsense. This gossip prevails only among those not in a position to know. When word gets around that John is coming for a visit, the better people want to throw a party for him." Eugene admits his brother hasn't gotten back often, maybe three or four times since he hit the big time. The last trip home was a couple of years ago when their mother was buried in St. Patrick's No. 3 Cemetery.

"Yet we get to see him," Eugene said. "His brothers and sisters pop in at Quogue or Princeton once in a while." Not many others get into his sprawling French manor house in Princeton. In choosing friends, O'Hara is very selective. Some of his neighbors say he's mean, a man of violent temper and repulsive personality. O'Hara is aware of this. He says he hates hateful people, and that there are so many around "I'm going to be busy for a long time."

Those who get to see the author never do until mid-afternoon, for he sleeps late, putters around, reads, refuses interviews, then puts on the coffee pot to go to work. From midnight until 6 a.m., or even later, he pounds the typewriter. He's got a lot on his mind and he's trying hard to get it all off while he has the health. The pace is frantic, the output a-mazing. He rarely rewrites. He simply types it, mails it to eager editors and deposits the checks.

Brother Eugene recalls John's taking him to Florida in the early Forties. "We stopped at a motel in Norfolk," he said. "Just as John was hopping into bed, he hopped out and uncovered his typewriter. In twenty minutes, he knocked out a story. He put it in an envelope, and I mailed it. A couple of months later it was in the *New Yorker*.

Friends—and he does have friends—say O'Hara likes a good time but hates his good times to be arranged.

His third wife is the former Katherine Barnes Bryan, whom he married in 1955. His second wife, by whom he had his only child, Wylie, died in 1954, and when Belle died O'Hara said "it was the only dirty trick she ever pulled on anybody."

O'Hara has received many honors. In May of 1964 the American Academy of Arts and Letters gave him its Award of Merit. Even Philadelphia paid tribute to him, making him an honorary citizen in 1961, when his close friend, Richardson Dilworth, was mayor.

Now that he has all the money and fame he needs, O'Hara is looking for more ribbons, the really big ones. He makes no secret of wanting a Nobel Prize. When his friend, John Steinbeck, won the Nobel Prize in 1962, O'Hara cabled him: "Congratulations. You were my second choice!"

Ben Franklin and His Pen

The most world-renowned writer and editor to come from Pennsylvania remains Benjamin Franklin. His *Autobiography* is probably the most famous book ever written by a Pennsylvanian, either in non-fiction or fiction, for critics enjoy pointing out how Franklin used his vivid imagination to elaborate on his own wit and wisdom, stretching the truth more than once.

Franklin was a first-rate editor. He started his *Pennsylvania Gazette* in 1729, noting that a rival Philadelphia sheet was "a paltry thing, wretchedly manag'd, and no way entertaining." He told the story of an apprentice hatter about to enter business who planned a signboard for himself, "John Thompson, Hatter, makes and sells hats for ready money." Before ordering the sign made, he consulted his friends. They whittled away his text until all that was left was "John Thompson," with a figure of a hat.

It was probably Franklin who edited Thomas Jefferson's first draft of the Declaration of Independence. "We hold these truths to be sacred and undeniable," wrote Jefferson. Franklin substituted "self-evident" for the last three words. Jefferson wrote that foreign mercenaries were sent to "deluge us in blood." Franklin toned down the language to "destroy us."

A recently vanished past comes to life in
John Updike's
The Dogwood Tree: A Boyhood

John Updike grew up in Shillington (his fictional
"Olinger") and on his family's farm at Plowville,
not far from Reading (his "Alton"). He has
become one of America's foremost chroniclers
of the suburban, small-town, Protestant, white
middle class.

The class comments in the 1950 Shillington High School yearbook read:
"Uppy doubles as poet and cartoonist...fathered both class plays...calls
Stephen's home...pet hate: ketchup...love dat Buick!...basketball and pin-
balling big sports interests...the sage of Plowville hopes to write for a living."

John Hoyer Updike indeed did go on to write for a living, and to write very
well, earning comfort and fame. His fifth novel, *Couples,* in 1968 was a best-
seller, and he made the cover of *Time* magazine, this small-town Pennsylvanian, as the cartographer of "The Adulterous Society," as *Time* labeled
contemporary, supposedly promiscuous America.

Updike's record is sturdy enough and his potential so great that he is
clearly one of the most important figures working today in American literature, though he has yet to prove himself the F. Scott Fitzgerald or Ernest
Hemingway of this generation.

He was born March 18, 1932, in West Reading, the only child of Wesley
R. and Linda Grace Hoyer Updike. He grew up in Shillington (the "Olinger"
in his stories) and on his family's 84-acre farm at Plowville, not far from
Reading (Updike's "Alton"). His father earned less than $2,000 for many

years as a junior high school mathematics teacher, and Updike used him as a model for his character George Caldwell, the driver of an old Buick and the science teacher in *The Centaur.* "Though for thirty years a public school teacher, he still believed in education," Updike once remarked wryly of one of his short-story personalities. Updike's mother has had her short stories published, under her maiden name, in the *New Yorker* magazine since her son reached the top.

Updike was a high-spirited, small-town Pennsylvania youngster, an incessant reader, good student, and a copy boy on the *Reading Eagle* for two summers. The girl he took to the senior prom told Ellen Sulkis of the Philadelphia *Bulletin* fifteen years later, "I knew even then he'd be famous, and I'd be able to say that I went out with him. My father thought he was absolutely crazy, but when I looked at Johnny, I didn't notice that his hair was uncombed or that he wore funny clothes."

He grew up to be 6 feet tall, about 170 pounds, with hair uncombed over a distinctive, almost early-American-looking long face. He is still high-spirited and seldom can stop himself from salting his writings with humor. Solemnity is not his bit, though he has almost a professorial curiosity about the intricacies of theology. He can't be taken seriously when he told a reporter he wanted to write a play about President James Buchanan.

Updike graduated *summa cum laude* from Harvard in 1954, and then spent a year at the Ruskin School of Drawing and Fine Art at Oxford. While a Harvard undergraduate, he married Mary Pennington, a fine arts major at Radcliffe and the daughter of a Unitarian minister in Chicago. The Updikes now live in Ipswich, Massachusetts, and have four children.

Updike was a staff member of the *New Yorker* for two years, and in 1957 became a full-time writer on his own. Much of his early work concerns Pennsylvania, which he dearly loves though he complains that its pollen gives him hay fever. His first four novels all were set in Pennsylvania: *The Poorhouse Fair,* 1959; *Rabbit, Run,* 1960; *The Centaur,* 1963, and *Of the Farm,* 1965. *Rabbit, Run* was bought by the movies in 1961, and in the summer of 1969 scenes were filmed in Reading. Many of Updike's excellent short stories, such as "The Persistence of Desire," also take place in Pennsylvania.

In 1964 when Updike accepted the National Book Award for *The Centaur,* he said: "Every generation—and readers and writers are brothers in this— inherits a vast attic of machinery that once worked and decorative doodahs whose silhouettes no longer sing. We must each of us clear enough space in this attic so we in turn can unpack."

Updike early in his career had his portion of the attic cleared and his talents unpacked. He made his place with a recognized originality and inventiveness, a gusto and aliveness, and that rare gift for being versatile and expansive while at the same time being meticulously precise and perceptive about delicate details. Updike has perfect pitch. He never rings false and never—he is that good—resorts to clichés or conventional writing. He writes as if he has been a professional for twenty to twenty-five years—which, unofficially, he has. When he can pinpoint a young doctor as "venerable with competence and witnessed pain," he is indeed the "Andrew Wyeth of literature," as John Barth, the novelist who taught at Pennsylvania State University, called him.

Updike captivates readers with his lyrical prose and dazzling manner. Invariably—as all artists must—he frustrates readers too, but in his own way. He is excessive, self-conscious, inconclusive, victimized by his own easy brilliance, coy, and often just too playful or clever. Norman Mailer once said he was just too "wry-necked," and that might be it. He enjoys cataloging, just as his fellow Pennsylvanian John O'Hara does. The splendid incidentals he elaborates about—baseball, bees, Dwight Eisenhower, pigeons, pinball machines, psoriasis, and the byways of sex—shine like diamonds on the printed page, but somewhere among the nuances and fine style Updike usually has pushed aside his plot and characters. An Updike piece of writing often resembles the modern good movie: tuned in to the audience's emotion, with a stepped-up pace, constant information signals about people and their predicaments, unexpected truths flashed amidst the honest reportage, nothing cornball and no shortcuts, yet in the end disappointing because it is only a temporary experience and lacks a transcending quality. Updike is a short-distance man, perhaps deliberately, and he has not yet attempted the novel with a theme bigger than its creator, a novel with intense dramatic situations and characters who clear their own attic space in human experience.

He once wrote of fellow author J. D. Salinger that "the refusal to rest content, the willingness to risk excess on behalf of one's obsessions, is what distinguishes artists from entertainers." Yet perhaps to explain himself, Updike noted in writing of James Agee: "A fever of self-importance is upon American writing. Popular expectations of what literature should provide have risen so high that failure is the only possible success, and pained incapacity the only acceptable proof of sincerity."

Pennsylvanians would take to Updike even if he weren't a native son. What so many must find revealing is his familiarity with the American Protestant white middle class, suburban and small-town. He portrays that common mass of people who are heterosexual, job-holding, troubled, religious-imbrued if not always church-going every Sunday, and well-meaning yet nervous about their fallibility. The Lutheranism, Unitarianism, and Congregationalism in Updike combine with his Berks County heritage to add a vital firmness to his work. It is interesting that the other acclaimed writer from the Reading area, poet Wallace Stevens (1879-1955), while lacking Updike's gaiety, also had an elegance of imagery and beneath that a deep understanding too of human chaos, sensibilities, and inner thought. Updike once remarked about his section of Pennsylvania: "I feel that there's something particularly fruitful here for becoming a writer. I find there is a sense of human richness here. Puritanism didn't touch the area with a heavy hand.

You have more access to people's real selves and not their social masks—there's a richness and a brutality."

The following are five of the sixteen sections of "The Dogwood Tree: A Boyhood." Updike originally wrote this impressionistic biography for *Five Boyhoods*, edited and copyrighted by Martin Levin and published by Doubleday & Company. The piece was later reprinted in *Assorted Prose* by John Updike, published by Alfred A. Knopf.

The Dogwood Tree:
A Boyhood

by John Updike

When I was born, my parents and my mother's parents planted a dogwood tree in the side yard of the large white house in which we lived throughout my boyhood. This tree, I learned quite early, was exactly my age, was, in a sense, me. But I never observed it closely, am not now sure what color its petals were; its presence was no more distinct than that of my shadow. The tree was my shadow, and had it died, had it ceased to occupy, each year with increasing volume and brilliance, its place in the side yard, I would have felt that a blessing like the blessing of light had been withdrawn from my life.

Though I cannot ask you to see it more clearly than I myself saw it, yet mentioning it seems to open the possibility of my boyhood home coming again to life. With a sweet damp rush the grass of our yard seems to breathe again on me. It is just cut. My mother is pushing the mower, to which a canvas catch is attached. My grandmother is raking up the loose grass in thick heaps, small green haystacks impregnated with dew, and my grandfather stands off to one side, smoking a cigar, elegantly holding the elbow of his right arm in the palm of his left hand while the blue smoke twists from under his mustache and dissolves in the heavy evening air—that misted, too-rich Pennsylvania air. My father is off, doing some duty in the town; he is a conscientious man, a school teacher and deacon, and also, somehow, a man of the streets.

In remembering the dogwood tree I remember the faintly speckled asbestos shingles of the chicken house at the bottom of our yard, fronting on the alley. We had a barn as well, which we rented as a garage, having no car of our own, and between the chicken house and the barn there was a narrow space where my grandfather, with his sly country ways, would urinate. I, a child, did also, passing through this narrow, hidden-feeling passage to the school grounds beyond our property; the fibrous tan-gray of the shingles would leap up dark, silky and almost black, when wetted.

The ground in this little passage seems a mysterious trough of pebbles of all colors and bits of paper and broken glass. A few weeds managed to grow in the perpetual shadow. All the ground at the lower end of the yard had an ungrateful quality; we had an ash heap on which we used to burn, in an extravagant ceremony that the war's thrift ended, the preceding day's newspaper. The earth for yards around the ashpile was colored gray. Chickens clucked in their wire pen. My grandmother tended them, and when the time came, beheaded them with an archaic efficiency that I don't recall ever witnessing, though I often studied the heavy log whose butt was ornamented with fine white neck-feathers pasted to the wood with blood.

A cat crosses our lawn, treading hastily on the damp grass, crouching low with distaste. Tommy is the cat's name; he lives in our chicken house but is not a pet. He is perfectly black; a rarity, he has no white dab on his chest. The birds scold out of the walnut tree and the apple and cherry trees. We have a large grape-arbor, and a stone birdbath, and a brick walk, and a privet hedge the height of a child and many bushes behind which my playmates hide. There is a pansy bed that in winter we cover with straw. The air is green, and heavy, and flavored with the smell of turned earth; in our garden grows, among other vegetables, a bland, turniplike cabbage called kohlrabi, which I have never seen, or eaten, since the days when, for a snack, I would tear one from its rows with my hands.

My boyhood was spent in a world made tranquil by two invisible catastrophes: the Depression and World War II. Between 1932, when I was born, and 1945, when we moved away, the town of Shillington changed, as far as I could see, very little. The vacant lot beside our home on Philadelphia Avenue remained vacant. The houses along the street were neither altered nor replaced. The high-school grounds, season after season, continued to make a placid plain visible from our rear windows. The softball field, with its triptych backstop, was nearest us. A little beyond, on the left, were the school and its boilerhouse, built in the late 1920s of the same ochre brick. In the middle distance a cinder track circumscribed the football field. At a greater distance there were the tennis courts and the poor farm fields and the tall double rows of trees marking the Poorhouse Lane. The horizon was the blue cloud, scarred by a gravel pit's orange slash, of Mount Penn, which overlooked the city of Reading.

A little gravel alley, too small to be marked with a street sign but known in the neighborhood as Shilling Alley, wound hazardously around our property and on down, past an untidy sequence of back buildings (chicken houses, barns out of plumb, a gunshop, a small lumber mill, a shack where a blind man lived, and the enchanted grotto of a garage whose cement floors had been waxed to the lustre of ebony by oil drippings and in whose greasy-black depths a silver drinking fountain spurted the coldest water in the world, silver water so cold it made your front teeth throb) on down to Lancaster Avenue, the main street, where the trolley cars ran. All through those years, the trolley cars ran. All through those years Pappy Shilling, the surviving son of the landowner after whom the town was named, walked up and down Philadelphia Avenue with his thin black cane and his snow-white bangs; a vibrating chain of perfect-Sunday-school-attendance pins dangled from his lapel. Each autumn the horse-chestnut trees dropped their useless, treasurable nuts; each spring the dogwood tree put forth a slightly larger spread of blossoms; always the leaning walnut tree in our back yard fretted with the same tracery of branches the view we had.

Within our house, too, there was little change. My grandparents did not die, though they seemed very old. My father continued to teach at the high school; he had secured the job shortly after I was born. No one else was born. I was an only child. A great many only children were born in 1932; I make no apologies. I do not remember ever feeling the space for a competitor within the house. The five of us already there locked into a star that would have shattered like crystal at the admission of a sixth. We had no pets. We fed Tommy on the porch, but he was too wild to set foot in the kitchen, and only my grandmother, in a way wild herself, could touch him. Tommy came to us increasingly battered and once did not come at all. As if he had never existed: that was death. And then there was a squirrel, Tilly, that we fed peanuts to; she became very tame, and under the grape arbor would take them from our hands. The excitement of those tiny brown teeth shivering against my fingertips: that was life. But she, too, came from the outside, and returned to her tree, and did not dare intrude in our house.

The arrangement inside, which seemed to me so absolute, had been achieved, beyond the peripheries of my vision, drastically and accidentally. It may, at first, have been meant to be temporary. My father and grandfather were casualties of the early Thirties. My father lost his job as a cable splicer with the telephone company; he and my mother had been living—for how long I have never understood—in boardinghouses and hotels throughout Western Pennsylvania, in towns whose names (Hazleton, Altoona) even now make their faces light up with youth, a glow flowing out of the darkness preceding my birth. They lived through this darkness, and the details of the adventure that my mother recalls— her lonely closeted days, the games of solitaire, the novels by Turgenev, the prostitutes downstairs, the men sleeping and starving in the parks of Pittsburgh—seem to waken in her an unjust and unreasonable happiness that used to rouse jealousy in my childish heart. I remember waiting with her by a window for my father to return from weeks on the road. It is in the Shillington living room. My hands are on the radiator ridges, I can see my father striding through the hedge toward the grape arbor, I feel my mother's excitement beside me mingle with mine. But she says this cannot be; he had lost his job before I was born.

My grandfather came from farming people in the south of the country. He prospered, and prematurely retired; the large suburban house he bought to house his good fortune became his fortune's shell, the one fragment of it left him. The two men pooled their diminished resources of strength and property and, with their women, came to live together. I do not believe they expected this arrangement to last long. For all of them—for all four of my adult guardians—Shillington was a snag, a halt in a journey that had begun elsewhere. Only I belonged to the town. The accidents that had planted me here made uneasy echoes in the house, but, like Tilly and Tommy, their source was beyond my vision.

We were Democrats. My grandfather lived for 90 years, and always voted, and always voted straight Democrat. A marvellous chain of votes, as marvellous as the chain of Sunday-school-attendance pins that vibrated from Pappy Shilling's lapel. The political tradition that shaped his so incorruptible prejudice I am not historian enough to understand; it had something to do with Lincoln's determination to drive all the cattle out of this section of Pennsylvania if Lee won the Battle of Gettysburg.

My parents are closer to me. The events that shaped their views are in my bones. At the time when I was conceived and born, they felt in themselves a whole nation stunned, frightened, despairing. With Roosevelt, hope returned. This simple impression of salvation is my political inheritance. That this impression is not universally shared amazes me. It is as if there existed a class of people who deny that the sun is bright. To me as a child Republicans seemed blind dragons; their prototype was my barber—an artist, a charmer, the only man, my mother insists, who ever cut my hair properly. Nimble and bald, he used to execute little tap-dance figures on the linoleum floor of his shop, and with engaging loyalty he always had the games of Philadelphia's two eighth-place teams tuned in on the radio. But on one subject he was rabid; the last time he cut my hair he positively asserted that our President had died of syphilis. I cannot to this day hear a Republican put forth his philosophy without hearing the snip of scissors above my ears and feeling the little ends of hair crawling across my hot face, reddened by shame and the choking pressure of the paper collar.

Roosevelt was for me the cap on a steadfast world, its emblem and crown. He was always there. Now he is a weakening memory, a semi-legend; it has begun to seem fabulous—like an episode in a medieval chronicle—that the greatest nation in the world was led through the world's greatest war by a man who could not walk. Now, my barber has retired, my hair is a wretched thatch grizzled with gray, and, of the two Philadelphia ball clubs, one has left Philadelphia and one is not always in last place. Now the brick home of my boyhood is owned by a doctor, who has added an annex to the front, to contain his offices. The house was too narrow for its lot and its height; it had a pinched look from the front that used to annoy my mother. But that thin white front with its eyes of green window sash and its mouth of striped awning had been a face to me; it has vanished. My dogwood tree still stands in the side yard, taller than ever, but the walnut tree out back has been cut down. My grandparents are dead. Pappy Shilling is dead. Shilling Alley has been straightened, and hardtopped, and rechristened Brobst Street. The trolley cars no longer run. The vacant lots across the town have been filled with new houses and stores. New homes have been built far out Philadelphia Avenue and all over the poorhouse property. The poor-house has been demolished. The poorhouse dam and its aphrodisiac groves have been trimmed into a town park and a chlorinated pool where all females must sheathe their hair in prophylactic bathing caps. If I could go again into 117 Philadelphia Avenue and look out the rear windows, I would see, beyond the football field and the cinder track, a new, two-million-dollar high school, and beyond it, where still stands one row of the double line of trees that marked the Poorhouse Lane, a gaudy depth of postwar housing and a Food Fair like a hideous ark breasting an ocean of parked cars. Here, where wheat grew, loudspeak-ers unremittingly vomit commercials. It has taken me the shocks of many returnings, more and more widely spaced now, to learn, what seems simple enough, that change is the order of things. The immu-tability, the steadfastness, of the site of my boyhood was an exceptional effect, purchased for me at unimaginable cost by the paralyzing calamity of the Depression and the heroic external effort of the Second World War.

I was walking down this Philadelphia Avenue one April and was just stepping over the shallow little rain gutter in the pavement that could throw you if you were on roller skates—though it had been years since I had been on roller skates—when from the semi-detached house across the street a boy broke and ran. He was the youngest of six sons. All of his brothers were in the armed services, and five blue stars hung in his home's front window. He was several years older than I, and used to annoy my grandparents by walking through our yard, down past the grape arbor, on his way to high school. Long-legged, he was now running diagonally across the high-crowned street. I was the only person out in the air. "Chonny!" he called. I was flattered to have him, so tall and grown, speak to me. "Did you hear?"

"No. What?"

"On the radio. The President is dead."

That summer the war ended, and that fall, suddenly mobile, we moved away from the big white house. We moved on Halloween night. As the movers were fitting the last pieces of furniture, furniture that had not moved since I was born, into their truck, little figures dressed as ghosts and cats flitted in and out of the shadows of the street. A few rang our bell, and when my mother opened the door they were frightened by the empty rooms they saw behind her, and went away without begging. When the last things had been packed, and the kitchen light turned off, and the doors locked, the three of us—my grandparents were already at the new house—got into the old Buick my father had bought—in Shillington we had never had a car, for we could walk everywhere—and drove up the street, east, toward the poorhouse and beyond. Somewhat self-consciously and cruelly dramatizing my grief, for I was thirteen and beginning to be cunning, I twisted and watched our house recede through the rear window. Moonlight momentarily caught in an upper pane; then the reflection passed, and the brightest thing was the white brick wall itself. Against the broad blank part where I used to bat a tennis ball for hours at a time, the silhouette of the dogwood tree stood confused with the shapes of the other bushes in our side yard, but taller. I turned away before it would have disappeared from sight; and so it is that my shadow has always remained in one place.

introducing
Paul B. Beers'
Pennsylvanians in Fiction

John Dos Passos, Christopher Morley, Thomas
Wolfe, F. Scott Fitzgerald, Sinclair Lewis, H. L.
Mencken, Theodore Dreiser, John O'Hara, and
John Updike are among the many authors who
have created memorable Pennsylvanian fictional
characters.

Have you ever noticed how many leading characters in famous novels are
Pennsylvanians? Here is a gallery of rogues, heroes, and people in between,
who enliven the pages of some of America's brightest contemporary fiction,
as reprinted from the "Reporter at Large" column, Harrisburg *Evening News,*
November 25, 1966.

Pennsylvanians in Fiction

by Paul B. Beers

Pennsylvania long has been a fertile field for fictional characters. Novelists, short story writers, dramatists, movie writers and television gagmen have made ample use of Pennsylvania. Why? It is difficult to say, except to observe that they've found Pennsylvanians to be an interesting breed.

John Dos Passos, in his classic novel, *USA,* has one of his major characters, J. Ward Moorehouse, start out in Philadelphia as an editorial writer for the old *Public Ledger.* Moorehouse comes home one night to find his bride, Annabelle, in the arms of a disreputable young architect. Moorehouse leaves Annabelle, quits his job and belts out for Pittsburgh in one of those peregrinations Dos Passos can describe so well.

Kitty Foyle, of Christopher Morley's 1939 classic of the same name, is an Irish-American Philadelphian with lusty instincts. Throughout the novel much of what she sees and hears reminds her of Pennsylvania. The fountain in Rockefeller Plaza is like a Pocono waterfall. She is on a subway headed for the old World's Fair, and whom does she meet but a bunch of kids wearing signs labeled "Harrisburg *Patriot.*" They are carrier boys off to the Fair, and Kitty cringes at the name Harrisburg because the first time she visited it she and a boyfriend over-celebrated.

Father Gant, the tombstone cutter in Thomas Wolfe's *Look Homeward, Angel,* was from the farmland near Gettysburg, as was Wolfe's real father. The hero of F. Scott Fitzgerald's final and incomplete novel, *The Last Tycoon,* was Monroe Stahr, of Erie. Stahr's advanced education was limited to a night school course in stenography, but he went on to be one of Hollywood's great directors in the Golden Era of the movies. Stahr had the "kind of eye that can stare straight into the sun," Fitzgerald wrote. He also had an eye for ankles.

Late in his career, Sinclair Lewis spent sixteen days traveling through Pennsylvania to get material. He was in his dry period at the time, but nevertheless he stayed up most of the night in Harrisburg to hear political tales.

H. L. Mencken wrote about "The Little Girl from Red Lion, P.A.," who went to the big, bad city of Baltimore. Humorist S. J. Perelman had a character named Joe Carbondale, no relation to Bill Scranton. Damon Runyon had Scranton Slim, the gambler who sings in the chorus of "Guys and Dolls." James Gould Cozzens stocked two of his novels, *The Just and the Unjust* and *By Love Possessed,* with characters from county bar associations in Pennsylvania.

Theodore Dreiser created an ugly set of political characters in his Philadelphia-based novel, *The Financier.* One is Judge Wilbur Payderson, "willing and anxious to do whatever he considered that he reasonably could do to further the party welfare and the private interests of his masters."

Warren Eyster, a native of Steelton, fills his 1955 novel, *No Country for Old Men,* with Pennsylvania figures. One is Tad Stevens, a county political boss. "Every ounce of his lean, bony figure was proud of his reputation, the good and the corrupt, and many people were proud of him. He raked his tithe, doubled it in good years, did not deny it, and in turn could be trusted to do what really needed to be done."

J. D. Salinger in his famous *Catcher in the Rye* created Pencey Prep, which by now is Pennsylvania's most world-renowned preparatory school, fictional or non-fictional. Salinger in real life went to Valley Forge Military Academy.

The novels of John O'Hara, Conrad Richter, John Updike and James Reichley, all native-born Pennsylvanians, are, of course, filled with Pennsylvania figures.

O'Hara created Julian English with his Kappa Beta Phi key and his "waxed-calf shoes." Al Grecco is the classic hustler in *Appointment in Samarra.* He drives down rich Lantenengo Street in Gibbsville early one Christmas morning, rolls down his car window and shouts, "Merry Christmas, you stuck-up-bastards, Merry Christmas." Then there is the politician Mike Slattery. "He had the look of a man who spent a great deal of time with the barber, the manicurist and the bootblack." And "Paul Donaldson from Scranton who was always referred to as Paul Donaldson from or of Scranton....In the list of directors of his New York bank his name was down as Paul Donaldson, Scranton, Pa., instead of Paul Donaldson, attorney-at-law, or the name of the firm." Of course, "Gentleman Joe" Chapin, of Gibbsville, is a superb O'Hara creation. Chapin sought to buy the Republican nomination for lieutenant governor and failed.

In his novel about Harrisburg, *A Rage to Live,* O'Hara has a few memorable characters. There is the disreputable Grace Caldwell Tate. There is the dentist, Dr. George W. Walthour, who is made mayor and whose lofty ambition is to have a bridge at Washington Street named after him while he is still alive. And there is the governor, Karl F. Dunkelberger, of Allentown, whose wife bought him the office. "No matter where they went it would always be nice to be able to mention that Karl had once been governor. It was a nice thing to be able to say," O'Hara writes. Meanwhile, Dunkelberger had trouble with his kidneys.

Richter has created a saint of this world in the Rev. Harry Donner, a humble Lutheran minister. In *A Simple Honorable Man,* Donner recalls riding a Johnstown trolley and smelling garlic on everyone's breath.

Updike captures a humble but persevering Pennsylvania school teacher, George Caldwell, in *The Centaur.* Probably no one has observed the Pennsylvania middle class as well as Updike.

Reichley has many Pennsylvanians in his *The Burying of Kingsmith* and *Hail to the Chief.* His best character might be Dan Shimonis, a big-shot nothing who "liked slobs" and said, "Howyadoin, fellows," to every street-corner gang. There must be a half-million Shimonises between the Delaware and the Ohio, wandering in the paths of unrighteousness and studying high school football, pretty girls, ward-heelers and wisecracks. Their dads were immigrant laborers who did more work in one week than the sons do in a lifetime.

W. C. Fields' Other Names

W. C. Fields (1879-1946) was born Claude William Dukinfield, possibly in Darby, but probably at 6320 Woodland Avenue in Philadelphia in a house now demolished. During his career of comedy he used hundreds of names, many of which have been traced back to old Philadelphia residents.

Charlie Muckle, Charlie Bogle, Mahatma Kane Jeeves, Effingham B. Huffnagle, Ambrose Wolfinger, Cuthbert J. Twillie, Godfrey Daniel, Egbert Souse, and Otis Criblecoblis found their way into Fields' comedy and came, in whole or in part, from Philadelphia.

Fields' parents are buried in Philadelphia's Greenwood Cemetery. On their stones are: "Kate Dukinfield—A Sweet Old Soul" and "James Dukinfield—A Good Scout." Fields himself is buried at Forest Lawn. Contrary to the legend, he has no epitaph, not even his gag line, "Rather here than Philadelphia."

Part IV
Pennsylvania in Politics: Past and Present

introducing
S. K. Stevens'
A Shot Is Heard in Pennsylvania

No one is better qualified to write about Pennsylvania's significant role in the American Revolution than Dr. S. K. Stevens, State Historian and president for three years of the Pennsylvania Historical Association.

Dr. Sylvester K. Stevens might well know more about the history of Pennsylvania than any other person. Certainly no other native Pennsylvanian has written as many words on Pennsylvania history as Dr. Stevens. He has more than a dozen books to his credit, and his two major works, *Pennsylvania, Birthplace of a Nation,* and *Pennsylvania, The Heritage of a Commonwealth,* total 1,754 pages and for their breadth of information are unduplicated.

In a career of forty years as a historian, Dr. Stevens has not let the gathering of facts, a concern for interpretation, nor heavy administrative duties submerge his lively wit. "I believe I understand equally Philadelphia and Eastern Pennsylvania, and Pittsburgh and Western Pennsylvania, but I am sure they do not yet entirely understand each other," he quipped in the foreword to *Birthplace of a Nation.*

Dr. Stevens, the grandson of a Pennsylvania pioneer, was born in 1904 in Harrison Valley, Potter County. He earned his bachelor and master degrees from Pennsylvania State University and taught there. He received his doctorate in 1945 from Columbia University for, ironically, a study of the newest state, Hawaii. He also has received honorary degrees from Susquehanna University, and Lebanon Valley and Moravian colleges.

He has not been an ivory tower scholar. In 1937 he was named State Historian and then in 1956 the executive director of the Pennsylvania Historical and Museum Commission. He has battled persistently for adequate appropriations for historical sites, publications, and scholarly endeavors. He was one of the founders of *American Heritage* magazine and was its business manager during its early years. He twice has served as president of the American Association for State and Local History and for three years of the Pennsylvania Historical Association. He has been in the forefront of Pennsylvania's fight for rightful recognition as the birthplace of the nation for the 1976 Bicentennial. For two and a half years in court he successfully defended the right of all historians to make unflattering assessments of dead national figures. Though the American Historical Association and the Society of American Historians supported Dr. Stevens in the Frick case in the Cumberland County Court of Common Pleas, essentially it was Dr. Stevens's fight and he, as always, made the most of it.

The great monuments to the career of S. K. Stevens are, of course, the books he has written. They will remain important to scholars, students, and general readers for years to come.

The William Penn Memorial Museum and Archives Building in Harrisburg, headquarters of the Historical Commission, is a monument to the efforts of Dr. Stevens too. He was the one man who worked decades to get this $10 million facility, and he has been amply rewarded by the public response it has received since its opening in April of 1965. The five-story, circular structure with its 18-story archives tower is one of the most impressive state historical facilities in the nation.

"A Shot Is Heard in Pennsylvania" is adapted from the seventh chapter of *Pennsylvania, Birthplace of a Nation,* published by Random House in 1964.

A Shot Is Heard in Pennsylvania

by S. K. Stevens

The first shots of the American Revolution were fired by embattled colonial villagers and farmers and British redcoats at Lexington and Concord on April 19, 1775. These shots lighted the fires of rebellion, but they had been fed hundreds of miles away in many colonies other than Massachusetts.

No colony of Britain had been a more central point for the sparking of the first flames than Pennsylvania—land of peaceful Quakers. A year earlier the First Continental Congress had met at Philadelphia in Carpenters' Hall in September, 1774, to assert the colonists' rights to "life, liberty, and property" and indeed to all the "rights, liberties, and immunities" of Englishmen. From this gathering in the largest city of the colonies, one with a population of 30,000, the colonials left to organize their local "committees of safety and inspection." These were the groups that collected the fagots with which to build the fires. The winter of 1774-75 determined whether they would be touched off. Even as the muskets sounded in New England, in April delegates from the several colonies once more were on their way to Philadelphia to meet on May 10 to discuss major and common issues developing from the unsettled dispute with the mother country. They arrived to realize that a shot had been fired which literally would be heard around the world.

Colonial Pennsylvania inevitably had to be the seed ground for the revolutionary movement. From its earliest history, dating back to William Penn, it had had a continuing drive for greater democracy. The rapid growth of the frontier in Pennsylvania, which had larger quantities of land open for easy settlement on its frontier than did any other single colony, kept this spirit of democracy alive and alert. Wrote Gottleib Mittelberger in 1750: "Liberty in Pennsylvania extends so far that everyone is free from all molestation and taxation on his property, business, house and estates." Little wonder that a protest on taxation without representation in Parliament should meet with support in Pennsylvania, even though many a Quaker and German opposed the use of force on religious principles.

When the mother country tried to make the colonials pay some of the costs of the burdens of their defense for the French and Indian War, the Stamp Act in 1765 brought united condemnation from all factions in Pennsylvania. John Dickinson, for whom Dickinson College is named, became the principal author of the protest resolutions drawn up at the Stamp Act Congress of October, 1765, in New York. In the "Declaration of Rights" and "Petition to the King," it affirmed the right of British subjects to be taxed only by their own consent or that of their "legal Representatives," and taxation otherwise to be "unconstitutional and subversive of their most valuable Rights."

As a colony with an expanding frontier, Pennsylvania had been shaken even earlier by the Crown's Proclamation of 1765 which tried to close the frontier to further settlement. The Currency Act of 1764 forbidding colonial paper money and providing that taxes must be paid in gold or silver did not sit well either with Pennsylvania merchants. Pennsylvanians in 1765 took an active part in organizing non-importation agreements along with Sons of Liberty societies.

In 1766 Parliament repealed the Stamp Act, but a year later the Townshend Acts levied new indirect taxes by attempting to collect import duties on tea, glass, lead, and paint colors. Writs of assistance authorizing arbitrary search and seizure of suspected violators possessing smuggled goods were also put in force. Philadelphia had its own Tea Party on November 27, 1773, but in the form of a protest meeting to which the captain of the British tea ship was invited. He anchored on the Delaware and saw and heard enough to lead him discreetly to withdraw his ship without an attempt to unload its cargo. In the meantime, John Dickinson, the noted Philadelphia lawyer, had unlimbered his pen once more to write in 1767-68 his famous "Letters from a Farmer in Pennsylvania," which appeared in the *Pennsylvania Chronicle* and were reprinted throughout the colonies. They presented a carefully reasoned case against the British policies and had great influence in organizing colonial resistance to them.

In the spring of 1774, petitions to Governor John Penn, the grandson of William Penn, to call a session of the Assembly to deal with revolutionary issues were ignored, and led to a huge citizens' meeting in Philadelphia on June 18 attended by some 8,000 people. Out of it grew an all-important call to establish throughout the province county committees of correspondence as citizens' organizations. Representatives of these committees were called upon to gather in Philadelphia on July 15.

The existing machinery of the colonial government was ignored on the grounds that it had refused to heed the petition of the people to act. The resulting Provincial Convention met at Carpenters' Hall with seventy-five delegates present and representing no less than eleven counties. Thomas Willing, 43, a banker and trustee of the University of Pennsylvania, was elected chairman. Charles Thomson, 45, a native of Ireland, friend of Ben Franklin, recent master of William Penn Charter School, later secretary of the Continental Congress for fifteen years and the man who notified George Washington that he was selected President, was elected secretary.

The Convention sat for seven days and adopted sixteen resolutions, along with some "Instructions" for the local committees. All of this activity was outside the bounds of legal governmental process and highly revolutionary in nature. The anti-revolutionary Pennsylvanians now rallied behind Governor Penn and the regularly elected Assembly, which also met in July. The revolutionary forces soon captured partial control of that body and it endorsed a proposal for a congress of all the colonies to consider how to cope with British threats to their rights.

The First Continental Congress opened September 5, 1774, at Carpenters' Hall at the suggestion of the city, though the State House, or "Independence Hall," had been offered by the Assembly. This was itself a victory of the Pennsylvania revolutionary element, because its organization had been perfected in these same halls.

Joseph Galloway typified the frightened conservatives whom he termed men of "loyal principles" with large fortunes, who now feared actual revolution on the part of those who were "congregational and presbyterians or men of bankrupt fortunes," and who were "overwhelmed in debt to British merchants."

Political turmoil ensued in Pennsylvania. The Assembly was the first colonial legislature to meet following the dissolving of the Congress October 26. Its action was of the greatest importance. On December 10, thanks to John Dickinson, Pennsylvania ratified despite much conservative opposition the action of the First Continental Congress in asserting colonial rights, reviving non-importation, and approving the further organization of Committees of Correspondence. On December 15 the Assembly approved appointments of seven delegates to the Second Continental Congress, already called for May 10, 1775.

In May of 1775, Governor Penn asked the existing Assembly to approve a plan for reconciliation with England, which it rejected, though at the same time refusing to approve a Philadelphia petition for colonial defense monies. The leaders of the revolutionary movement at once revived Franklin's voluntary militia, or Associators, of the French and Indian War days. When John Adams arrived to attend the Second Continental Congress, he found the martial spirit "astonishing" and some

2,000 Philadelphians marching about in daily drills. Even Quakers, he noted, were to be found in the ranks. By November of 1775, revolutionary feeling was so strong that those who refused to join this militia were made subject to a special tax. When in 1776 the Assembly was called upon to appoint two brigadier generals to command the now recognized Associators, the volunteers themselves took the initiative in defying the Assembly on the ground that it did not have "a proportional representation" and the militiamen elected their own leaders. The provincial Assembly was now utterly without power in the face of the revolutionary forces of the last several months. The tide of revolution had become so strong that even John Dickinson now emerged as a conservative opposing actual violence.

The last colonial Assembly was elected in October of 1775. Revolution against Britain was now tied inseparably with revolt against the government headed by the last of the Penns, as well as the wealthy landholders and merchants allied with the proprietor and the Church of England as the "establishment." This, of course, was not different from the general pattern of 18th Century revolutionary movements. It is noteworthy that throughout the period, debates in the Assembly stressed on the part of the revolutionary leaders the fact that the provincial government itself was guilty of taxation and formation of policy without the adequate representation of all of the people. The colonial Assembly adjourned on June 14, 1776. Four days later the second of the Provincial Conferences met at Carpenters' Hall to represent the revolutionary committees. Every possible effort was made by the supporters of what some persons now openly termed the "radicals" to secure full and proper representation at this meeting. Franklin, Dr. Benjamin Rush and Thomas McKean were among the best-known members. It agreed that the existing government was incompetent.

The crucial Declaration of Independence was approved on July 2 by the Continental Congress with the aid of a 3-to-2 vote of the Pennsylvania delegation present and voting. Franklin, James Wilson and John Morton cast the affirmative votes, while such notables as Robert Morris and John Dickinson abstained. It was proclaimed to the public in front of the State House on July 8.

The Declaration was drafted in Philadelphia by 33-year-old Thomas Jefferson, who rented two second-floor rooms in the home of Jacob Graff, Jr., a bricklayer, at Market and Seventh Streets. Jefferson's first draft was edited by Franklin and others, and later when Jefferson asked the 70-year-old Franklin why he hadn't written the document, Franklin replied,"I have made it a rule to avoid becoming the draftsman of papers to be reviewed by a public body." Franklin, of course, signed the Declaration of Independence and later the Constitution, one of the few Americans to have his signature on both historic papers. Nine Pennsylvanians signed the Declaration, the largest delegation to do so.

Pennsylvanians, of course, were in actual combat outside their colony well before the Declaration was promulgated. John Harris III, the son of the founder of Harrisburg, was an officer in the Harris Ferry riflemen's unit and was killed in the attack on Quebec six months before the signing of the Declaration of Independence.

The Pennsylvania Convention and the Continental Congress both met in the crowded 40-feet-by-40 east room of Independence Hall, normally used by the Pennsylvania Assembly. By September 28, 1776, the Pennsylvanians hammered out a new frame of government for an independent state. Because of conservative reaction, the first state constitution was hastily pushed through to adoption without reference to the votes of the people. Twenty-three members did not sign it, for better or for worse. Pennsylvania was first to adopt a formal constitution.

The Pennsylvania Constitution of 1776 ended the proprietorship of the Penns, which had started back on March 4, 1681, when Charles II gave the charter to William Penn. The new document relied heavily upon Penn's liberalism as expressed in the Charter of Privileges of 1701 and the thinking behind England's revolution of 1688. It contained a Declaration of Rights, which was carried through with little change into the three later Pennsylvania constitutions. The Declaration is a brilliant statement of the social compact and natural-rights theme justifying even today the "inalienable and indefeasible right" of the people "to alter, reform or abolish their government in such manner as they may think proper." Few Pennsylvanians today appreciate the fact that their state government is so subject to change.* Religious liberty was

---

*Pennsylvania has had constitutions of 1776, 1790, 1838, and 1874, with major amendments adopted in 1968, and still on the first page (Article I, Section 2) is found: "All power is inherent in the people, and all free governments are founded on their authority and instituted for their peace, safety and happiness. For the advancement of these ends they have at all times an inalienable and indefeasible right to alter, reform or abolish their government in such manner as they may think proper."

In actuality, however, the government of Pennsylvania is not as subject to change as the Constitution permits. There were not even any provisions for amending the Constitution until 1838, and then the rule was established, and is still in effect today, that a proposed amendment must pass two successive legislatures before the people can vote on it. In the 94 years following adoption of the 1874 Constitution, more than 1,000 amendments were proposed, but only 86 got on the ballot and then 27 of these were defeated. The people, not only the politicians, have been reluctant to accept change. They defeated proposed constitutional conventions in 1891, 1921, 1924, 1935, 1953, and 1963, and accepted a convention with only limited authority in 1967. The amended Constitution approved in 1968 scarcely alters Pennsylvania government, though the outmoded $1 million debt limit was discarded and governors can run for a second successive term. The governors provision ironically was rejected by the people at the polls in 1961.

In almost 200 years of constitutional government, Pennsylvanians have seldom chosen to exercise their fundamental rights.

extended by removing such oaths as prohibited Catholics from holding office. Quaker morality called for laws encouraging "virtue" and aimed at preventing "vice and immorality," beginning the tradition of the Pennsylvania "Blue Laws." Property qualifications for suffrage were ended but paying a poll tax was required to vote, a feature of Pennsylvania government which lasted until the 1930s. A unicameral legislature, or People's Assembly, was set up, reflecting long-standing distrust on the part of the supporters of democratic movements against an upper house which commonly represented an aristocracy in the population.

The new Assembly was elected annually, with six members from each county. Distrust against "kingly" power was also evidenced by the creation of a Supreme Executive Council rather than a single governor as the executive authority. The Council was elected every three years, with two men from each county and one from Philadelphia. The head of the Council was known as the President, and Pennsylvania had this official rather than a governor until its second constitution in 1790. Ben Franklin from 1785 to 1788 was the sixth President of Pennsylvania; he was never governor.

In general, the Pennsylvania Constitution of 1776 was one of the most liberal and truly influential products to come out of the American Revolution. It divided the conservative and liberal forces sufficiently to produce the first real strength of the Tory, or Loyalist, movement. Perhaps one-third of the population turned Tory, and it included many who had been earlier supporters of strong protest against imperial policy, notably Joseph Galloway. Many merchants and large landholders failed to see the necessity for revolution and looked upon it as a radical manifestation of what they termed the "rabble." Quakers and many German sects were pacifist by religious principle and opposed armed revolt, though many deserted this conviction. It is a mistake to label all the wealthy, the able and the well-born as Loyalists. There were Quakers like Timothy Matlack who could write, "I have ever considered personal liberty and safety as the first object of civil government, and possession and security of property the next." There were many notable scientists, lawyers, manufacturers, merchants and landholders who were stalwart patriots.

Pennsylvania in 1776 was not only the seat of the united colonial movement for independence and of its continued revolutionary government, but also a powerful force in winning that independence by war. It was the third largest colony, with a population of 275,000. Its troops took part in almost all the campaigns of the Revolution.

By the autumn of 1776 at least 35,000 Pennsylvanians were enrolled in the Continental forces. Thirteen regiments under "Mad Anthony" Wayne were in the Pennsylvania Line, mostly on an annual enlistment basis. The "Pennsylvania Navy," consisting of twenty-seven ships, was organized to defend the Delaware. The United States Navy and the Marine Corps both had their birthplace in Philadelphia, mainly because of the urgency of defending the Delaware as an avenue of attack by the British on the "nest of rebellion" which Philadelphia so completely represented. Pennsylvania riflemen were at Bunker Hill from as far west as Carlisle. They were also in the campaigns in Canada.

In 1776 General Washington with his feeble army was forced back from Long Island and across New Jersey into Pennsylvania on November 28. The British were talking now of a "total end to the war." British officers were convinced the so-called patriots were a mere rabble with "scarce a pair of breeches." Washington had perhaps 3,000 men and the numbers were dwindling under the one-year enlistment policy.

At the Thompson-Neely house in what is today Washington Crossing State Park, Washington planned the strategy which took him across the ice-choked Delaware on Christmas night to strike the British at Trenton and capture more than 1,000 Hessian prisoners. Pennsylvania riflemen and militia brought to Washington's aid gave him new strength for this maneuver and for another brilliant movement through which he surprised Cornwallis, leaving his campfires burning to deceive the enemy, and the next day badly cut to pieces three British regiments at Princeton. He then retired to the hills of Morristown, N. J. From this point he was able to raid British communications with New York, and here Washington spent the critical winter of 1777, in a considerably better position than at the close of 1776.

In the late summer of 1777, General William Howe landed his army of 18,000 troops at Head of Elk, Md. His strategy was aimed at cutting off Pennsylvania from the southern colonies. If the total British campaign had been successful, it could well have ended the Revolution. Washington was unable to halt the British and lost the Battle of the Brandywine on September 11, as Cornwallis executed a flanking movement he may have learned earlier that year from Washington at Trenton. Wayne's corps was nearly wiped out on September 20 in the "Battle of the Clouds" at Paoli. In Philadelphia the dread cry, "The British are coming," was heard at every street corner as both the Congress and many citizens fled the city, which Howe occupied on September 25. Attacking the British early on the foggy morning of October 4 at Germantown, Washington again failed to win victory. Howe was left free to occupy Philadelphia without hazard and settled down for a pleasant winter of wining and dining with its Tory society. When informed in Paris that Howe had taken Philadelphia, Franklin is said to have replied, "No, Philadelphia has captured Howe."

Washington withdrew his beaten, hungry and tattered army to Whitemarsh and finally to Valley Forge. He did test the British again in November and Howe advanced to Whitemarsh in December, where, though he outnumbered the Continentals by two to one, he decided not to press an attack.

Valley Forge, on the west bank of the Schuylkill and 21 miles from Philadelphia, was an excellent protective position which placed Washington's army between the British and possible raids upon the iron furnaces and powder mills of the interior. The lack of proper supplies and food at Valley Forge reflected the low ebb of the patriot cause. It brought to light the resulting unwillingness of some fair-weathered patriots, as well as about one-third of Pennsylvanians who had never committed themselves one way or the other, to aid the cause of liberty. Food and clothing were to be had, but there were all too few who were willing to sell it for Continental money as opposed to British gold. Congress, sitting at distant York, helped little with its bungling efforts. The result was an army at times almost starving and without adequate clothing encamped at Valley Forge in the midst of plenty.

But there were some brighter lights in the darkness. Prussian drillmaster General Baron von Steuben arrived. There were patriots who did provide food and clothing, sometimes without any promise of money. Pennsylvania's popular General Thomas Mifflin, later its first elected governor, met with some success in recruiting. Best news of all was that of the treaties of commerce and of alliance with France signed on February 6, 1778, and in the negotiation of which Franklin had so large a role. Spain and the Netherlands also came to the support of the American cause.

The first feeble steps toward a new national government were taken by Congress at York as it endorsed the Articles of Confederation. On June 16 the British left Philadelphia, and with them went some 3,000 Tories. Washington marched out of Valley Forge on June 19, 1778, now celebrated as "Evacuation Day." The major campaigns for Washington's army were then outside Pennsylvania.

In Pennsylvania itself the problem of protection of the frontier against the British-incited Tories and Indians was a major concern of not only the state but also the Congress. Both Congress and the British sought Indian support, but here again Continental currency and a feeble treasury could not cope with British gold and liberal supplies of guns, powder and rum. By tradition, the Iroquois in New York were friends of England. Besides, Pennsylvania frontiersmen who pressed westward after 1763 had not endeared themselves to the Indians.

By 1778 the notorious Colonel John Butler emerged as a leader of Tory and Indian raids in the upper Susquehanna Valley. In June of 1778 these attacks forced settlers to flee in the "Great Runaway" from this region. In July, Butler's minions fell upon the defenseless region around Wilkes-Barre and perpetrated the infamous Wyoming Massacre on July 5. Pennsylvania fought back with an expedition led by Colonel Thomas Hartley which left Fort Muncy September 21. Hartley marched overland and destroyed the Seneca town of Queen Esther Montour just south of the present Athens. Hartley returned to Fort Muncy on October 1, after marching some 300 miles in about two weeks and fighting another rear-guard battle with the Indians near Wyalusing Rocks.

In the spring of 1779, Washington announced tersely: "It is proposed to carry the war into the heart of the country of the Six Nations, to cut off their settlements, destroy their next year's crops, and do to them every other mischief which time and circumstances will permit." General John Sullivan was ordered to organize an army at Easton at the forks of the Delaware. On June 18, 1779, Sullivan began his long march northward toward Wilkes-Barre and Tioga Point. Old Fort Wyoming at Wilkes-Barre was rebuilt as a base. Sullivan marched on and arrived at Tioga Point, now Athens, on August 11. There he built Fort Sullivan. General James Clinton came with a second army from Cooperstown, N.Y., and joined Sullivan at Tioga Point. The combined force now amounted to 4,000 men. The Indian and Tory forces were encountered and defeated just south of Elmira, N.Y., in the Battle of Newtown. The expedition then marched into the heart of the Seneca and Cayuga country in New York, destroying at least forty major Indian villages and their all-important cornfields.

The Sullivan-Clinton expedition had a healthy influence in weakening for the remainder of the war the ability to incite Tory-Indian raids on the American frontier in the Susquehanna Valley. Western Pennsylvania, however, despite the American outpost at Fort Pitt, continued to be the victim of bloody raids from Indians in the Ohio country. The state and local citizens resorted to settler forts on the frontier, similar to those of French and Indian War days, in an effort to protect themselves against the enemy.

Pennsylvania made many contributions to American success in winning independence. Military leaders of more than average note included Thomas Mifflin, Ephraim Blaine, "Mad Anthony" Wayne, Arthur St. Clair, Edward Hand, John Armstrong, William Irvine and Peter Muhlenberg. Pennsylvania riflemen, trained on the frontier in the use of the long rifle, were among the most expert sharpshooters of the Revolution. The vigorous fighting abilities and the numbers of Scotch-Irish from the Pennsylvania frontier in the Continental Army led more than one Hessian and British soldier to feel their presence and refer to the Revolution as an "Irish" uprising. Franklin's achievements in European diplomacy, which won France and others to the patriot cause, deserve his recognition as one of the truly decisive individual leaders influencing the outcome of the Revolution. James Wilson, Dr. Benjamin Rush, Joseph

Reed, George Bryan, Thomas McKean, Robert Morris and Haym Salomon all played distinctive roles in trying areas of government and finance in those crisis years from the start of the Revolution until its end.

Pennsylvania's resources always have been important in wartime, and the tradition goes back to the Revolution. The fact that Pennsylvania as early as 1750 had won leadership in the iron industry in itself was a prime factor in determining the outcome of the Revolution. Philadelphia was a center of wealth and enterprise in colonial America and, while many of its more wealthy merchants turned Tory, there was never any doubt that the major influence of Pennsylvania's economy and its leadership was thrown behind the patriot cause. Few ironmasters, for example, were ever counted as Loyalists. Samuel Wetherill was a "fighting Quaker" merchant and manufacturer who supplied clothing for the Continental Army without too much regard to payment.

Delaware shipyards provided vessels for the first American Navy. There were at least sixty powder mills in the state at the end of the Revolution. Lead mines in Central Pennsylvania, not far from today's Altoona, provided so important a lead supply as to necessitate building Fort Roberdeau to insure their protection. Riflemakers of the Lancaster and York county region provided their vital wares in abundance, while Pennsylvania furnaces cast cannon and balls. Their product was important enough to justify the use of Hessian prisoners to bolster the labor supply on the iron plantations. Armies move on their stomachs, and Pennsylvania wheat provided much of the needed flour. Philadelphia was a major port from which many supplies moved to other states for wartime use. Its financial resources made it possible for Robert Morris and Haym Salomon to become the financiers of the Revolution.

All in all, Pennsylvania not only gave birth to the Revolution in terms of providing the locale for the Declaration of Independence and the seat for the work of the Continental Congress, but also in a variety of other ways which reflected its position of influence at the end of America's colonial era.

The Revolutionary War stopped in America on October 17, 1781, when General Charles Cornwallis surrendered to Washington at Yorktown, Va. The British and French did not actually stop fighting until June 28, 1783, at Cuddalore, India. Washington announced the armistice on April 19, 1783, the eighth year of the war, and the formal peace treaty was signed that September 3.

Pennsylvania was the birthplace of the federal Constitution. The Articles of Confederation, approved by Congress while sitting at York and ratified by the states during the Revolution, had not provided the strong bonds of union needed to meet the problems of the new nation. A national convention to draw a constitution was held in Philadelphia in

May of 1787. Pennsylvania was very much of a key state in the calling of the convention. Virginia feared New England as supporting even more disunity and wanted Pennsylvania on its side. Some Pennsylvanians leaned toward New England's idea of continuing a decentralized government. On the other hand, Philadelphians were desirous of securing the national capital for their city and willing to cooperate with southern states on certain issues in order to get it. This paid off when in the first session of Congress a compromise was arranged to have the capital at Philadelphia until 1800 when it would be moved to Washington.

The Constitutional Convention got underway on May 25, 1787. There were seventy-four delegates appointed, of whom nineteen did not attend. The dean of the Pennsylvania delegation was 81-year-old Benjamin Franklin, who did not take an active part in the debates but whose sound wisdom and kindly humor at times held the meetings together in the face of possible disruption. James Wilson, a former Carlisle lawyer, was one of the great legal minds influencing the new Constitution and was second only to Virginia's James Madison as its major architect. Gouverneur Morris, a Philadelphian, was one of the stylists who helped to write the document in proper form. Also present were Robert Morris, Thomas Mifflin, George Clymer, and Thomas Fitz-Simons. Admittedly, it was a delegation which favored conservative thinking.

Ratification of the completed Constitution became the most spirited political issue in Pennsylvania since 1776. It was understood generally that Philadelphia and the eastern counties were for it, and the western counties against it. The ratifying convention met in Philadelphia from November 21 to December 15, 1787, and with the efforts of Dr. Benjamin Rush and James Wilson, Pennsylvania approved the Constitution, 46 to 23. The following day members of the convention marched in colorful procession with officials of the state, city and university to the courthouse to announce the decision to the people. Pennsylvania was the second state to ratify, led by only a few days by Delaware. It was the first large state to ratify, and thus boosted greatly the final triumph of the Constitution.

Pennsylvania opponents to the Constitution, including Albert Gallatin, the Swiss-born Western Pennsylvanian, were instrumental in securing the early adoption of the Bill of Rights, the first ten amendments to the Constitution.

The Commonwealth itself changed its own government shortly after the new federal Constitution was adopted. The Constitution of 1790, the second state constitution, provided for a bicameral assembly and a governor with the power of veto. James Wilson, Thomas McKean, William Findley, Albert Gallatin and Thomas Mifflin were among those who drafted this state frame of government. It was one of the most advanced in the new nation, and Kentucky in 1792, for one, took a large part of its constitution from Pennsylvania.

Pennsylvania through its contributions and leadership during the Revolutionary era demonstrated its place as the keystone state in a new nation.

discover the youthful James Buchanan in
Roger Steck's
The Mischievous Future President

Pennsylvania's only native-born son to be elected
President held several important state and
national posts earlier in his career. Despite the
mark he made in politics, however, he was
something of a cutup in college.

It is paradoxical that Pennsylvania, the third largest state and one that takes
its politics with gusto, should have but one native-born son, James Buchanan, make it to the White House. Furthermore, Pennsylvania has had but one
Vice President, George Mifflin Dallas, the Philadelphian who served under
President Polk.

It is true that Dwight D. Eisenhower, the son of a Pennsylvanian, had his
home at Gettysburg when he was elected President and that Richard M.
Nixon came from Pennsylvania stock, but neither were native Pennsylvanians.

Pennsylvania has been a keystone of national politics. Its delegation
strength and electoral vote are important at the conventions and in the campaigning. Of the forty-two Presidential elections from 1800 through 1968,
Pennsylvania has been on the winning side thirty-four times. Every candidate
considers the Pennsylvania vote a necessity.

Yet Pennsylvania politicians, for all their skills in political combat within the
commonwealth, have been notoriously inept at pushing favorite sons or making their votes count at national conventions. There is no solid explanation
for this dismal historical fact. "Bull" Andrews from Crawford County, an old
Matt Quay henchman, expressed the sentiment at the 1908 GOP convention. "As usual," observed Senator Andrews, "Pennsylvania gets only the
smell from the kitchen."

Pennsylvania's tradition of machine politics and bossism long worked against its getting Presidential and Vice Presidential candidates. To the national leaders, Pennsylvania was easily categorized as "in the bag" or "impossible to win." From 1800 to 1860, the state was solidly Democratic; from 1860 to 1934, solidly Republican. It went Democratic again from 1934 to 1938, but swung back to Republicanism from 1938 to 1954. Only in the last fifteen years has it had outright competitive politics, but, unfortunately, in this period it has had but one serious Presidential prospect, William W. Scranton.

James Buchanan is not rated highly as a President. As the pre-Civil War chief executive, he was the victim of a crisis that could scarcely be resolved by anything less than war. He took office in 1857, fifty days short of his sixty-sixth birthday. Only Eisenhower was an older President. Buchanan's own ingrained conservatism offset his ample experience of forty-two years in public life and contributed to his ineffectiveness. When Lincoln succeeded him and the Civil War began, Buchanan retired to his home at Wheatland in Lancaster, happy to be rid of the burden of the Presidency.

He was born on April 23, 1791, at Stony Batter, in Gove Gap, Franklin County, the son of an immigrant Scotch-Irish merchant and farmer. He was raised in Mercersburg, graduated from Dickinson College, practiced law in Lancaster, and then launched a political career in 1814. He served two terms in the State Legislature, ten years in Congress, was minister to Russia for President Jackson, refused the governorship in 1838, served eleven years in the U.S. Senate, was Secretary of State for President Polk, and then minister to Great Britain for President Pierce. He was considered for the Vice Presidency in 1832 and for the Presidency in 1844, 1848, and 1852. Finally in 1856 in Cincinnati, Buchanan got the Democratic nomination. The Republicans held their first convention in Philadelphia and selected John C. Fremont, while the Know-Nothings met in Pittsburgh and named former President Millard Fillmore. Buchanan carried his own state by 27,152 votes—the last time Pennsylvania went Democratic until 1936—and he won the national vote handily.

Two days after Buchanan was inaugurated, Chief Justice Roger B. Taney, a Dickinson College graduate of 1795, announced the Dred Scott decision, which overruled popular sovereignty on the slavery question. Justice Robert C. Grier, of Williamsport and Pittsburgh, a Dickinson graduate of 1812, was the lone Northerner to concur in the ruling. From that time forth, Buchanan had a troubled administration. Contributing to his difficulties were his own habits of temporizing, his overlegalistic mind, and his wrongheaded belief that while it was illegal for the Southern states to secede, it also was illegal to prevent them by use of force. As Attorney General and then Secretary of State, Jeremiah S. Black, a native of Somerset County and a former State Supreme Court Justice from York, shared his boss's indecisiveness. At the end of his administration, Buchanan appointed Black to the U.S. Supreme Court, but the appointment was blocked in the Senate.*

Buchanan was the nation's only bachelor President. He was a tall man with a pink complexion and eye trouble which caused him to tilt his head. He had a good sense of humor and a keen mind, as his biographer, Dr. Philip S. Klein of Penn State, has pointed out. He was right as a state politician when he warned against Pennsylvania's starting an expensive canal system, and he was right again when he wanted Cuba annexed a century before Castro came on the scene.

Buchanan's first lady was his niece and ward, Harriet Lane, a beautiful young woman of twenty-seven who became the fashion leader of Washington during her uncle's administration. Miss Lane married after Buchanan left the White House.

The old President died on June 1, 1868, within months of the passing of two other prominent Pennsylvanians, his rival in Lancaster, Thaddeus Stevens, and David Wilmot. In the twilight of life, Buchanan would attend a

---

*Pennsylvania has had remarkably few family dynasties in politics. Jeremiah Black (1810-1883) probably could have been governor if he had so chosen. His son, Chauncey F. Black, was lieutenant governor and in 1886 lost a gubernatorial election.

In his novel, *Hail to the Chief,* A. James Reichley has a Senator Weaver explain: "We have our aristocratic families in Pennsylvania, too, but we just tell them when to get out their checkbooks and every once in a while we put one of them on the ticket for the sake of atmosphere." Another character, Emmaline, adds: "Pennsylvania is different. In Pennsylvania the organization is everything and the first families have been out of politics except to make campaign contributions since before the Civil War. In Massachusetts the old families have remained a power in their own right."

Francis Rawn Shunk married one of the daughters of Governor William Findlay and twenty-five years after his father-in-law left office became governor himself, in 1845. Shunk's grandson, Francis Shunk Brown, was the Republican machine candidate against Gifford Pinchot in the 1930 primary and narrowly lost. No other direct descendant of a governor has ever run for that office in modern Pennsylvania history.

Andrew Gregg served sixteen years in Congress, six years in the U.S. Senate, was Secretary of the Commonwealth, and then lost the governorship in 1822. His grandson, Andrew Gregg Curtin, was the famous Civil War governor.

George, Edwin, and Bill Vare maintained a Vare seat in the State Senate from 1897 to 1923, with Edwin's widow Flora also being a senator for three years. The Philadelphia Vare brothers "pyramided a garbage concession into a political dynasty," as Senator Joe Guffey said. Bill, the most noted of the three, also was in Congress for sixteen years and in 1926 defeated Pinchot for the U.S. Senate; but, as governor, Pinchot declared the election "partly bought and partly stolen" and the Senate refused to seat Vare. "I was stopped at the threshold of the chamber as though I were some common thief," Vare complained.

The most recent of the political dynasties have been the Greens of Philadelphia. Bill Green II, the Democratic boss, served in Congress from 1945 until his death in 1963 and was succeeded by his 25-year-old son, Bill Green III. The voters made the transfer and it was above board, not similar to Simon Cameron's ordering the 1877 Legislature to approve the giving of his Senate seat to his son, J. Donald Cameron.

Presbyterian Church in Lancaster. Upon leaving, he inevitably was greeted by a lady at the door who would say, "A good sermon, Mr. President?" and he would reply, "Too long, madam, too long."

The most unlikely but true story of Buchanan's expulsion from Dickinson College was written for the news media on November 20, 1968, by Roger H. Steck, a native of York, former newspaperman and Dickinson's public relations director since 1948.

The Mischievous Future President

by Roger Steck

James Buchanan, fifteenth President of the United States, may have been one of those early college protestors against rules and regulations. He attended Dickinson College and by his own admission engaged in "every sort of extravagance and mischief" and was expelled. But with the help of a Dickinson trustee who knew his father, James got things straightened out with the faculty and graduated in 1809 with fine grades.

At sixteen, the youngest member of his class, the boy was tall and fair. He was also brassy and boisterous and further displeased the faculty by swearing and smoking cigars—serious infractions in those days.

Years later Buchanan attributed his "disorderly conduct" at college to a desire to be considered "a clever and spirited youth." In the Dickinson records are his own description of his first year as a student. "There was no sufficient discipline, and the young men did pretty much as they pleased. To be a sober, plodding, industrious youth was to incur the ridicule of the mass of students. Without much natural tendency to be dissipated, and chiefly from the examples of others, and in order to be considered a clever and spirited youth, I engaged in every sort of extravagance and mischief in which the greatest proficients of the college indulged. However, I was always a tolerably hard student, and never deficient in my college exercises."

The college advised James not to return for his second year but relented, he wrote later, after "I pledged my honor to behave better than I had. I returned to college without any further questions being asked; and afterwards conducted myself in such a manner as, at least, to prevent any formal complaint."

As his commencement approached, the brash young man let it be known that he deserved and expected to be graduated with the first honor. "I had set my heart on it," he wrote. But the faculty had other ideas and gave the top honor to another boy, reasoning that it would be unwise "to confer a high distinction of the college on one who had shown so little respect for the rules of the college and for his professors."

This action riled members of Buchanan's literary society—founded in 1782 and still active today—and they proposed to demonstrate in his behalf by boycotting the commencement exercises, but the future President wouldn't let them do that "on my account especially as several of them were designed for the ministry."

Although he lived to be seventy-seven, Buchanan never forgot his failure to win the first honor. "I have scarcely ever been so much mortified at any occurance of my life as at this disappointment," wrote the man who served in Congress and the U.S. Senate and as Ambassador to England and to Russia before entering the White House in 1857.

Political Advice

One of James Buchanan's friends in 1847 was the rising politician Simon Cameron. Buchanan was then Secretary of State for President Polk and Cameron succeeded him in the U.S. Senate. It was a gubernatorial election year, and a political hack named Seth Salisbury was giving both President Polk and Governor Francis Rawn Shunk a bad time by publishing abusive articles about them.

Six months before the election Cameron wrote Buchanan about Salisbury. "He is as poor as a rat and as enterprising as a monkey," wrote Cameron. "If you don't give him bread, his facility for scribbling and his acquaintance with the printers, together with his persevering industry, will keep the whole state in ferment....There is no tire in him. I say make him watchman (at the capitol). This will feed him, and a man with a full belly is not half as troublesome as a hungry one."

sit in with
A. James Reichley's
The Boys

The Pennsylvania brand of politics and political
reporting has often been fierce and sometimes
funny. A. James Reichley—reporter, novelist,
and serious student of politics—has perceptively
analyzed what makes politicos tick.

Perhaps nowhere in America have politicians and the press played such hard
politics as in Pennsylvania. The often fierce, more than occasionally funny,
and sometimes underhanded scrimmaging has produced a distinct Pennsyl-
vania-brand politico, as well as much lively political writing.

The head-butting and fratricidal slugfest in the public arena goes back
well before 1895, when the Pennsylvania Legislative Correspondents Association was founded as the nation's first state-house press corps. The fun
and anguish were here in Benjamin Franklin's day, and, appropriately enough,
Pennsylvania's greatest citizen was both a politician and a newspaperman,
and never dull at either trade.

After Franklin was elected a Philadelphia alderman in 1751, his mother
complimented him but said she didn't know "what the better you will be of
it beside the honor of it." After he himself was the target of opposition
editors, he called newspapers the "Supremest Court of Judicature in
Pennsylvania." Franklin jested that the Legislature was composed of "plain
people, unpracticed in the Sleights and Artifices of Controversy, and have
no Joy in Disputation."

For the plain people of the 1969 State Senate, the Rev. Richard L.
Huggins, a 31-year-old Presbyterian minister from McKeesport, opened a
session with a prayer: "Well, God, here we are again, asking your help in
another week when we look at the frustrations and frenzy in running a state.
The hell of it is, God, we are not sure that we really want your help. We feel

self-sufficient. But we really are not. Help us anyway. Strengthen our minds and our abilities for the commonwealth. Amen."

Lincoln Steffens used to tell of the Philadelphia politician who had Independence Hall in his ward. One day while campaigning, the candidate recited the names of the signers of the Declaration of Independence. "These men, the fathers of American liberty, voted down here once. And," he added with a sly grin, "they vote here yet."

In 1965 the chief clerk of the State House, a Westmoreland County politico, refused a patronage job for a fellow Democrat from Mayor Jim Tate's Philadelphia. "Can he type?" asked the chief clerk. After the 1968 election, the chief clerk himself had to seek reappointment, but now Mayor Tate was a political power. When the chief clerk's name came up at a patronage session, Tate with his long memory asked straight-faced, "Can he type?"

There are politicians without a sense of humor, but they are a rarity. The many pressures and situations in politics lend themselves to levity and wit. An Erie County legislator interrupted matters on the House floor in 1969 to say, "Mr. Speaker, if there had been another speech on mental health, I would have been able to finish my entire box of Girl Scout cookies."

Pennsylvanians read 276 newspapers with a total circulation of 9.7 million. Their daily journalism varies from the stalwart conservative and the rural homespun, for both of whom taxes for any purpose are an abomination, to the moderately progressive papers that are willing to consider social change and even on occasion to recommend new ideas.

The newspapers, like the politicians themselves, aren't as lively as they once were, but usually they are much more responsible than they are given credit for being. Simon Cameron and James Buchanan had patronage jobs, such as postmasterships, for their newspaper friends. President Nixon did give a Philadelphia publisher a prized ambassadorship, but otherwise the blatant favor-swapping among politicians and the press has just about expired. Outright political partisanship in newsprint is almost gone too. The late Joe Grundy, the Bucks County tory and foe of the New Deal, instructed the editor of his newspaper to run the story of President Roosevelt's 1936 re-election on the back page. Editorially, the Republicans in Pennsylvania still do better than the Democrats, but news coverage, with few exceptions, is objective and fair.*

---

*Editorial endorsement of Presidential candidates in Pennsylvania comes close to being predictable. In 1960, Richard Nixon was backed by 53 newspapers with a circulation of 2,856,550, as compared to John Kennedy's endorsement by just five papers with a circulation of 534,184. With 91 percent of the newspaper support, Nixon got 49 percent of the popular vote. In 1968, Nixon was backed by 39 papers with a circulation of 1,875,593, while Hubert Humphrey got just four papers with a circulation of 387,539. Once again Nixon had 91 percent of the press's support, but got 42 percent of the vote. The lone major papers to be for Kennedy and then Humphrey were the *Pittsburgh Post-Gazette*, the *Scranton Times*, and the *Lancaster In-*

The day of the fighting-mad editor is gone. In the last century the *Pittsburgh Times* editor asked a friend for his opinion of an editorial. "It's a gem in its way," the friend said. "You begin by calling him an s.o.b. and then gradually become abusive." The immodesty of the press, however, is not gone. Often with little knowledge and less wisdom, the press will talk *ex cathedra* about problems, especially those in the behavioral sciences, of which it has a minimal understanding.

Pennsylvania's newspapers have won a fair share of Pulitzer prizes, and there are enough conscientious publishers and editors so that most urban areas have civic-minded newspapers. In general, Pennsylvania metropolitan newspapers in the 1950s and 1960s were abreast of such subjects as honesty in government, the tax revolt, industrial development, and urban renewal. Not all the swords were bent, as evidenced by the Northampton County delegate to the 1968 Constitutional Convention who complained for the official record: "I don't believe we should let nitwit editorial writers who have never had the privilege of serving the state tell us how to vote." But the newspapers also were late to recognize and often insensitive to, if not irrelevant about, such issues as civil rights, the generation gap, poverty, and cultural advancement.

Not unlike the press in other states, the fourth estate in Pennsylvania is intermittently courageous, enlightened, and contemporary-thinking. Similarly, at times it can backslide, cower beneath the forces of authority, and exhibit a narrowness of sympathies that dismays intelligent readers. The lapses would be cheerfully ignored in many other places, but Pennsylvanians still are preoccupied by their newspapers and politics. There is one important new counterbalance to the written word, and that is the infant Pennsylvania educational television statewide network, which is becoming an increasingly persuasive media.

A. James Reichley came out of the *Pottsville Republican* to be a novelist, political backshopman, pundit, and now a writer for *Fortune* magazine. He was born in 1929 in St. Clair and lived at 1610 Mahantongo Street in Pottsville, just up the road from where John O'Hara had lived. Reichley earned

---

telligencer Journal. Nationally, Nixon received 77 percent and 81 percent of the support of the press, respectively.

Noncommitment is becoming increasingly popular in Pennsylvania. There were 31 noncommitted papers in 1960, including the *Easton Express, Hazleton Standard-Sentinel, Hazleton Plain Speaker, McKeesport News, Pottstown Mercury, Pottsville Republican, Reading Eagle, Williamsport Sun-Gazette,* and *York Gazette and Daily.* Without the religious overtones of 1960, the 1968 election had ten fewer noncommitted papers, including the *Allentown Call, Allentown Chronicle, Bethlehem Globe Times, Reading Times, Reading Eagle,* and the papers in Easton, McKeesport, and Pottsville.

This information was taken from the surveys made by *Editor and Publisher* magazine.

degrees at the University of Pennsylvania and Harvard and was a Congressional Fellow. He has two novels to his credit, *The Burying of Kingsmith,* 1957, and *Hail to the Chief,* 1960, and in 1964 he authored *States in Crisis.* He was legislative assistant to Senator Joseph S. Clark and to Congressman Kenneth B. Keating of New York and Congressman William W. Scranton. He followed Scranton to Harrisburg in 1963 to be his legislative secretary.

Reichley was called the "intellectual in residence" in the Scranton Administration. He helped devise schemes for school financial aid and for political reapportionment. He organized "Scholars for Scranton" to formulate policy in the 1964 Presidential effort. Theodore H. White praises Reichley in *The Making of the President 1964* for his insight into the mystique of Barry Goldwater in the GOP and the decline in influence of such pragmatists as Scranton. Reichley wrote Scranton's unusually fine valedictory message to the legislature in 1967, and he was in charge of drawing up Raymond P. Shafer's 1966 gubernatorial platform.

Reichley, who now lives in Bucks County, maintains that party organization and the professionals, or "boys," are a productive and ideologically respectable part of American politics. One of his most perceptive works is *The Art of Government,* a study he did for The Fund for the Republic in 1959 on the decaying Philadelphia Democratic reform movement. The following excerpt is from that Reichley report.

The Boys

by A. James Reichley

What manner of men are these who make politics their life's work? In the first place, the majority of them don't; the "bad" committeemen and most of those in the independent wards generally have some other means of gaining a livelihood and play at politics for the extra dollars, prestige, and fellowship that it may bring to them. The professionals, the "boys," are a breed apart from these, as they are a breed apart from most of the human race. Keeping hours that often resemble a doctor's schedule, managing negotiations with the government that would make even a lawyer shudder, listening to gales of shapeless oratory that might try the wits of a clergyman, they are men with a vocation as certain as any on this earth.

To begin with, they are men not especially fond of hard labor as a rule; they have, that is, a hankering for a soft life in the sense of not keeping regular hours, not doing much actual work, remaining more or less permanently in the pleasant morasses of conversation. Their claim that they give more time and more nervous energy to their jobs than most men do is nevertheless valid. Their task of bridging the gulf between the individual and his government, or at least of seeming to do so, forces on them endless small duties which take them to all corners of the city at all hours of the day and night.

They are usually gregarious, vocal, good-natured, as one would expect, although every now and then one runs across a committeeman, often effective in his own division, who is close-mouthed or possesses a sour disposition. Many of them are suspicious of strangers—perhaps in memory of some comrade who opened his mouth or his books too freely to treacherous journalists, reformers, or congressional investigators— and as testy as a gang of feudal knights about the deference and perquisites to which their positions entitle them, reflecting the rigid hierarchy in which they exist. Often they have inherited their trade from fathers, uncles, and grandfathers who were magistrates, congressmen, city commissioners.

They are one and all men who, as one of the most able of them told me after searching his mind for the reason why he had chosen his profession, "love politics."

What does it mean to "love politics"? It might mean just to love people or it might mean to love the special skills that are involved in successful government; in some cases it does mean one or both of these things, but in most cases it means something more.

The "boys," when one thinks of them, are strikingly different in their origins—Irish, Jewish, Italian, Negro—but yet they are strangely homogeneous as a group. There may be more significance to the predominant absence of white Protestants from their number than the Protestant concentration on the rewards of private enterprise would indicate. It may be that Northern European Protestants by and large lack or else have suppressed the motivation that causes men to "love politics." What could this motivation be? Money? In part, certainly. The "boys" as a rule, if they manage to stay on the winning side, make money out of politics—out of petty graft, out of pay-offs from the racketeers, out of their insurance or contracting or legal businesses that benefit from their knowledge of how the government is spending its money and their ability to manipulate the direction of its expenditures, out of the salaries which for some public offices are by no means meagre.

But one has heard them complain often enough and with apparent sincerity that if only they would devote the time to selling insurance or practicing law that they give to politics they would be far wealthier and see more of their wives and families besides, and one cannot believe that money alone keeps them in public life. Why, then, don't they get out? "Because," they say, "I love politics." What can it mean? The game, the maneuvering, the excitement? Partly. But there is more to it than that.

One explanation of their motivation would locate the "boys'" essential urge in the factor known as "prestige." The truth is, many intellectuals and many members of the upper class who have come in contact with politicians argue that, for the Irish, Jewish, Italian bright boys who pursue it, politics is a "status-conferring" occupation. The Bill Greens and the Victor Blancs and the Aus Meehans, they point out, could no doubt have earned wealth and even the respect of their fellow-men by selling insurance, practicing law, and the like. But the one thing that they could not earn in these ways is "place" in the community. Politics gives them that. As successful politicians, they can demand deference from the greatest capitalists, the toughest union leaders, the oldest of the old families. The Protestants, on the other hand, the argument continues, have "place" conferred upon them as their natural birthrights, and many may rise in society through the practice of the more normal professions; it is for this reason that so few Protestants are to be found in the dirty trade of politics.

There is much truth, I believe, to this theory: It explains the remarkable similarity between the Irish, Jewish, and Italian faces gathered around the tables in the Bellevue at lunch time; it explains the difference of these men from the folks who remain back in the neighborhoods from which they have come and also from their ethnic brothers who have risen in the world through business or the professions; it explains the financial sacrifices that many of them actually make to remain in public life. They constitute a separate class—very nearly a governing class—in most of our large cities. They form a circle of consciously powerful men, united in their determination to hold control over the community and in their conviction that loyalty to the organization is the way in which this control is most readily achieved.

Status hunger alone cannot explain the satisfactions the "boys" seem to gain from their work. Let us look more closely at the concept, "love politics." What, after all, is politics? Politics, we are told, is who gets what, when, and how. Viewed in one light, no doubt. But if that is politics, then what is economics? Is not economics also who gets what, when, and how? Are politics and economics then identical? Hardly, since there are clearly economic activities—like selling automobiles and buying cucumbers—that are not political activities. Is politics, then, a division within the general class of economics? One thinks not. The feeling of frustration associated with reform, for instance, seems to have little economic basis, and neither does the feeling of camaraderie that is so valued by the "boys."

Is not politics more truly defined, all things considered, as the expression of the will of the individual within the society of his fellows, or, more completely, the participation of human beings in the activities of conserving, distributing, and improving the values that are created by a civilized community? In short, is not politics the "art of government"? And if this is true, is not the question of why human beings should "love politics" similar to the question of why men should love women? Is not the answer to both, that is, that it is the nature of the beast? Is it not true, then, that political activity is a normal manifestation of human nature, and the real question is: Why should there be men who do not love politics?

introducing
James Welsh's
Portrait of a Not-So-Dark Horse

William W. Scranton is the rare nonpolitical type who has been extremely successful in politics and with politicians. The youthful governor's tardy entry in the 1964 race for the Republican Presidential nomination earned him the sobriquet "the Hamlet of Harrisburg."

When William Warren Scranton in 1962 ran for the governorship against Philadelphia Mayor Richardson Dilworth, Pennsylvanians had the unusual choice between two wealthy public servants from families distinguished enough to have towns named for them—Dilworthtown in Chester County and Scranton in Lackawanna County.

Scranton, Pennsylvania, formerly Slocum's Hollow, was named for the governor's great-grandfather Joseph Scranton, an entrepreneur in anthracite, railroading, banking, and utilities. When Bill Scranton went to Congress in 1960—winning his district by 16,915 votes while Democrat John F. Kennedy carried it by 14,963 votes for the Presidency—he was following in the footsteps of two previous Scrantons who had served in the U.S. House of Representatives.

There are remarkable similarities between Governors Scranton and Gifford Pinchot. Both were the most talked-about Pennsylvania politicians of their eras. Both were born in their families' summer residences in Connecticut, but both came from old Pennsylvania establishments of wealth, with the Scrantons estimated to be worth $50 million. Both were liberal Republicans with an understanding of education, welfare, and civil rights, as well as the needs of the business community—though Pinchot made a career of purposefully antagonizing the Old Guard, while Scranton used soft soap and charm and had "an apparently instinctive talent for ingratiating himself with the conservative party chieftains," as pundit Robert Novak wrote.

There is one major other difference. No one ever found a way to stop Gifford Pinchot from running for office, while today no one can offer the right enticement to lure Scranton back into the political arena.

Scranton could have been a U.S. Senator in 1968, but he let Congressman Richard S. Schweiker win the post. He turned down President Nixon's offer to be Secretary of State. Many Republicans think—and many Democrats fear—that Scranton might make a second bid for governor, and dislodge Pinchot's distinction as the lone two-term occupant of the Governor's Office in the twentieth century.

Before Scranton left the governorship in January of 1967, he announced that he would not run "ever again for any public office under any circumstances." Later, after serving as a delegate to the 1968 Pennsylvania Constitutional Convention and as President Nixon's fact-finder to the Middle East and Western Europe, he commented: "I enjoyed the governorship because it was a place to get things done, but personal politics has never appealed to me very much. I'm interested in what you can do with power in government, programming, and problem-solving."

Scranton is the rare nonpolitical type who has been extremely successful in politics and with politicians. Senator M. Harvey Taylor, for thirty years a political baron in central Pennsylvania, called him "the smartest damn governor" he ever saw.* The late George Draut as editorial chief of the Harrisburg *Patriot-News* wrote that Scranton was the "most out-and-out political realist we've had in the Governor's Office in years," and that this "young pro played a much rougher game of party-line politics than did his old-pro predecessor, Governor Lawrence."

The record of the Scranton Administration is much too recent for a fair historical judgment, of course. On the negative side, its activism during the most prosperous years in Pennsylvania history, 1963 through 1966, accelerated mandated spending programs that helped make a continuing tax crisis for the succeeding Republican administration. The bare bones of the Scranton Administration are impressive: it almost doubled aid to education, passed two teacher pay increases, started state scholarships, revised unemployment compensation, more than doubled Civil Service, extended

---

*Maris Harvey Taylor of Harrisburg has been the most successful of the many local bosses in Pennsylvania, including Mike and Joe Lawlor of Scranton, Henry W. Lark of Sunbury, John S. McClure of Chester, Fred Peters of Ardmore, and John R. Torquato of Johnstown. Taylor, born June 4, 1876, is nine years older than Uncle Dan O'Connell, the Democratic boss of Albany, N.Y., who is generally regarded as the proprietor of the oldest established political machine in the nation. Taylor won his first election as a city councilman in 1907, was GOP state chairman in 1934, served in the State Senate from 1941 to 1964, and was president pro tempore for a record nine sessions. For three decades Taylor called all the shots in Dauphin County. One of his rewards was a special invitation in 1969 to sit in President Nixon's White House chair. "Now isn't that something?" Taylor remarked.

fair housing and fair employment legislation, established the nation's first Department of Community Affairs, passed a $500 million conservation bond issue, built six new state parks, encouraged tough strip-mining regulations, established Pennsycare medical aid and the Council on the Arts, got a 5 percent sales tax, and in four years spent $5.1 billion in General Fund appropriations, or $1.3 billion more than the Democrats did in the previous Lawrence Administration.

Scranton, born July 19, 1917, learned politics from his mother, Mrs. Marion Margery Scranton, the Pennsylvania GOP national committeewoman from 1928 to 1951 and the national party vice chairman in the 1940s. "The Duchess," as she was called, was "the only person in the world who could wear an orchid corsage into a coal mine and still win votes," Thomas E. Dewey supposedly said. She had her one son be a college volunteer for Wendell Willkie in 1940, but she probably didn't care for his dating, briefly, the late Kathleen Kennedy, a sister of John F. Kennedy.

Scranton's win of the governorship was a masterpiece his mother would have enjoyed. After such names had been advanced as Thomas S. Gates Jr., State Senator George N. Wade, Superior Court Judge Robert E. Woodside, Congressman James Van Zandt, Elkins Wetherill, U.S. Senator Hugh Scott, Walter Alessandroni, and Congressman Schweiker, the Republicans finally guaranteed the reluctant Scranton the support of 66 of 67 county chairmen, and this was before the primary.

The 1962 election was the century's first gubernatorial contest in which Pennsylvania Democrats outregistered Republicans, and by a wide gap of 195,935. Scranton overcame the handicap to carry 62 counties and win by 486,291 votes, the biggest ever for a man in a party out of power and with a registration deficit.

He ran a superslick campaign and outshone Dilworth in the state's first television debate, making the 64-year-old mayor look more than just nineteen years his senior. Age was a difference, and Scranton—just two months younger than President Kennedy—pressed his advantage. In getting 45-year-old State Senator Raymond P. Shafer as his running-mate, Scranton had a youthful-looking, appealing ticket, the youngest Republican slate in state history. The women's vote also was critical, because for the first time they outnumbered male voters. In 1958 the men led by 40,048 registrations; in 1962, the women led by 88,321. And it is certain that Scranton captured a majority, if not a large majority, of the woman's vote.

The "Scranton-for-President" boomlet began the day after he won the governorship and got serious the day after President Kennedy was assassinated in 1963. Not since 1920 and Democrat A. Mitchell Palmer had a native-born Pennsylvanian made a concerted effort to be a Presidential candidate. Scranton himself refrained from tossing his hat into the ring, and his nonchalance as the "Hamlet of Harrisburg" irritated many in politics and the press. Finally, on June 11, 1964, at 8:23 P.M. at the Governor's Summer

Mansion at Indiantown Gap, Scranton acquiesced to Senator Scott's challenge to oppose Barry Goldwater. The next day at the Maryland State Republican Convention in Baltimore, Scranton announced his candidacy. He had thirty-one days of running time, sixteen fewer than Willkie had in 1940. He spent $750,000 and traveled through twenty-five states, only to have Ohio Governor James A. Rhodes and Illinois Senator Everett M. Dirksen throw their bloc of controlled votes behind Goldwater. On the first ballot at the San Francisco Cow Palace, Goldwater won, 883 votes to 214, though the Gallup Poll had Republican voters favoring Scranton by 60 percent and independents by 61 percent.

The Scranton story did not end with that Presidential boomlet, and it still isn't ended, though the highwater mark of his public career probably was in 1964.

The *New York Times Magazine* on January 12, 1964, was one of the many national publications to profile Scranton. "Portrait of a Not-So-Dark Horse" is by James Welsh, at that time editorial writer of the *Patriot-News* and now urban affairs reporter for the *Washington Star*. Welsh, born in 1929 in Baltimore and a Yale man like Scranton, has had numerous articles in national publications about current events and politicians.

Portrait of a Not-So-Dark Horse

by James Welsh

A few weeks ago, Pennsylvania's Governor William W. Scranton, an amateur skier of no great renown, sloshed through the mud to dedicate a new ski center, Ski Roundtop, about 15 miles south of Harrisburg. Looking up at a photographer, he asked innocently: "You say this is the closest ski slope to Washington?"

It was decidedly tongue-in-cheek, for in serious conversation Scranton would have you know that Washington, together with the White House and the Presidency, are just about the farthest things from his mind. In fact, over the last year, he has become one of the most assiduous non-candidates for President ever to appear on the American political scene.

But things are not as they were when Scranton first established that posture. The assassination of President Kennedy transformed him instantly from a very dark horse into a fairly bright prospect for the Republican Presidential nomination—and he knows it.

As short a time ago as May, 1962, Scranton was unknown to most Pennsylvanians. That was when, as a freshman congressman, he became his party's choice to run for governor. Even today, after a full year in office, he remains something of a puzzle to those who have tried to take his measure. Nine days out of 10, he fits the picture that is often drawn of him—correct and reserved, instinctively averse to flamboyancies. On the 10th day, he'll be as cornball as they come, riding a mule, shooting a Kentucky rifle, sitting in a canoe, blowing a bugle or wearing any funny hat a photographer hands him. In his politics and programs, he swings from bold to cautious, from stubborn to conciliatory. He is very good at keeping people off balance.

Said a veteran observer of the Pennsylvania scene: "To me, Bill Scranton is an enigma. I still cannot decide whether he has been a good governor. I can't make up my mind if he has the qualifications to be President. And I can't be sure what he's going to do about all this President business. You just can't generalize about the guy."

Is he going to run for President? Here is Scranton the sincere: "I think I've made myself very clear on this matter. I am not a candidate for any national office. I do not want to be." Here is Scranton the semantically meticulous: "I would be a favorite son, but not a favorite-son candidate." And here is Scranton the self-joshing, as when a reporter asked if he were a possible candidate: "Possible, no; impossible, yes."

For all his dancing disclaimers, he is plainly leaving the door open. He's not running, but he's available. What's more, he believes he can do the job.

In the externals, Scranton meets a good many of the stereotyped political requirements. A lean 6-footer, he is handsome, though not in a rugged way. At forty-six, he is comparatively young. He has energy and stamina. He has a happy, attractive family. He is easy to meet, with a pleasant, urbane manner. He has the kind of assurance that F. Scott Fitzgerald called the identification badge of the firmly established rich. And he has the money to back it up—$9 million by his own estimate, representing the fortune amassed by four generations of Scrantons in coal, iron and other industries in the Pennsylvania city that bears the family name.

Best of all, according to the people who see in him a possible champion on the national scene, he is a proven political winner. In 1960, he bucked the Kennedy tide and the Democratic inclinations of his home district to win a seat in Congress. His victory for the Pennsylvania governorship, reversing eight years of Democratic rule, was by a massive 486,000 votes.

Here is how he describes his political philosophy: "I've always been one of those people who thinks government has a real part in our national life, not only in obvious areas like defense, but where the private sector is unable to find the answers to human problems. Government should seek to supplement what's being done in the private sector, preferably at the local level, and if not there, then at the state and federal levels. Where does that place me in the scheme of things? I don't know how to describe myself. I believe in sound fiscal policy, which I guess makes me a fiscal conservative. But I tend to be quite liberal in the area of civil rights and I suppose moderate on other matters."

In his one term in Congress, Scranton compiled a voting record that fits very well within these loosely drawn political coordinates. He voted against several spending proposals, notably the big 1961 public-works bill. But he went along with the Kennedy Administration on a number of issues, including urban renewal, aid to depressed areas, minimum-wage legislation, the Peace Corps and expansion of the House Rules Committee.

Everything got more complicated when Scranton moved to the State House in Harrisburg. Operating as governor and head of a political party in a big state is not the neat and tidy way of life of a freshman congressman. And the Pennsylvania governorship in particular is no soft touch for anyone in search of a showcase record. The state is in deep economic distress. It has a backlog of expensive needs. It is chronically short of new revenue and chronically averse to new taxes. Its legislature remains oriented to rural conservatism and a brand of politics that is not for the faint-hearted. And neither party commands enough of an edge to allow a governor to plot a clear course of action.

Before Scranton entered office, there were two diametrically opposed predictions going around as to how he would fare. One was that the legislature, especially the ruling dinosaurs of his own party, would ignore his requests or, worse, cut him to political ribbons. It didn't happen. With bare legislative majorities, he had to deal and compromise, but he wasn't ignored or shoved around. He remained unflappable in difficulty and emerged with a fairly high legislative batting average.

"The thing is," explained one of his young aides, "that Bill Scranton really likes politicians and they like him. They learned that, one, they can trust him and, two, he doesn't look down on them."

A second prediction was that the Governor, who went into office remarkably unbeholden to any segment of his party, would remold state government and the party into a more progressive image. Little has come of that, either. In outlook, method and style, Scranton remains way out in front of the run of Pennsylvania Republicans. So far, the party remains comfortably unreconstructed. Theirs is a marriage of convenience, with terms of coexistence.

The Scranton method of operating leans more to direct personal involvement than to strict delegation of authority. He is on the phone a great deal to his administrative aides, cabinet officers and bureau chiefs. At times he gets restless in his high-ceilinged, oak-paneled office and goes roaming through capitol corridors to see whom he wants.

An 8-to-6 man in the office, he seldom goes home to dinner alone. Accompanying him usually are one or more aides to thrash out a particular problem. Scranton is no intellectual. Neither is he a bear for facts and statistics. But he does plenty of homework on policy and legislative matters, and he goes over his budgets line by line with the fiscal experts.

As a politician, Scranton operates best in small groups. A fund-raising dinner, for instance, will find him moving easily from table to table, deploying charm and first names, talking and listening equally well and leaving everyone thoroughly impressed. As for getting people to do the thing he wants done, Scranton has ample powers of persuasion.

For all the genuine activity going on around Scranton, his administration is a bland one. There is little color. There are few anecdotes.
Pressed for "Scranton stories," the people closest to him just sit and
stare. They have none to tell. The Scranton legislative record contains
ironies. Many of the victories he is credited with are more apparent than
real and some of his achievements fall short of what he might have obtained by fighting hard. Yet the point on which he is most vulnerable—
an increase in the sales tax from 4 to 5 percent—was virtually unavoid-
able.

It is an article of faith among Republicans, of course, that all Democrats are wild and wasteful spenders. As a candidate, Scranton rode this
theme hard in slamming the records of the two preceding Democratic
administrations. Actually, Scranton's immediate predecessor, David L.
Lawrence, was more of a fiscal conservative than most Eastern Republicans dare to be. For his last three years in office, Lawrence held the line
on taxes and exhausted just about every bookkeeping gimmick for
stretching the state's budget dollars.

The Scranton team made a noble try at economizing. His budgeteers
cut and trimmed where possible, even to the point of denying Harrisburg's capitol-park squirrels their annual handout of $100 in nuts. It
wasn't enough. Even without going ahead on badly needed teacher salaries, school subsidies and other campaign promises, Scranton had to
have a tax increase. The increase he got represented a moderate step.

Although he likes to refer to himself as "contentious," Scranton has
clearly established himself as a soft-talker and compromiser. On one
major issue, though, he waged a long, uphill struggle, with his prestige
clearly on the line, and he won. The issue was civil service reform.
Scranton had made much of the state's wide-open spoils system in his
campaign, and he introduced a bill to extend civil service status to 17,000
state employes. Republicans and Democrats alike were against the step,
and a month before the end of the session, Scranton was given little
chance of getting any kind of meaningful legislation.

He pulled out all the stops. He made major addresses on the subject
and brought in groups of businessmen, civic leaders and newspaper editors to ask their help. More directly, he summoned Republican legislators in batches of twos and threes and turned on the charm. One re-
calcitrant Republican, upon emerging from the Governor's office, was
confronted by a reporter: "Did he ask for your vote?" The legislator
replied: "I don't recall being exactly asked for my vote, but I do recall
promising it." When the votes were counted, Scranton got his bill and
the satisfaction of knowing that not one Republican voted against him.
It was a remarkable victory.

In a fight over reorganizing Pennsylvania's patchwork of small school
districts—an essential if the state is ever to get anywhere in education—

Scranton compromised well before he had to and wound up with a program that means very little. And while talking a good game of traffic safety, he looked the other way while the political professionals systematically weakened what had been a fine traffic-safety program.

Scranton had other victories, among them a legislative reapportionment bill, strip-mine controls and the beginnings of an industrial development program. He lost a big opportunity by remaining partially aloof from a campaign to get a new state constitution, only to see a November proposal to call a constitutional convention lose by a very narrow vote margin. For all that, the Governor feels he had a successful first year in office. And he believes Pennsylvania's big task in the next few years will be "to continue upgrading our education system and our technological resources, and to do a better job of salesmanship in industrial development."

Scranton's personal life presents an exemplary picture. His wife Mary, a hometown girl he married while a wartime Air Corps pilot, is a lively down-to-earth woman and a tireless performer on the campaign trail. "Hello, I'm Mary, Bill's wife," became a byword of the 1962 state campaign. She was reportedly stopped but once—by a man who replied: "Glad to meet you, I'm Tony, Dorothy's husband." The Scrantons have four children, Susan, William, Joseph and Peter. Father, mother and children all enjoy each other's company. They like to hike, ski, swim and play tennis. At Christmas and other special occasions, they and dozens of other relatives gather at the family home of Marworth, the 22-room hilltop centerpiece of a 240-acre estate ten miles north of Scranton.

Any portrait of William Scranton sooner or later veers into a comparison with the late President Kennedy. Cool and sophisticated, having great wealth and an Ivy-League background (Yale '39), Scranton has been called a Kennedy Republican and a Republican Kennedy. It's misleading. There are too many differences. But there are similarities enough to fascinate those Republicans who want a progressive Easterner.

tracing the President's family tree in
Harry McLaughlin's
Richard M. Nixon and Pennsylvania

> Surprisingly, Richard M. Nixon twice failed to carry the Keystone State, where his great-grandfather Nixon died fighting for the Union at Gettysburg and where his parents owned a farm in Menges Mills.

Richard Milhous Nixon surprisingly has never carried Pennsylvania, the state where his Grandfather Nixon and his Great-grandfather Milhous were born and where his Great-grandfather Nixon died fighting for the Union at Gettysburg.

In 1960 Nixon lost Pennsylvania to John F. Kennedy by 116,326 votes, and in 1968 he lost it again to Hubert H. Humphrey by 134,046 votes. Should the President decide to run for re-election in 1972, it would be crucial, perhaps imperative, that he win the electoral votes of Pennsylvania, the home of 36 of Nixon's forebears.

Pennsylvania no longer is the political keystone of the nation, as it was in Thomas Jefferson's day when its 20 electoral votes comprised a vitally important chunk of the 89 electoral votes needed to name a President. Today it takes 270 electoral votes, but Pennsylvania's 29 (soon to be reduced to 27) represent the second most important vote bloc coming out of the urban Northeast. A man can win the Presidency without Pennsylvania's support, as Nixon did in 1968, but it isn't recommended.

Prior to the mid-1950s a candidate like Richard Nixon—an orthodox Republican, a party man, a moderate conservative, and a small-town champion—would have had little trouble carrying Pennsylvania. The Commonwealth in those days was solidly Republican. Furthermore, it submitted to benevolent but oligarchic rule and, with rare exceptions, was counted as "regular." Its people were "a well-drilled body of voters marching in perfect and obedient order to the polls," as Senator Boies Penrose, the cynical Republican boss, observed.

The change to an unpredictable, ofttimes exciting two-party state came when the Republicans lost—more so than the Democrats won—control of Philadelphia and the State Capitol. Though the Democratic bosses could be every bit as bossy and self-serving as the Republican ones, 37-year-old Governor George M. Leader from York County, ironically Nixon country, evoked an image of independence and responsible government. The new brand of politicians like Leader and Senator Joseph S. Clark—plus the better educated and more discriminating voters, rapid urbanization, the impact of television, and other factors—made the once tried-and-true Pennsylvania into a two-party, swing state.

In 1956 the GOP still held a voter registration lead of 446,911. Four years later, for the first time ever, the Democrats went ahead, by a mere 2,965 registrations. They increased their edge to 124,831 in 1964, but then in 1968 the Republicans recaptured the lead by 59,949. Nixon in 1968 had a registration advantage and a Shafer Republican Administration with patronage working for him, but still he could not carry Pennsylvania.

Ticket-splitting is the new and happy political sport of Pennsylvanians. It is incredible that in the five major elections from 1956 through 1968 where ticket-splitting was possible the voters eagerly exercised their privilege.*

The registration fluctuation and ticket-splitting are indicative that today's Pennsylvanians are increasingly more interested in attractive candidates, industrial development, urban renewal, civil rights, taxes, and cultural ad-

---

*Here's the rundown. 1956: President Eisenhower carried Pennsylvania by 603,483; Philadelphia's Democratic mayor, Joe Clark, ousted Republican Sen. Jim Duff by 17,970. 1958: Pittsburgh's Democratic mayor, David L. Lawrence, won the governorship by 76,083; Republican Cong. Hugh Scott beat outgoing Democratic Gov. Leader for the U.S. Senate by 112,765. 1962: Republican Cong. William W. Scranton won the governorship by 486,291; Democrat Clark retained his Senate seat by a 103,734 margin over Cong. James E. Van Zandt. 1964: President Johnson took Pennsylvania by 1,457,297; Senator Scott defied the odds and defeated Miss Genevieve Blatt, three-term Secretary of Internal Affairs, by 66,135. 1968: Hubert Humphrey carried Pennsylvania by 134,046; Cong. Richard S. Schweiker dumped Senator Clark by 169,795.

Though Pennsylvania politics has been almost exclusively reserved for males, Miss Blatt, a protégé of Dave Lawrence, holds the distinct record of having run in more statewide elections than any other Pennsylvanian in history, six all told. Four Pennsylvania women previously sought the U.S. Senate seat, but Miss Blatt was the first to be a candidate of a major party, and she won that right without her party's endorsement in the 1964 primary. Scott's high-polished political skills and Pennsylvania's undercurrent bias against women in high office contributed to her defeat in the general election.

Schweiker, 43, a Main-Line businessman, in 1968 pulled an amazing reversal, and appropriately enough on Joe Clark, who himself had managed two upset wins to be a U.S. senator.

vancement than they are in any allegiances to machine politics. No state in American history for so long had such strongly organized and usually unresponsive political parties as Pennsylvania, but the old order passeth. Party and patronage still mean a great deal, but even Raymond P. Shafer conducted his governorship from 1967 through 1970 more as an independent than as a true-believing Republican who had never been beaten in an election.

Party labels will still be around in 1972, but President Nixon, as did Kennedy and Johnson, is more likely to campaign in the state as a man of "all the people" than as an organizational warhorse.

One recent development bears watching, because for the first time since the death of Penrose in 1921 the Pennsylvania Republicans have a strong leader in Washington. In September of 1969, following the death of Illinois' Senator Everett M. Dirksen, Senator Scott became the minority leader in the U.S. Senate.

Hugh Doggett Scott, Jr., is not cut from the mold which produced such previous intransigent Republican Senate figures as Simon Cameron, J. Donald Cameron, Matthew Stanley Quay, and Boies Penrose. He is a gifted compromiser and bargainer, something of a conservative, moderate, and liberal all in one, and the best Republican-Democrat vote winner in Pennsylvania history.*

---

*Scott served 16 years in the U.S. House of Representatives, and in 1948 as a congressman was the Republican national chairman for the Thomas E. Dewey election. He has been in the Senate since 1959. His relatively limited length of service is typical for Pennsylvania, which by tradition has followed the principles of rotation in office and retiring the elderly. The late Cong. Francis E. "Tad" Walter (D-Easton) holds the Pennsylvania record of 30 years of Congressional service. Many legislators, especially southerners, have exceeded that seniority. Cong. Robert J. Corbett (R-Pittsburgh) and the late Cong. William D. "Pig-iron" Kelley (R-Philadelphia) achieved 28 years. Cong. James G. Fulton (R-Mount Lebanon) and Cong. Thomas E. Morgan (D-Fredericktown) have 26 years of service. Dr. Morgan, a surgeon, is the distinguished chairman of the House Foreign Affairs Committee. The two most important historical figures, Cong. Samuel J. Randall (R-Philadelphia) and Cong. Thaddeus Stevens (R-Lancaster), had 27 and 14 years respectively. The record in the Senate is even less impressive. Penrose of Philadelphia served 24 years; J. Donald Cameron and his father, Simon Cameron, both of Harrisburg, served 20 and 14 years respectively; Quay of Beaver served 16 years, and James "Puddler Jim" Davis of Sharon served 14 years. All were Republicans.

The Camerons retired from the Senate. Quay and Penrose died in office. Sen. Joseph F. Guffey (D-Pittsburgh) was defeated for re-election at age 76; Sen. James H. Duff (R-Carnegie) lost re-election at age 73, Puddler Jim Davis lost at age 71, and Sen. Joseph Clark was defeated at age 67. James Buchanan, who served 10 years in the House and 11 in the Senate, is the only Pennsylvanian to step from Congress to a higher office.

Senator Scott, born November 11, 1900, faces the prospect of overturning two Pennsylvania traditions in length of tenure and age, but Scott, unlike most of his predecessors, is an accomplished underdog.

Scott, like Thaddeus Stevens, is one of the exceptions in Pennsylvania politics in that he was born and educated outside of Pennsylvania. Scott is a native Virginian, a descendant of President Zachary Taylor. He is also an exception in that he is an expert on Oriental art, has written four books, and has lectured at Oxford on American politics.

Scott's own politics are deceptively remarkable. He has seldom initiated any legislation. He has been above the brawl in state issues, yet has been a master manipulator in Pennsylvania GOP organizational matters. On national policy, he has been for civil rights, open housing, foreign aid, moderate welfare and redevelopment programing, and the interests of business. He has served in the Senate all through the Vietnam crisis, but deliberately kept in the background of the debate. He has been neither a hawk nor a dove, but a ruffed grouse (the Pennsylvania state bird). In short, by being a facsimile of the pastel, low-keyed Pennsylvania voter attitudes on postwar national issues, Scott has made himself the leading Pennsylvania politician of the era and a figure to be reckoned with in both national and state politics.

Harry McLaughlin, born in York in 1922 and bureau chief there for the Harrisburg *Patriot-News* since 1959, has known the Nixon family since 1952. He interviewed Mrs. Hannah Nixon in 1952 at the time of her son's "Checkers Speech" crisis, and he got the national story of Mrs. Nixon's saying, "My Richard is honest." In a 20-mile triangle were the Nixon and Eisenhower farms and the summer home of diplomat-scholar George Kennan at East Berlin, Pennsylvania. McLaughlin, winner of four Pennsylvania Newspaper Publisher awards, covered them all. He has worked on the *York Gazette and Daily, Stars and Stripes,* and the *York Dispatch.* His piece, "Richard M. Nixon and Pennsylvania," appeared in the *Sunday Patriot-News* of November 10, 1968.

Richard M. Nixon and Pennsylvania

by Harry McLaughlin

President Richard Milhous Nixon has deep family roots in Pennsylvania, especially in York County. His late parents, Mr. and Mrs. Frank Nixon, owned and operated a farm in Menges Mills, near Hanover and Spring Grove, from 1947 to 1954, before returning to their home state of California. A younger brother, Edward, also lived on the farm. He graduated from West York High School in 1948 and his famous brother, then a United States congressman, was the commencement speaker.

Edward Nixon and his wife campaigned in York County in October of 1968, revisited the 57-acre farm and were welcomed by more than 100 former friends and neighbors.

The President's great-grandfather, George Nixon III, is buried in the National Cemetery at Gettysburg. He was born in Washington County, was married there and then moved to Ohio. At the age of forty in 1861, with eight children, he enlisted in the Union Army as a private and was fatally wounded in the Battle of Gettysburg. In 1953 Richard Nixon as Vice President toured the cemetery and placed flowers at his great-grandfather's grave.

The President's uncle, the late Dr. Ernest L. Nixon, was known as the "Potato King" because of his promotion of the food product during his twenty-three years as a professor at Pennsylvania State University. He is the author of *The Principles of Potato Production,* published in 1931. Ernest was the first Nixon to get a college education. He worked his way through school, earning a Ph.D. from Columbia in 1927. It was Uncle Ernest who encouraged Richard to get an education. The two Ernest Nixon children still reside in Pennsylvania. They are, of course, the first cousins of the President. Leland W. Nixon operates his father's potato farm, and Mrs. C. J. Noll is a librarian at Penn State.

Richard Nixon until the week of his election as President was his New York law firm's representative for Harsco, an international corporation headquartered in Harrisburg.

On Nixon's mother's side, the former Hannah Milhous, the ancestry associations with York County are even more prominent, according to Mrs. Florence Sterner, a retired York genealogist and companion of the late Mrs. Nixon. Mrs. Sterner was requested by the family to research the family tree.

The President has thirty-six direct forebears who were born or lived in Pennsylvania. His great-great-great-great-great-grandfather, William Griffith Jr., owned land in Warrington Township, York County, in 1769, although the township then was still part of Lancaster County. Griffith's father came to this country from Wales before 1690 and resided in New Castle on the Delaware. The young Griffith, born in 1714, moved to York County in 1735 and later died there. He married a second time after his first wife died, and in all he had twenty-two children. One of the sons born to the first wife was named Jacob. He married Lydia Hussey, also born and reared in York County. The couple in 1790 moved to West Pike Run Township in Washington County, where he founded the Clover Hill Friends Meeting group as a member of the Society of Friends.

One of Jacob Griffith's daughters, Elizabeth, born in 1829 in Washington County, married Joshua Vickers Milhous, an Ohioan, after he had moved back to Pennsylvania. Joshua's grandfather, William Milhous, had lived in Chester County. Joshua Milhous was the great-grandfather of the President, as was George Nixon III. Both were married in Washington County, George in 1843 and Joshua in 1847. Joshua later moved to Belmont, Ohio, and had a son, Franklin Milhous, born there in 1848. Joshua died in Indiana in 1893. After her husband's death, Elizabeth Milhous and her son Franklin moved to Whittier, Calif. There Franklin, the grandfather of the President, married Almira P. Burdg, of Cumberland County, Ohio. He died February 2, 1919, and she on July 23, 1943. Their daughter, Hannah Milhous, married Francis Anthony Nixon in 1908, and Richard, the second of their five sons, was born January 9, 1913, at Yorba Linda, Calif.

Nixon's father, Francis, was the second son of Samuel Brady Nixon, who had been the second son of George, the soldier killed at Gettysburg. (The President continued this line of second sons by being the second son of Francis Nixon.) Samuel was born near Midway, Pa., and his son Francis was born in Ohio in 1878. Francis—always called Frank—was first a farmer in Ohio, then a streetcar motorman in Columbus, Ohio, and after 1907 a motorman in Whittier, Calif. Frank later operated a ranch, was a carpenter and finally from 1922 a grocery store owner. The President's father died in 1956.

When President Nixon's parents resided at their York County farm, he and his family spent many weekends and summer vacations there. Julie and Tricia, his daughters, often joined their grandparents while their famous parents traveled abroad or throughout the country. They were familiar figures, along with their Uncle Edward, at the combination Menges Mills community store and post office.

Menges Mills Postmaster Carl Stambaugh said, "The Nixon girls seemed to enjoy just sitting on the front porch of the store and talking." He recalled that the President, then still a congressman and later a senator, used the store telephone for calls to Washington and other places. "The Nixons were unable to get the York telephone company to install a phone, so he had to come to the store. I never eavesdropped, but I understand that later he told newsmen that he discussed the famous case involving Alger Hiss and Whittaker Chambers on our phone with out-of-town people. I can imagine some of the people on our party line who might have been listening in, trying to figure out what he was talking about."

The postmaster and his wife were invited to the 1953 and the 1969 inaugurations by the Nixons.

The farm is now owned by Mr. and Mrs. Sterling Myers, who also bought the community store from Stambaugh. In the living room of the farmhouse was the piano that Nixon often played for relaxation. For a long time it was in need of tuning. Nixon's mother, after selling the farm, frequently returned for visits, and in 1961 she made the present owners promise to give the Nixon piano to a museum "if my son is ever elected President of the United States." (The piano has been sent to the Nixon Presidential Museum at Yorba Linda, Calif. When the President on August 5, 1969, made a surprise visit to the farm, his first visit there since the early 1950s, he asked about the piano and was told it is in his museum.)

Frank Nixon farmed the land and loved to raise potatoes by merely placing potato eyes on the ground and covering them with straw, rather than planting them. The main reason the elder Nixon sold the farm and returned to California in 1954 was a tractor accident. He was plowing the fields when he fell off the tractor and fractured his left arm. It was set, but failed to heal properly and it was rebroken and set a second time.

During the following winter months, the 76-year-old Nixon suffered great pain in the arm, and he was advised to return to the warmer California climate.

The late Mrs. Nixon recalled several times for this reporter, and it was confirmed later by the President, that during the Hiss-Chambers controversy, "Richard spent many hours of those hectic weeks in week-end strolls on our farm, just meditating and trying to determine whether

Hiss or Chambers was lying. He never discussed the case with me, or anyone else around here, but he did say he wanted to be sure who was telling the truth." Later, as history shows, he sided with Chambers and often stopped to visit Chambers, a resident of Westminster, Md., when he drove from Washington through Westminster to the York County farm.

The Nixons are sports fans, and Edward was an athlete at West York High School. In the spring of 1948, he was the York County high school high jump champion, and credits C. C. Richards, his coach and still a social studies teacher at West York, for helping him win the county title. "Coach Richards tried to make me an athlete," he said, "but I couldn't follow his instructions too well, although I tried." The 6-foot-4 Edward Nixon now laughs when he recalls his high school athletic exploits.

The York County voters like Richard Nixon. In 1960, with a Democratic registration majority of 16,000, York voters gave Nixon a 17,000-vote edge. In 1968 they gave him an 18,000 majority, believed to be the best record on a per-capita basis in any of the Pennsylvania counties.

Bob Hoffman, the famous Olympic weightlifting coach from York and a friend of Nixon, at his seventieth birthday party following Nixon's Presidential election donated a 177-acre farm to the York County Board of Parks and Recreation for a public park. Hoffman asked that it be named "Richard Nixon County Park," and the county board honored his request. It is the first public facility to be named for President Nixon. A school in California was named for him when he was Vice President.

Part V
Pennsylvania
Success Stories

meet
Paul A. W. Wallace's
Milton Hershey

The Mennonite millionaire who made his chocolate bar a household word was in the tradition of the genuine Pennsylvania millionaires—like Andrew Carnegie, Stephen Girard, and the Mellons—who worked hard at getting money and equally hard at giving it away.

At the time of the Revolution, Pennsylvania was the richest colony. Today it ranks but seventeenth in per capita income, about $3,200 a year and not much better than the national average. It is the poorest per capita of the mideastern states. Yet in 200 years immense wealth has been accumulated in Pennsylvania. With typical Pennsylvanian exaggeration, the citizens of Williamsport, for example, call their town the "City of Millionaires," and their high school football team is the only one in the world known as "The Millionaires."

The genuine Pennsylvania millionaires have made a tradition of hard getting and then equally hard giving away. Andrew Carnegie (1835-1919) espoused what he called "The Gospel of Wealth," that a man should first concentrate on accumulating dollars and then on distributing dollars. As a young man in his early twenties, Carnegie earned $4 a week as one of the first telegraphers. When he was in his sixties, he had a personal income of $25 million a year as a steel magnate. In 1900 he sold out to J. P. Morgan's U.S. Steel for $250 million in 5 percent, 50-year gold bonds, and in the following twenty years proceeded to give away $350 million. He started 1,946 libraries; yet he scorned the use of the name "philanthropist" to describe himself.

Benjamin Franklin, as usual, was one of Pennsylvania's first philanthropists, though he wasn't a millionaire. At his death in 1790 he left $4,440 each to Philadelphia and Boston, stipulating that the funds were to provide

$300 at 5 percent interest to "married artificers" under age 25. "Good apprentices are most likely to make good citizens," he said. The fund in Philadelphia has now grown beyond $300,000. Franklin willed that his trust be terminated in 1990, with the money divided between his beloved city and commonwealth.

Stephen Girard, merchant, mariner and banker, came to Philadelphia from France in 1776. He lent his adopted nation $5 million in the War of 1812 to tide it over. He had millions and he had genius, but he was taciturn, blind in one eye, partially deaf, personally unattractive (he wore the same overcoat most of his life), and in perpetual grief because his only child, a daughter, died in infancy and his wife was institutionalized for mental illness for twenty-five years. When he died in 1831, he left an estate of $10 million and from that came Girard College, for 100 years the world's leading school for orphan boys.

The extraordinary Mellon family of Pittsburgh has a continuity of more than 100 years and is said to be worth at least $3 billion. Since World War II, the Mellons have given away in excess of $700 million. Andrew W. Mellon (1855-1937), the U.S. Secretary of the Treasury from 1921 to 1931, was the genius, said by some to be the greatest businessman America has ever produced.

Milton Snavely Hershey remains one of the most fascinating of the Pennsylvania breed. His life was one of contradictions. He came from Mennonite stock, but at age 41 married Catherine Sweeney in St. Patrick's Cathedral on Fifth Avenue. After he died, October 13, 1945, services were conducted by five Protestant ministers and a Catholic priest, and eight seniors from his boys' school were his pallbearers.

"Milton, you have always been a good boy. Don't let your money spoil you," his mother once told him. He listened to his mother, as well as to good lawyers, chemists, and salesmen.

David Rubinoff once played Hershey, Pennsylvania, with his $100,000 Stradivarius. "It's $100,000 to you, but I wouldn't pay that for it," Hershey told him. In 1936 he was asked to contribute to the National Rose Garden in Washington. He thought it over, and decided to plant his own rose garden in his own town. Today it is one of the world's great gardens, with 1,200 varieties and 42,000 roses. In the 1930s, Hershey had Italian sculptor Giuseppe Donato do the "Dance of Eternal Spring." When Donato produced three nude maidens, Hershey at first refused to pay for it. Eventually he relented, but gave the statue to the city of Harrisburg.

He was a magnificent businessman; yet in October of 1929, the month of the great crash, he began negotiations to merge his chocolate company with the Kraft-Phoenix Corporation and the Colgate-Palmolive-Peet Corporation. That December he wisely called the deal off. Since his death, the now Hershey Foods Corporation has purchased H. B. Reese Company, San

Giorgio, Delmonico, David and Frere, and the Cory Corporation. Sales have gone from $5 million in 1911 to $246 million in 1968.

The Hershey company did not begin mass consumer advertising until 1970, and earned a national reputation for its abstinence from the ways of Madison Avenue. The commonly told story is that whenever Milton Hershey saw an empty candy wrapper on the ground, he would kick it over so that its label showed. To him that was mass consumer advertising. One of his slogans was, "A sweet to eat, a food to drink." When demand for his chocolate was soon forthcoming, Hershey reasoned that he didn't need advertising and eliminated it.

Hershey had little education or liking for social life, but his philanthropies went for these. His boys' school was started in 1909. During the Depression, he built a community center, two theaters, the state's biggest swimming pool, four golf courses, an outdoor stadium, and a hockey arena. When he died, he didn't even own the house he lived in; that had been given to his employees for a country club. From 1938 to 1963 there was the Hershey Junior College, succeeded by the $50 million Milton S. Hershey Medical Center, which is the medical college of Penn State and the first new one in Pennsylvania since Temple Medical School was founded in 1901.

"His deeds are his monument. His life is our inspiration," the inscription reads on the statue of him that his orphan boys had erected.

"Milton Hershey" is a profile taken from *Pennsylvania, Seed of a Nation,* by Paul A. W. Wallace, published by Harper & Row in 1962. Dr. Wallace (1891-1967) was a native of Canada who for twenty-five years was chairman of the English Department at Lebanon Valley College. He edited *Pennsylvania History* magazine for seven years, and in 1957 after retiring from Lebanon Valley joined the Pennsylvania Historical and Museum Commission. Dr. Wallace was an authority on Colonial Pennsylvania, early American Indians, the Pennsylvania Dutch, and Milton S. Hershey, whom he knew personally. He wrote a number of books, including a study of the Iroquois, *The White Roots of Peace,* 1946, which is in the White House Library.

Milton Hershey

by Paul A. W. Wallace

Milton S. Hershey, founder of the Hershey Chocolate Corporation and the Milton Hershey School for orphan boys, was distinctively a Pennsylvania product. This does not mean that he was a mere provincial. On the contrary, he was of national importance, both as one of the first Americans to master the techniques of mass production—some years before Henry Ford—and as one of the leaders in the modern movement for the decentralization of industry.

It is not, however, as an economic portent that he best deserves to be remembered, but as a representative of a distinctively Pennsylvanian ethos. In him the religion of the Pennsylvania Dutch plain sects was taken out of its local context and injected into the world of big business—with some surprising results.

Milton Hershey came of Swiss Mennonite stock on both his father's and his mother's side. Exactly where in Switzerland his forebears came from is not known. Martin H. Brackbill, of Harrisburg, traced Hershey's descent from a Christian Hirschi of Schangnau in the Emmenthal, Canton Bern. There could hardly have been a better place for a chocolate manufacturer's genealogy to begin. Emmenthal is good dairy country, and its people make the most famous of Swiss cheeses, the Emmenthaler, which is as big as a cartwheel and, for all its holes, weighs up to 300 pounds. Only ten miles of foothills separate Schangnau from Interlaken and the most dazzling sight in the Alps—the Jungfrau, presiding in splendor over the black peaks and white glaciers of the Bernese Oberland.

Christian Hirschi of Schangnau and some 700 of his compatriots were expelled from Switzerland in 1672. They were members of a sect known then as the Swiss Brethren, and later as Mennonites or followers of

Menno Simons, who had incurred the hostility of the Bernese authorities because, among other things, of their refusal to bear arms. After spending some years in the German Palatinate, Christian Hirschi—Milton's great-great-great-great-grandfather—emigrated to Pennsylvania in 1717. With his friend Hans Brubaker he took out a warrant for 1,000 acres of land on little Conestoga Creek just west of the present city of Lancaster. The section included the site of President Buchanan's future home, Wheatland.

From this Christian Hirschi the line is unbroken through Bishop Bentz Hershey, a second Christian Hirschi, Isaac Hershey, Jacob Hershey, Henry Hershey, and finally Milton, who was born at the Hershey homestead in Derry Township, Dauphin County, on September 13, 1857. Milton's mother, Veronica, known as Fanny, also traced descent from the first Christian Hirschi, and her line, like her husband's, was strictly Swiss Mennonite. Her own father, Abraham Snavely, was a bishop of the Reformed, or New, Mennonite Church, a body which split off from the parent stem because it found the orthodox Mennonites not strict enough in discipline.

Milton Hershey's astonishing blend of generous daring—as seen in his Cuban venture*—and miserly caution—as seen in his mania for turning out office lights—was a gift from his parents. His father, Henry, was a man of infinite zest and unfathomable curiosity, who entered and failed in—by his son's count—seventeen separate careers, including those of farmer, oilman, inventor, journalist, preacher, horticulturist, steelworker, carpenter, and still-life painter. In his old age he was rescued by his millionaire son from near destitution in Colorado where, according to rumors then circulating, he was driving a dump truck, selling secondhand books and peddling horse powders of his own invention to small farmers in the foothills of the Rockies. His last years were spent in ecstatic content at the Hershey homestead, where his son had

---

*Hershey was a widower for 31 years. After his wife died in 1914, he vacationed often in Cuba. Because of the scarcity of sugar during World War I, he decided to extend his business there. Eventually he owned seven raw sugar mills and a refinery, about 100,000 acres of land 40 miles from Havana, and had 3,500 employees. He had tried to buy one town, but politicians asked for $50,000 under the table. He then built his own town, Central Hershey, usually known as Hershey, Cuba. Hershey built a second hotel in Cuba and even a second orphans' school, though the school wasn't a success and he closed it. All in all, Hershey practiced business in Cuba with unusual daring, especially since he knew he paid too much for his plantations and that their operating costs were too high. Even with the sale of Hershey sugar in the United States, Hershey was not reaping just profits from his investments. In months prior to his death in 1945, he authorized the sale of the Cuban properties. It was another smart Hershey move, because in little over a decade Fidel Castro confiscated the properties. After the sale, the Hershey trade name continued to be used in Cuba, but by the late 1960s the Hershey Corporation in Pennsylvania was able to restrict its use to its wholly owned operations.

prepared a good library for him, filled with his own choice of books on history, religion, nature study, and experimental science.

Milton's mother was a frugal, cautious, but determined little woman whose one great passion in life was to help her unlucky son Milton succeed as his father had not. Her own father, Bishop Abraham Snavely, was blest with great riches, and she found it hard to live with a mate who would rather read a book than earn a meal. One day when the larder was bare, she presented an ultimatum to her husband, "If you go on reading books, I will leave you." They separated, and thereafter she had herself listed in the Lancaster city directory as "widow of Henry Hershey," although the "widower" continued to visit her now and then, for at heart they were really very fond of each other.

Fanny Hershey was with her husband at the time he died in the Hershey homestead, and she saw to it that in death the barrier that had separated them should be finally removed. She had workmen take all his books out of the library and burn them in the experimental chocolate-factory furnace. Fifty years later Harry Tinney recalled the scene: "Monroe Hershey hauled the books out in a wheelbarrow. I opened the (furnace) door and slung them in. Monroe went back a couple of times to the house to fetch them out. She stood back a little and watched, but she didn't say anything."

Milton Hershey had very little schooling. Starting at the Derry Church School, where his uncle Elias was teacher, he went to a succession of one-room schools, six in about eight years. By his own estimate, he never got beyond the fourth grade. Country schools in those days were open for only a few months in the year, and there was no compulsory attendance law to make it seem wiser to a boy and his parents to spend daylight hours on a school bench rather than out in the fields catching skunks — a sport in which Milt Hershey was malodorously adept — or doing chores about the barn. The result was that his formal education left him with little to show beyond an elementary ability to read and write and a hearty dislike for books.

To the end of Milton's days, abstract ideas and scientific reasoning meant little to him. But he had a good memory and what is called an "experiencing" nature. Everything he heard, saw, felt, smelled or tasted had meaning for him and was remembered. From his father he learned to experiment. From his mother he learned industry and patience. In developing his chocolate formula, he worked on no abstract theories and attempted no scientific short cuts. He used instead the trial-and-error method, inching his way untiringly through failure after failure to a final and triumphant success.

From earliest childhood he had known the taste of failure, and this inoculation saved him from discouragement in his mature years. When he was four or five years old, his parents took him to the oilfields in the neighborhood of Titusville, where his father tried to sell drilling machinery, shortly after the oil boom had ended. When Milton was fourteen, his father—who had always wanted to be a writer himself—tried to start the boy in that direction by apprenticing him as printer's devil on a pacifist weekly, the *Waffenlose Waechter (Weaponless Watchman)*. When one day Milton dropped his hat into the press—thus adding a heady element to the *Watchman's* potpourri of German and English prose and poetry—the printer and his devil parted.

Next he got a job with Joe Royer of Lancaster, who made candy and ran a restaurant famous for its "ice cream and lemon squares." Joe set the boy to holding horses for his customers and turning the handle of the big ice-cream freezer. He failed in this latter job because he lacked the necessary physical strength. Joe accordingly sent him to the kitchen to help make candy, and there he found his life's work.

After a few years spent tinkering with candy recipes there, Milton resolved to set out on his own. Like his father, he allowed his imagination to shoot skyward, and he began a series of ambitious failures that carried him well into manhood. He started in Philadelphia in 1876, hoping to profit from the crowds in the city attending the Centennial Exhibition. Though the competition was killing, he held on for several years, during which time the family rallied to his side: his mother by cooking and wrapping candies, his father—in his inimitable, dubious way—by inventing a brand of H. H.—Henry Hershey—Cough Drops and a patented Medicated Candy Cabinet to exhibit them in.

Milton sold candies on the street by day and cooked fresh batches by night, becoming so exhausted that he was known to fall asleep on his feet. In the end he broke down. His creditors refused to carry him further, and the business collapsed.

At the urging of his father, who had followed the mining rush to Colorado, Milton went out to Denver, only to find that his father as usual had missed the boat. The silver mining boom had burst, and Denver was filled with unemployed. Milton somehow got a job with a candy-maker, who taught him how to make caramels with real milk. That recipe turned out to be the key to Hershey's subsequent success.

In Denver, Milton Hershey learned a lot of other things too. He learned to steel himself against both the threats and the enticements of a world not much talked about by Dauphin County Mennonites. At that time in 1882, Soapy Smith—who was to die in Alaska of well-earned gunshot wounds incurred on the Trail of '98—was one of the kings of the underworld, and Baby Doe was one of the queens. The year Hershey was there, Buffalo Bill was robbed of $2,000 worth of jewels.

Bishop Abraham Snavely's grandson carried a revolver in that haunt of wickedness, and he used it on one occasion to get himself out of a jam. He had seen a Boy Wanted sign in a shop window and went in to apply for a job. Finding himself in suspicious company, he tried to leave but found the door locked. Only the sight of Milton's drawn revolver persuaded the boss to let him go. Denver did not fill Milton Hershey's pocket with gold pieces, but it taught him self-reliance and gave him fresh stamina to withstand the failures that lay ahead.

The Hersheys, father and son, went to Chicago. There Henry Hershey got a job as a carpenter, while Milton hired himself out to a candy-maker. They pooled their resources, but when father Hershey put his name to an unlucky friend's note and had to pay, the Hershey balloon was again deflated.

"If you want to make money," said Henry Hershey to his son, "you must do things in a big way."

They went to New Orleans, planning to borrow money, buy machin-ery, and take the Southern market by storm. Finding, however, that the machinery they wanted was made in New York, they decided to save the cost of freight by going themselves to New York, hub of the candy uni-verse, and storming the biggest market of all.

In New York they borrowed money and set up an expensive cough-drop machine. Milton manufactured caramels and H. H. Cough Drops, while his father drove a candy wagon round Manhattan and across the new Brooklyn Bridge. But the candy market was a hard one to break into. A day of reckoning came. Milton's creditors demanded payment. In desperation Milton hired a wagon, filled it with cough drops, and drove round the alleys trying to sell the stuff to small dealers. While he was inside one place dickering with a prospect, some boys threw fire-crackers under his horse. Hearing the tumult that erupted on the cobble-stones, Milton rushed out, only to see horse and wagon disappearing in a shower of cough drops. After that, he remained in New York only long enough to earn money, by doing odd jobs, for train fare back to Lan-caster.

In Lancaster, Milton was icily received by most of his relatives. But being as incorrigibly optimistic as his father, he borrowed money from an aunt, Mattie Snavely, hired a room with a stove, bought some sugar, and started all over again. His mother and Aunt Mattie wrapped candies, while Milton peddled them round the streets—at the wrong end of town—in a pushcart. The pushcart rivalry was really tough. Milton, now about 30, pushed his luck too far along South Dorwart Street on Cab-bage Hill one day and was stoned out.

An English candy importer visiting the United States tasted Milton Hershey's fresh-milk caramels and recognized their superior quality. He gave Hershey a sizable order. Milton realized that his future depended on his ability to fill this order. He had neither the equipment nor the staff to make caramels in the mass, and the banks turned him down when he tried to borrow money on his prospects. One man, however, Mr.

Brenneman, cashier of the Lancaster National Bank, became interested. He was not impressed with Milton's establishment, a small noisy room in a building that housed a carriage factory and a carpet-beating concern. On the other hand, Milton Hershey's quiet, confident manner and his complete devotion to his work made the banker believe for the moment in the Horatio Alger type, and he put his personal name to the young man's note.

The candies were made, shipped to England, and paid for. When Milton received the English check, he rushed down to the bank, still in his candy apron, to pay off his note.

Once Milton's luck turned, it turned completely. Thereafter to the end of his life he never ceased to be surprised at the way money makes money. In a very few years he owned a large factory in Lancaster, where he made his Crystal A. Caramels: the aristocratic Lotus, Paradox, and Cocoanut Ices, all made of cream, and the plebeian Icelets, Empires, and Melbas, made of skim milk.

Milton had a sharp eye for the market, anticipating changes before they occurred. Chocolate was then on the horizon. His father had apparently been reading up on the subject and was thinking of going to Brazil to grow cacao trees for an expected boom in chocolate candy and cocoa. Milton caught his father's enthusiasm. Caramels were a passing fad, he thought, but chocolate—"A sweet to eat, a food to drink," as he was one day to advertise in New York—must be in never-ending demand. He was sure that the first man to exploit fully the immense new market for a popularly priced chocolate would make a gigantic fortune.

At the World's Columbian Exposition at Chicago in 1893 he saw a machine for making chocolate candies, bought it, hired chocolate experts, and set aside a part of his huge factory for experiment. After long tests and many failures, he settled on a milk chocolate bar—made with fresh milk—as the thing to concentrate on, and he assembled all the instruments of mass production to turn it out at a price everyone could afford. With roasters and hullers and milling machines, agitators and condensing kettles, plow machines, chasers, melangeurs, and longitudes, he made the Hershey Chocolate Bar, next to the Stars and Stripes, the most widely known American product in the world of his day.

In 1900 he sold his caramel business for $1 million. Examining sites for the mammoth chocolate factory he now planned to build, he rejected Baltimore, Yonkers, and Kingston, N.Y., and selected his own birthplace, Derry Church, Pa. It was not mere sentiment that dictated the choice but penetrating insight into the future. For one thing, this was good dairy country, and fresh milk was the secret of his success. There was also a good water supply. Best of all, in Derry Township of Dauphin County he had available a dependable labor supply: a countryside inhabited by the industrious, home-loving Pennsylvania Dutch folk to whom he belonged and who could be trusted to be loyal to their own.

He built his factory in a cornfield and in 1903 laid out the town of Hershey. There, from a rural base, he set out on the course of mass production and national distribution which soon made him a millionaire many times over.

Milton Hershey's philanthropies were not an afterthought. Though he had rejected the theological doctrines of the Reformed Mennonites, the vision of life they had shown him—especially through the example of his mother and his uncle, Bishop Elias Hershey—remained with him to the end. The Golden Rule was his article of faith. He plowed his fabulous millions back into the community around him in many ways: by using his capital in time of depression to erect public buildings, thus giving employment at the time and providing future benefits to his people; by building a great residential school for orphan boys, in which the weaknesses of mass education were avoided by housing the youngsters in small "family" units or farm cottages; by providing amusement parks, golf courses, swimming pools, theaters, and athletic fields as the best means of healthy recreation; by giving financial assistance to all local churches, whatever their denomination; by helping the public schools; by setting up a junior college; by providing a good library and a museum to help keep the community from the mental stagnation that sometimes afflicts the carefree and the prosperous.

The first thing that impresses a visitor in the town of Hershey is the untroubled—but by no means slack—expression on the faces of its citizens. The next is the natural way in which the town has been allowed to grow, the healthy individuality of the houses on the streets, and the absence of any corrosive uniformity. Milton Hershey had a horror of the neat rows of identical houses he had seen in some company towns. He was interested in the Garden City movement in England.

Even the ambitious Hotel Hershey, perched above the town on Pat's Hill, is a strictly individual affair. In the flush of his first multimillions, Milton Hershey and his wife planned it to be a replica of the grandiose Heliopolis Palace at Cairo. But the passage of time altered his perspective, and in the end he chose a more modest model. He gave the architect, D. Paul Witmer, a picture postcard showing a small, 30-room, end-turreted hotel that he and his wife had once enjoyed on the shore of the Mediterranean. He told the architect to blow it up to 200 rooms. When shown that the hill could not accommodate so many, he reduced the number to the 150 rooms the Hotel Hershey has today. He wanted the lobby to have a Cuban look, to remind him of his beloved plantation, Rosario, near Havana. He wanted the dining room to be without pillars, so that the diners could all enjoy the view of the Blue Mountains on the horizon. Other suggestions came out of a notebook he had kept on his travels. The hotel and the town of Hershey below it may not be the best places in which to study classic architecture, but they are definitely monuments to Mr. Hershey's individualism.

The Milton Hershey School is now the chief beneficiary of the Hershey Chocolate Corporation. Into it Mr. Hershey poured millions for up-to-date buildings, qualified teachers, and the latest equipment, in order to give the boy students the better opportunities he had missed as a child. His own failures and frustrations had not left him bitter. They had given him an overwhelming compassion.

"I would give everything I possess if I could call one of these boys my own," he said to a friend visiting one of the school dormitories with him. His wife was an invalid, and they had no children of their own. Today thousands of "Milton Hershey's boys," graduates of the Milton Hershey School, many of them in high positions, honor him as the man who was more than a father to them.

Hershey was, of course, like all entrepreneurs of the day, something of an autocrat. To get his full flavor, we should not compare him with the "organization man" of today but with the financial tycoons of his own day. He did not fully understand labor problems or the emerging concept of property as being in part the possession of the labor force that helped to create it. He was a hard trader, and not everybody had occasion to like him. But he loved his labor force and did his best, according to his lights, to help them. "Well," said one of his competitors, who had watched him putting millions into his two beautiful towns—Hershey, Pa., and Hershey, Cuba—"if he likes to give money away, that's his affair."

In labor's attempt to unionize the workers of America one of the toughest nuts to crack was the Hershey Chocolate Company. This was in part owing to the unwillingness of the factory workers to join a union, many of them being members of plain sects whose religion forbade them to do so. In part also, it was because Milton Hershey had shown so generous a public spirit that most of his employees, and certainly the Pennsylvania Dutch community behind them, supported his benevolent autocracy.

In the great Hershey sit-down strike of 1937 the farmers of Dauphin and Lebanon counties and the students of Lebanon Valley College in nearby Annville joined forces to break the strike, making a sudden rush into the factory that brought many of the sit-downers tumbling out of the windows. This marked the end of an era of sit-down strikes throughout the country. It marked also a change in Mr. Hershey himself. He was bitterly grieved that any of his employees should have turned against him, but he was also led to reappraise the relations between employer and employed, and he came in the end to accept the principle of collective bargaining.

presenting
Gifford Pinchot's
Time like an Ever Rolling Stream

Gifford Pinchot—author, athlete, forester,
lifelong nonconformist, and Pennsylvania's
only two-term governor in the twentieth
century—carved a special niche for himself
in American politics and conservation.

Gifford Pinchot (1865-1946), the only two-term governor of Pennsylvania in
the twentieth century, was America's first professional forester and certainly
its most famous conservationist. "I have been a governor, every now and
then, but I am a forester all the time," he remarked late in his life.

Pinchot was a millionaire and traveled most of the world, but he came
from a Pennsylvania family and in heart and spirit he never left this state.
The forests, streams, mountains, and especially the people of Pennsylvania
were exciting to Pinchot, and he always remained in his enthusiasms something between a woodsman and a grown-up boy about his state.

Pennsylvania even yet isn't all asphalt and urban blight. It has 9,500 miles
of streams, hundreds of lakes and ponds, and forests that still cover 57 percent of its acreage. It has almost 700,000 licensed fishermen, 200 species of
fish, and there is trout in 60 lakes and 4,500 miles of streams. It is the leading hunting state in the nation, issuing nearly 1.1 million permits a year, well
ahead of second-place Michigan. The annual harvest is 250 bears, 3 million
rabbits, almost 1 million ringneck pheasants, 142,000 whitetail deer,
70,000 wild duck, and even 18,000 wild turkey.

Pinchot lived at Milford in Pike County, seven miles west of Port Jarvis,
New York. He fished for trout in the Sawkill, a limestone-rich stream similar
to the chalkwater streams of Hampshire, England, where anglers began 200
years ago. Often his companion was Edward R. Hewitt, the New Yorker and
one of the leading trout authorities. Hewitt was the grandson of the famous

inventor Peter Cooper. Pinchot's wife was Cornelia E. Bryce, whom that famous sportsman, President Theodore Roosevelt, had introduced to him. Cornelia was the great-granddaughter of Peter Cooper.

The article, "Time like an Ever Rolling Stream," is the final chapter of *Just Fishing Talk,* which Pinchot wrote for Stackpole Books in 1936. The son he introduces to fishing is his only child, Giffie, now Gifford Bryce Pinchot, M.D., of Johns Hopkins University.

The Pinchot home was the 41-room French chateau, Grey Towers, at Milford. It and ten acres were given by Dr. Pinchot for the U.S. Forest Service Institute of Conservation Studies, and was dedicated in his father's memory by John F. Kennedy in 1963 in the President's last visit to Pennsylvania.

"The distinction between men," Pinchot once said, "is much more in their will than in their ability." He believed in hard work and hard play. "He seemed to have a terror of the temptation to self-indulgence," wrote political pundit Mark Sullivan. Teddy Roosevelt in his autobiography praised his close friend Pinchot for his "tireless energy and activity, his fearlessness, his complete disinterestedness, his single-minded devotion to the interest of the plain people, and his extraordinary efficiency."

Pinchot was born to the aristocracy. His grandfather was forced to flee France after the Battle of Waterloo because of his outspoken republicanism. His father, James Pinchot, earned a fortune in the manufacturing of wallpaper and married into the even wealthier Eno family of New York with millions from real estate. James built Grey Towers in 1885. Gifford married the 5-foot-10 Cornelia, daughter of a former New York state senator and worth perhaps $18 million herself. If anything, red-haired Cornelia was more of an activist than her husband. She battled for woman suffrage, Prohibition, and better labor conditions, and she dressed in red corduroy so she wouldn't be missed on a picket line. She ran in three Pennsylvania Republican Congressional primaries, but lost all three. She actually filed to run for governor to succeed her husband in 1934, but then withdrew. At age 72 she was playing excellent tennis. As a campaigner and organizer of the Pennsylvania State Council of Republican Women, she was immensely popular and equally controversial, a sort of Eleanor Roosevelt of Pennsylvania. She certainly thought her husband qualified to be President in 1924 and 1932, and it didn't take much encouragement for Gifford, who adored her, to believe himself fit.

Pinchot's often-repeated motto was "The public good comes first." He could have devoted his life to being a rich playboy or accumulating more dollars, but he was too highstrung and possessed with an inner light for service. "Life is something more than a matter of business," he said. "No man can make his life what it ought to be by living it merely on a business basis. There are things higher than business."

His zest for action and his moral absoluteness about causes could be the despair of others. Harold Ickes called him "a self-appointed Messiah" and a "zealot." Governor David L. Lawrence remembered him as "an opportunist in many respects but very colorful, extremely colorful." His fellow Republican, Senator Boies Penrose, pronounced his name scornfully as "Pin-shot" and called him a "tree surgeon" and "millionaire carpetbagger." Historian S. K. Stevens noted that Pinchot often could be pontifical and a "personal dictator whose 'GP' scrawled in heavy black pencil on any state paper was a demand that this request be taken care of without question as to proper procedures." Republican Senator David A. Reed called him "a common scold," but Democratic Senator Joe Guffey acclaimed him as the best governor since the Civil War. Governor George M. Leader in 1958 when he dedicated Pinchot State Park in York County said, "My respect and admiration for Gifford Pinchot are boundless." Pinchot for his part said "bully" when he was pleased and called his enemies "yellow dogs" when he was angry. Once before the legislature he exclaimed, "They're gangsters first and Republicans as a matter of convenience." He, of course, was always a Republican, but a special Pinchot Republican.

Indeed, the man was extremely colorful. "The eyes peered out above appropriately hollowed cheeks, over a truculent nose that hovered above ferocious muleskinner mustachios, and the head was attached to as lean and spare a frame as ever suggested austerity and rigor," scholar James Penick has written. "The total effect was magnificent."

He wrote his platform on a postcard so that his friends with short attention spans would know why they were voting for him. He wore blue shirts in a day when men wore only white shirts. His floppy black hat was his trademark. He didn't drink or smoke, and he kept every animal not dangerous enough for a zoo. He'd breakfast at a prison and throw parties in the Capitol for state employees. At Christmastime he sent out 40,000 cards with Grey Towers on them. When in 1935 he left the governorship and public office for the last time, he walked from the inaugural stand through Capitol Park, while the secretaries standing at their windows cheered him. Then suddenly, in a typical Pinchotian dramatic gesture, he turned to the Capitol, swept off his hat, and bowed gracefully to the end of his career and to the girls.

Pinchot was a madcap athlete all his life. At Yale, though only 161 pounds on a 6-foot-1 frame, he captained the freshman football team and boasted he had the second highest lung capacity of anyone. He once played President Teddy Roosevelt six straight sets of tennis in January and then raced him to the White House. At a picnic while he was governor and in his sixties, he won a 75-yard dash against an astounded cabinet member. He was an expert horseback rider, and he took his student pilot's license while governor. He was a sailor, and fishing he thoroughly enjoyed. "From one sin I may boast I have so far been free," he wrote. "No shark has ever struck my hook and got away alive with my consent." All forms of recreation mattered to him. "The man who thinks about nothing but work is inevitably consumed by it. In a sense, our best work is done in play time," he said.

Pinchot served under Presidents McKinley, Roosevelt, and Taft as U.S.

Forester. He made a record that insures him the title as the greatest practicing conservationist in American history. "A nation deprived of its liberty may win it," he wrote. "A nation divided may unite, but a nation whose natural resources are destroyed must inevitably pay the penalty of poverty, degradation, decay."

Pinchot and his younger brother, Amos, helped write the 1912 Bull Moose platform. Two years later he ran in the first direct election for U.S. senators, but was badly beaten by incumbent Penrose, though he did finish ahead of Congressman A. Mitchell Palmer. He served as state forester and then in 1922 formed his own Republican Party within the GOP and ran for governor. He won the primary by a mere 9,259 votes but swept the general election. Pinchot served as governor from 1923 to 1926, lost another race for the U.S. Senate, and in 1930, with his foe, Boss Bill Vare of Philadelphia, quoting odds of 100-1 against him, he won his second GOP primary, this time by a close 20,099 votes. He served his second term from 1931 to 1934, and proceeded to lose his third bid for the U.S. Senate. In 1938 at the age of 73 he ran again for governor, but this time was overwhelmed in the primary by Arthur H. James.

There has never been a maverick in Pennsylvania politics, not even Thaddeus Stevens, the equal of Gifford Pinchot. He spent his own money, wrote his own speeches, denounced his own Republicans, formed his own county committees, shook everyone's hand, and was the first candidate to use the radio. Had there been television, Pinchot with his magnetism probably never would have been defeated. He was not beyond making deals with the powerful Joseph R. Grundy, the founder of the Pennsylvania Manufacturers Association, and he paid his political debts faithfully. "Farm support, labor support, plus the echoes of 'Onward Christian Soldiers,' made Pinchot governor," the *Nation* reported.

He knew what people wanted. His 1922 campaign took place the first time women could vote. He won almost all their votes and went ahead and appointed seventy-nine women to public office, including Dr. Ellen C. Potter, the first woman cabinet officer. He fought for health and safety standards, woman's suffrage, the graduated income tax, workmen's compensation, aid to education and agriculture, and, above all, high moral principle and conservation. Though he was fifty-seven when he first became governor, the younger voters invariably were his greatest supporters.

The novelist Owen Wister once remarked that Pinchot's eyes always looked as if they gazed upon "a Cause." Pinchot was incapable of heeding his own advice that "if you succumb to espousing every good cause, you keep building up the number of your enemies. Soon they reach such proportions that you cannot possibly be reelected."

Pinchot's achievements in Pennsylvania have been lasting: permanent voting, the State Administrative Code, standardized state salaries, Civil Service, the Liquor Control Board, the nation's first Sanitary Water Board to fight pollution, paved rural roads, charity hospitalization, the state mental hospital system, the Milk Control Board, the State Planning Board, and Old-Age and Public Assistance. "The public welfare cannot be subserved merely by walking blindly in old ruts," he said early in his career. "Times change, and the public needs change with them."

He wrote a number of books, his last one, *Breaking New Ground,* when he was eighty, a year before his death from leukemia. Something of the flavor of Pinchot shows in *Just Fishing Talk.* Ironically, though Pinchot is second only to Benjamin Franklin as Pennsylvania's most sparkling public figure and though a number of scholarly studies have been done on aspects of his career and interests, especially on conservation, no biographer yet has captured the charm and exuberance of "Ole Hoss," as he often was called.

Time like an Ever Rolling Stream

by Gifford Pinchot

Men may come and men may go, but the Sawkill brook flows on—feeding its trout, protecting its insect, molluscan, and crustacean life—a home and a hiding place for myriads of living creatures—a thing of beauty and a joy forever.

Along its banks giant pines and hemlocks have germinated and grown, flourished and died, decayed and vanished, uncounted generations of them, each leaving its contribution to the richness and glory of the place—and in their branches other uncounted generations of squirrels and birds have fed and quarreled and mated and carried on the business of their world.

Under the shade of little needles on great limbs, deer and bear drank and listened as they drank. About their roots cubs, fawns, and baby otters romped and rested and romped again. In winter their cones and leaves strewed the snow after every breeze, and on sunny days melted little cavities for themselves, and froze there as the shadows fell across them.

Buffalo, moose, elk, wolves and panthers left their tracks beside the semi-human tracks of bears and coons, the webbed tracks of beaver, and the triangular imprints of mink.

Great flocks of passenger pigeons hid the sun, and where they settled the branches of stout trees were broken off and crashed to earth, to the thunder of innumerable wings.

Kingfishers clattered up and down the gorge in high water and low, as through the years the weather and the water shaped the rocks and the floods ground out great potholes with their in-arching rims.

Century upon century of millenniums passed over the Sawkill and left it very much as they found it. At times great pines and hemlocks fell across the stream, at times the rush of the torrent after great rains moved them away to new positions, to be moved again or to disintegrate where they lay by the slow action of the elements. Now and again a sandbar changed its place, a pool was deepened by a fall of rock or shallowed by the cutting of a new channel. Great trout grew fat and lazy in the slow current of beaver dams, and the full-fed water snakes sunned themselves where countless forebears had coiled in comfort before them.

When the redmen came, the life of the brook changed, but only a little. For they were no slaughterers, but conservationists, blood and bone, and took no more than the natural increase. Each family had its hunting grounds in which no other family might hunt except for food while passing through, and the penalty for breaking that game law was sometimes death.

Now and again through the centuries a forest fire set by lightning swept one or the other bank, or maybe both, and changed the lives of land and water dwellers for a few or many generations.

For uncounted ages the redmen hunted on the Sawkill, and still the greater and lesser tribes of wood and stream lived with them, not one destroyed, not one dangerously reduced in numbers by anything the Indians did. Then came the change.

White men appeared. With new weapons of destruction, new zeal for slaughter, new appetite for conquest, they made new demands on nature for the means to live a new kind of life. With their coming the axe began to modify the face of the earth, and the days of the wilderness were numbered.

The slow and uneventful march of the centuries over the Sawkill changed almost over night to the rush of oncoming civilization. The old order, grown out of thousands of generations of adjustment, and the old balance, painfully won through the life and death and internecine struggles of myriad forms of life, suddenly found themselves powerless before a new and strange attack, against which they had no time to develop a method of resistance.

The Indians gave way before it, and disappeared. The buffalo, the elk, and the panther followed them. The primeval forests went down before the need for houses and 10,000 other needs for wood. The white man was reaping where he had not sown, and nature paid the price of the better living, the faster thinking, and the more stable existence of the heirs of all the ages.

Hemlocks that overhung the riffles and pools of the Sawkill when Columbus discovered America were still vigorous trees when the first Pinchot to set foot in Pennsylvania twitched his first trout out of the Sawkill, and found it good. With him came his son, a boy of 19, who the year before had been on his way to join Napoleon's army as a recruit when the Battle of Waterloo put an end to his soldiering.

The son threw himself into the life of his new country with the vigor which distinguished him. The tribes of pine and hemlock along many streams paid him tribute, with the years much land passed into his keeping, and he prospered and grew strong, while the Sawkill hurried and tarried on its never-ending march to the sea.

His son, my father, was born and grew up in the little village which occupied the level plain between the Sawkill and the Delaware, and in the days when artificial flies were yet unknown, became so skillful an angler with more natural bait that few fly fishermen I have known could match him.

I in my turn became a lover of the Sawkill and its sister little rivers, and under my father's eye I learned the uses of the worm. I took full many a trout with it, and in due and early season graduated to the wet fly and the dry. But my best performance with any fly was far below the high craftsmanship of my father's handling of a worm.

When my son announced his participation in the affairs of this world by the barbaric yawp of infancy, his mother and I destined him to be a fisherman. Anxiously we waited for the time when he might take his first trout, and take an interest in taking it. At the age of 3, accordingly, we explained to him about fishing, which dissertation he obviously failed to comprehend, and asked him if he wouldn't like to catch a tiny speckled little trout. Being, like other youngsters, ready to try anything once, he assented—and the cortege moved in solemn procession to the stream. It was no light matter. The son and heir was about to begin his career—catch his first fish.

So I hooked a trout, handed Giff the rod and urged him to pull. He pulled; the trout struggled on the bank; and the boy, casting an indifferent eye on what should have engaged his whole I.Q., passed on with no interval whatever to matters of greater juvenile interest.

What a shock was there, my countrymen! I was struck with horror. I couldn't be consoled even by the fact that I had just taken several trout on a leader made by myself. Was it possible that the son of such parents could fail to love to fish? We couldn't believe it, and, what was more, we didn't intend to stand it.

And we didn't have to. We let nature take its course, and, because we did not press him, before he was 10 Giff was casting a workmanlike fly. From then to now on more than one occasion he has brought back more trout than his instructor and progenitor. And he loves to fish about as much as I do.

"Dad," said the fifth generation of Pennsylvania Pinchots on a day when everything was right, "how about fishing this afternoon?" "I thought I would," said I. "Hot dog!" replied this worthy son of a slang-infested father. "What rod you goin' to take?" "Well, I thought I'd take the 2 3/8-ounce Leonard. There's too much wind for the 1 3/4." "What fly you goin' to use?" "A spider," said I. "Hot dog!" said Giff again, out of the limited objurgatory vocabulary of youth.

So father and son settled the preliminary details, and when four o'clock came, off we went in the open car, up over the hill behind the house, past the little red Schocopee schoolhouse where I cast my votes at every election, to the brook I have been fishing for more than fifty years.

There we put our rods together, first carefully anointing the ferrules by rubbing them on our noses, as good fishermen do. Then we chose white and brown spiders, with long hackles and little hooks, out of my horn snuff box, with Napoleon's tomb carved in relief on the cover; made sure that the barbs had been broken off with a pair of sharpnosed plyers (we never fish for trout with barbed hooks anymore); tied leaders to spiders with the turtle knot; and oiled the hackles of our spiders with three parts of albolene* to one of kerosene. Then the war was on.

It was a good war, and a swift one. Before you could say Jack Robinson, Giff had a nine-inch native. Untouched by human hand, back into the stream he went, thanks to the debarbed hook, with nothing but a little healthful exercise to remember his adventure by. I always get great satisfaction out of that.

Then no more rises for a while, until, as the sun sank low, thick and fast they came at last—the little to swim away unhurt, and the less little to drop into the creel after they had been put to sleep with the back of a jack-knife. We had all we wanted long before it was time to quit. So we sat down on a log and held a session on the State of the Union.

"Dad, how long has this brook been here?" asked Giff, after long pondering.

So I told him, as best I could, and when we got home I tried to write it down. And that's what you've been reading.

* Albolene is a waxy substance which anglers once used to make their flies float.

a tribute to
Grantland Rice's
Jim Thorpe, the American Indian

"Pop" Warner's team of incredible redmen
from the Carlisle Indian School made football
history from 1900 to 1915. Star of
the team was Jim Thorpe, whom the Associated
Press poll of 1950 named the greatest
athlete of the first half of the twentieth
century.

James Francis Thorpe (1889-1953) spent the greatest years of his life, from 1904 to 1913, as a Pennsylvanian. He was a student at the Carlisle Indian Industrial School, making Walter Camp's All-American football teams for 1911 and 1912. The Associated Press 1950 poll named him not only the greatest football player of the first half of the twentieth century, but its greatest athlete.

"Sir, you are the greatest athlete in the world," King Gustaf V of Sweden said to Thorpe in 1912 at the presentation of Olympic medals. Though Thorpe's decathlon feats have since been surpassed, Finland's Paavo Nurmi, another Olympic great, declared, "Jim Thorpe could still beat them all."

Thorpe was born on a farm in Prague, Oklahoma. He had a predominance of Sac and Fox Indian blood, though he also was part Dutch, Welsh, and Irish. His mother called him Wa-Tho-Huck, or Bright Path.

Thorpe was sent to the Carlisle Indian School in 1904. The 311-acre school had been founded in 1879 by Captain Richard Henry Pratt, who desired to train the Indian in the white man's ways. It was the nation's first nonreservation school for Indians. Thorpe was there in its heyday, when it had 1,200 Indians from 79 tribes.

Marianne Moore, later to be the great poet, taught rapid calculation and handwriting at the Indian School from 1911 to 1915. She lived with her widowed schoolteacher mother, who resided in Carlisle for fourteen years. Miss Moore returned to the small Cumberland County town with a degree from Bryn Mawr. A few years ago a *New York Times* reporter heard how Miss Moore used to bicycle out from Carlisle to the Indian School, which is where the Army War College is today. He asked the poet if she had ever taught Jim Thorpe. "Yes," she said. "I always called him James."

Oscar H. Bakeless, later a distinguished professor at Bloomsburg State College, was academic head at the school. It was the policy that the Indian youths were integrated, no Cheyennes rooming with Cheyennes and no Sioux with Sioux. This was done deliberately to Americanize the Indians, but it also helped destroy their cultural background. John Bakeless, the dean's son, was the only white child to grow up at the Indian School. Because of the policy enforced by his father, he never was able to learn an Indian tongue, which was unfortunate because he went on to be the biographer of Daniel Boone for Stackpole Books and a well-known historian of the American frontier.

Glenn Scobey "Pop" Warner was the great coach of the Indians, from 1899 to 1903 and from 1907 to 1914. He later coached at Pitt, 1915-1923, and Temple, 1933, as well as at Cornell, Stanford, and San Jose. It was he who discovered Thorpe, then not much interested in sports. Thorpe was a substitute halfback in 1907 and a varsity star from 1908 through 1912.

What magnificent teams these were, with such stars as Thorpe, Thaddeus Redwater, Frank Mt. Pleasant, Wounded Eye, Joel Wheelock, and Asa Sweetcorn, the last of whom held up the Carlisle railroad station one day because he assumed that that was the way to get a train ticket. The Indians, all told, won 169 games, lost 87, and tied 13. From 1900 to 1915, they played Lebanon Valley College, whose team never scored a point. Against all their opponents, they scored 5,409 points and gave up 2,220. The great 1912 team, starring Thorpe and averaging less than 170 pounds a man, won 12 games, tied one, and lost only to Penn, 34 to 26. It shut out Lebanon Valley, Dickinson, Villanova, Syracuse, and Brown. Thorpe led the nation's scorers with 25 touchdowns and 198 points.

Pop Warner's Indians were a football power because they had enthusiasm and speed. Furthermore, they were innovators in the use of the spiral pass, and single-wing formation, the "Indian block," or flying block, and the running interference, or "Play No. 32," Warner's call to pull interior linemen for leading end sweeps and off-tackle slashes. The Indians never lacked for spectacular performers. Perhaps the nation's first real All-American was halfback Isaac Seneca, chosen in 1899 from Pop Warner's first Indian team.

The Indian School closed in August of 1918. Thorpe left in 1913 at the age of twenty-four. He was a professional baseball player until 1919 with the New York Giants and the Boston Braves and had a lifetime average as an outfielder of .252. From 1915 to the late 1920s he played professional football, and established a record for never leaving the field because of an injury. Thorpe's later life was not as happy. He lived in California, did bit parts in the movies, was in the Merchant Marine during World War II, married three times, and had five sons and three daughters. In 1951 Burt Lancaster starred in the movie, *Jim Thorpe, All American.*

After Thorpe's death, the voters of Mauch Chunk named their town Jim Thorpe. In the mid-1960s the name was retained at a referendum, though Thorpe probably never had even seen Mauch Chunk.

While some of Thorpe's marks—the 10-second 100-yard dash, the 4:35 mile, the 11-foot pole vault, and the 23 1/2-foot broad jump—are no longer exceptional, it should be remembered that this man not only excelled in track, baseball, and football, but also in lacrosse, boxing, basketball, hockey, archery, rifle shooting, canoeing, handball, swimming, skating, and what the Indians called "rough-and-tumble."

"Jim Thorpe, The American Indian" is taken from Grantland Rice's *The Tumult and the Shouting, My Life in Sport,* published by A. S. Barnes & Company in 1954. Rice (1880-1954) was a Tennessee boy and a Phi Beta Kappa from Vanderbilt University who became one of America's great sportswriters. He was a newspaperman in Atlanta, Cleveland, Nashville, and New York, and if Grantland Rice thought Thorpe the greatest American athlete, that's testimony enough for the Sac and Fox from Carlisle.

Jim Thorpe, the American Indian

by Grantland Rice

The Indian is a great natural athlete. Given the same chance, he has the white man lashed to the post. His heritage is all outdoors. His reflexes are sharp. He takes the game—in fact, every form of life—as it comes to him. He rarely gets excited or off balance.

An example was Chief Albert Bender, a Chippewa. A pal of mine, the Chief was a great pitcher, a fine shot and an able golfer. He strong-armed Connie Mack's pitching staffs from 1903 to 1914. Mack told me he was once undecided whether he should pick Christy Mathewson or Bender to pitch a game that meant a million dollars to him.

When Bender pitched for the Athletics against the Giants in the 1911 World Series, I noticed that he often quarreled with Eddie Collins at second or Stuffy McInnis at first. "What was the fuss all about?" I asked the Chief. "Well," he said, "they're young. In assists to first or second I was throwing them curves. I just wanted to let 'em know the World Series was just another ballgame."

I played a lot of golf with Bender from 1911 through 1914. Whatever the game, he was a great competitor. Nothing ever bothered him.

Bender brings up another, even greater Indian. His name is Jim Thorpe. In many ways, Thorpe was like Bender. Nothing ever bothered or upset him. Both Bender and Thorpe had the philosophy of the ages. At football Jim was a brilliant ball carrier, a fine passer, a good pass receiver, a place kicker, a drop kicker and a punter—and also a murderous blocker. Undoubtedly the game's greatest all-around kicker, he rated Camp's 1911 and 1912 teams as a halfback.

Old-timers may tell you Thorpe couldn't hit a curve, but he was a big league ballplayer. He was also a fine shot. And in 1912 he was a decathlon and a pentathlon winner at the Olympics in Stockholm. That was long before the long grind of training improved so many others who, as natural athletes, couldn't fan Jim's brow.

Thorpe did little training. Francis Albertanti who covered the 1912 Games for the old *Evening Mail,* told me that going over on the old Red Star liner *Finland,* Thorpe would sit alone while the rest of the track squad pounded a stretch of cork laid down on one of the decks. "What are you doing, Jim," asked Albertanti one day, "thinking of your Uncle Sitting Bull?" "No, I'm practicing the broad jump," replied Thorpe. "I've just jumped 23 feet 8 inches. I think that can win it." He did win, at five inches less.

John J. Hayes, the 1908 Olympic marathoner who helped train our 1912 team, tells of another anecdote concerning Thorpe and his Olympic chaperone, Warner. Pop, of course, had Thorpe at Carlisle. "Mike Murphy, who coached the Yale and later the Penn track teams for so many years, trained our boys along with Lawson Robertson and several others," said Hayes. "Mike was a martinet, at least for those days. One hot morning out on the track, Mike missed Thorpe for the third consecutive day. He blew his top and hunted him out. He found Thorpe asleep in a hammock behind the living quarters of our marathon team. Seated nearby and soaking up the Swedish sun was Warner.

"'Glenn,' said Mike, 'I've seen some queer birds in my day but your Indian beats all. I don't see him do anything except sleep.' Pop eyed Mike benignly. Then he said, 'Mike, don't worry. All those two-for-a-nickel events you've got lined up for Thorpe won't bother him. He's in shape. What with football, lacrosse, baseball and track back at school, how could he be out of shape? This sleeping is the best training ever, for Jim.'"

Hayes reflected that the few times Thorpe appeared for work he'd simply study the broad jump take-off or the high-jump pit, place a handkerchief out well past 23 feet, or on something higher than six feet, and then sit under a tree and study his marks. Jim's practice was 90 per cent concentration.

As Warner had prophesied, Thorpe shambled his opposition, the pick of the world's best. He won four of the five firsts in the pentathlon and four of the ten firsts in the decathlon. These included a winning 4:40.1 in the 1,500 meters, after he had competed in the dash, hurdle and other field events.

When King Gustav, a sincere sport fan, presented the gold medal following one of Thorpe's victories, the King uttered the accolade which Jim never forgot: "Sir, you are the greatest athlete in the world."

During his later and bitter years, Jim used to brood on that appellation whenever the subject was broached concerning the return of his Olympic trophies because of charges that he had violated his amateurism by playing semi-pro baseball prior to the Games. "At least they couldn't strip me of the King's words," Jim told me. "I played a little summer baseball while I was at Carlisle, for eating money. But whatever the competition, I played with the heart of an amateur, for the pure hell of it."

When Thorpe was running wild for Carlisle, the Indians played few games at home. Aptly called The Nomads of the Gridiron, they roved east, west and into the Southwest. "Carlisle's entire student body comprised no more than 250 boys," recalled Warner years later. "And bear this in mind, they were all youngsters, including Thorpe. None was more than sixteen or seventeen. They were really high school boys playing against college men, but my God how they could play!"

"Yes, Pop," commented Gene Fowler, "they may have been kids when they started playing for you at Carlisle, but they were old men when they stopped. Those Redskins played for years and years, with Carlisle as their home reservation." Warner's only reply was a chuckle.

It was around 1914 that I asked Thorpe, then out of college for a year or more, if he'd ever been hurt in football. "Who in hell can get hurt playing football?" scoffed Jim. "I never needed to call time out during any college game."

Thorpe liked to wrestle with anybody who would roughhouse. He and Jack Dempsey would have made a wonderful team for about fifteen hours a day. Both carried an enormous excess of energy, and Dempsey also had Indian blood in his veins.

McGraw had an iron-clad rule on the Giants that none of his ballplayers was to wrestle or "play" with Thorpe. Down at spring training in 1916—it was while the Giants were at Marlin, Texas—Jim went on a happy rampage one day and practically clobbered the whole team. All in play, he was as gentle as a wild African water buffalo.

You had to like Jim. He was a very decent human being. He rose to great fame in a hurry and then sank. He was a gentleman, but there were times when firewater got the better of their long feud. Years ago I went out to the ball park in Rocky Mount, N.C., one day with a local writer. On our way out he showed me a big iron can about five feet high. "This," said the writer, "is where Thorpe stood our sheriff on his head one day, just picked him up and dumped him in, upside down. The sheriff was trying to arrest Jim."

The one man Jim was leery of trying to handle, however, was Warner. When Carlisle played Brown on Thanksgiving of 1912, Thorpe and Pop got into a heated argument over a drink Jim had taken that morning to celebrate the pact between the Indians and white men in the Massachusetts Bay Colony. Pop gave Jim a hard riding. Late that afternoon I ran into the referee who worked that game. "I've just officiated at a game in which I've seen the greatest football player ever," he said. "Jim Thorpe defeated Brown 32 to nothing, all by himself. Runs of 50 and 60 yards were nothing, the Indian was a tornado. He wrecked the entire Brown team." The referee's name was Mike Thompson, one of the best.

In the 1912 game against a strong Army team, Carlisle was on its own 10-yard line. Thorpe dropped back to kick. Bill Langford, the well-known referee, dropped back with him. "They think I'm going to kick, both us and Army," Thorpe muttered to Langford. "But I ain't." After faking a kick, Thorpe ran 90 yards and the Indians broke open the game and won 27-6. "He was an unbelievable competitor," reflected Langford. "The game has never seen his like."

It was during Jim's junior or senior year at Carlisle that Lafayette was playing host to the Indians in a track meet. It had been well publicized and a welcoming committee, headed by Lafayette's coach Harold Bruce, met the train. All were stunned when a party of two alighted at Easton—Warner and Thorpe. "What's this?" demanded Bruce. "We expected the Carlisle track team." "Here it is," replied Warner, casually pointing to Thorpe. Jim racked up practically every blue ribbon on the field in a rout for Carlisle.

In street dress Thorpe, like Dempsey, wasn't particularly imposing. Both were so perfectly proportioned that nothing seemed unusual about either man—both scaled around 185 pounds at their respective peaks.

"In addition to having every physical asset, Thorpe had a rare spirit," reflected Warner in later years. "Nothing bothered Jim. When he was 'right,' the sheer joy of playing carried him through. When he wasn't, he showed it. For that reason I used to call him 'a lazy Indian' to his face. I'll admit, though, it didn't bother him. But when he was right, he was the best. The reason I picked Ernie Nevers over Thorpe as my all-time football player was because Ernie gave 100 per cent of himself always. In that respect, he was a coach's ideal. Thorpe gave it only on certain occasions. It was difficult to know if Jim was laughing with or at you."

Down the last fifteen years, when Thorpe was up but mostly down, the Circus Saints and Sinners in New York took an interest in him. Fred Benham, a New York publicist, was close to Jim. "We were talking one night," said Benham, "and I asked Jim if there was any material about him that hadn't been done to death in the papers. 'Yes, one thing,' grunted Thorpe. 'I'm a twin. My twin brother died when we were five or six.' 'How did it happen?' I asked. 'We were raised on canned condensed milk,' replied Jim seriously, 'and we ran out of cans.' "

No matter what the sport, Thorpe was the complete natural. He could play tennis, he was a whiz at billiards or pool, and he was adept at these games long after his pro football days were over. Thorpe was a cornerstone, badly used, but nevertheless a cornerstone of professional football from 1920 through 1926. His pro days started nearly eight years after he finished at Carlisle: the Canton Bulldogs in 1920; the Cleveland Indians in '23; with Rock Island in '24 and '25, the year he came to the New York Giants, and back to Canton for the '26 season, his last. With the exception of the Giants, those names may strike a weird note with neophytes, but pro football was built around those early franchises. In this respect, Thorpe was born at least thirty years too soon. In '20, when the league was formed, Jim was already a veteran, an old man in the strict competitive sense, slowing down for that last painful grind through the homestretch of his career. By '26 he was barely getting by on a pair of scarred and weary legs, legs that had carried him through more competitive miles than all the campaigns of the French and Indian Wars.

I can still see Thorpe as Pop Warner described Jim when he first came to Carlisle from the plain country of Oklahoma: a skinny Indian youngster weighing around 130 pounds, but moving like a breeze, no strain. He grew into 185 pounds of muscle, blue-steel ligaments, split-second reflexes and a keen competitive brain that gave him a supremacy in football and track and a high ranking in almost every sport he tried.

If ever an individual was pilloried by the shabby treatment he received from most of the press and the public, Jim Thorpe is that man. As a symbol of the greatest athlete of his day, if not all time, Thorpe should have been utilized by the Department of Interior where he could have helped his own people, not after he had become a broken down caricature but while he was a young man. Instead, he was allowed to live on the $5 a day he received as a movie extra, when and if.

The act that barred Thorpe could never be justified. Baseball and track and field are totally apart. Thorpe was truthful when he maintained that all he got from summer baseball at Rocky Mount, while he was at Carlisle, was barely enough to pay expenses. In those days, college ballplayers from all over the map, and particularly the Ivy schools, played on summer teams, including various hotel nines, for far more cash than accrued to Thorpe and were still held as clean, pure amateurs and passed for football, track and other college sports.

Since his death, Thorpe's body has been more in demand than it ever was during the last twenty years of his life. Civic do-gooders and Chamber of Commerce people, both in Oklahoma and in Pennsylvania, want his burial mound for a tourist shrine. Looking down on it all, old Jim must be chuckling an ironic chuckle.

It would be fitting that an effigy of the American Indian should stand prominently in the entry to the Indian wing at the Museum of Natural History in New York. That effigy should be a red copper, life-size, detailed likeness of Jim Thorpe—this country's, if not the world's, greatest all-around natural athlete.

The Playing Fields of Pennsylvania

There was only one Jim Thorpe, but over the years Pennsylvania high schools have produced many men and teams worthy to be on the same football field with Jim Thorpe. Probably no state has ever been as mad about football as Pennsylvania. Not only has high school and college football thrived, but professional football began at Latrobe in 1895 when Dr. John Brailler, a dentist and former college star, was recruited for $10 to play quarterback against the arch-rival team from Jeannette.

The top ten ranking teams in Pennsylvania in 1969 were: Harrisburg's John Harris, Canon-McMillan of Canonsburg, St. James of Chester, Abington, Erie East, Mount Lebanon, Gateway, Steelton-Highspire, Wyoming Valley West, and Farrell. Over the years the steel, mining, and railroading towns invariably produced good teams. Some of the outstanding are Aliquippa, Altoona, Ambridge, Beaver Falls, Bishop Egan in Fairless Hills, Butler, Johnstown, Monessen, Mount Carmel, Nanticoke, Neshaminy in Langhorne, Ridley, and Shikellamy in Sunbury.

The secret of Pennsylvania's football reputation is the seriousness with which the sport has been taken. Warren Eyster in his 1955 novel about Steelton, *No Country for Old Men,* describes how the football coach was paid more than the superintendent of schools and how football got the support, including the dollars, of all civic clubs, industries, poolrooms, and local businesses. "There was the money football brought into the school, and there was the promise of glory toward which every boy was striving," wrote Eyster.

Coach Howard Minnich of the champion John Harris Pioneers told sportswriter John Travers in 1969, "Some parents have asked me how we get our boys to remember all their plays. There's a difference between academic and athletic IQ." The coach was joking. More than thirty of his graduates that fall were playing college football, and many of them had high enough IQs to get them scholarships at some of the finest universities.

introducing
Marcia Davenport's
Music Will Out

Marian Anderson rose from humble beginnings
as a member of the choir of South Philadelphia's
Union Baptist Church to attain acclaim as
one of the world's greatest singers despite
the barriers of race.

Marian Anderson, the great contralto, was the first Pennsylvania Negro to
achieve world attention for artistic talent. With that deep-toned, haunting,
black-velvet voice, she might well be the finest singer to ever come from
Pennsylvania.

She was born on Webster Street in Philadelphia in 1902. Her father, John
Anderson, employed in the refrigerator room of the Reading Terminal Mar-
ket, was injured at work and died when she was ten. Marian's mother, Mrs.
Annie Anderson, raised her three daughters by taking in laundry and working
at Wanamaker's. Marian at thirteen was singing in the adult choir of the
Union Baptist Church, where her father had been head usher.

Her first great concert successes were in Europe in 1924. The following
year she won first prize at Lewisohn Stadium. It was her Lincoln Memorial
concert on Easter Sunday, April 9, 1939, that made her widely known beyond music circles. The District of Columbia denied her manager permission
to use a high school auditorium. The Daughters of the American Revolution
in January said she could not sing in Constitution Hall because it was booked
previously. Mrs. Franklin D. Roosevelt resigned from the DAR, and Secretary
of the Interior Harold Ickes and others arranged for the Lincoln Memorial
event. That weekend in Washington, Miss Anderson and her mother were
the house guests of former Governor and Mrs. Gifford Pinchot.

Marian Anderson told her life story in her book, *My Lord, What a Morning,*
published by The Viking Press in 1956. She harbored no rancor against the

DAR and, in fact, later sang in Constitution Hall a number of times. In 1955 she was the first Negro signed by the Metropolitan Opera. In 1958 she served as an alternate delegate to the United Nations, and in 1961 she sang at the inauguration of President Kennedy.

She held her farewell concert at Carnegie Hall on April 18, 1965, before an enthusiastic audience of 2,900. Jimmy Breslin in the next morning's New York *Herald Tribune* wrote: "They didn't even announce her name. They just opened a door and here she was, tall and sweeping, coming out onto the stage, and you knew that her business was singing and that she was one of the great ones."

Many Pennsylvania Negroes have become famous in the world of art, sports and entertainment.

Henry Ossawa Tanner (1859-1937) was America's first major black painter. Born in Pittsburgh, the son of a bishop of the African Methodist Church, he was raised in Philadelphia and studied under Thomas Eakins at the Pennsylvania Academy of Fine Arts. Most of his career was spent in Paris, and his son, a chemical engineer, is a citizen of France today. Tanner's work reflects his deep religious feelings and sense of serenity. In 1969 Washington's National Collection of Fine Arts held a Tanner exhibit, and at long last he received due recognition as an American master.

Horace Pippin (1888-1946) was the son of a West Chester domestic. He was a self-taught, primitive-styled painter who worked in a coal yard and a feed store, as a furniture packer and brakeshoe maker, and for seven years as a hotel porter. "Pictures just come to my mind, and then I tell my heart to go ahead," he said after he became famous in 1937. He was wounded in World War I and had to hold his right arm with his left hand to paint. In 1964 the William Penn Memorial Museum purchased Pippin's "Losing the Way," a covered wagon scene and the first work by a Negro to be in the state collection.

Henry Thacker Burleigh (1866-1949), grandson of a slave, was born in Erie and became one of the nation's most gifted baritones, performing as a soloist for decades in New York's churches and synagogues. The blinded Burleigh's reputation is for his concert arrangements of "Deep River," "Nobody Knows," "Steal Away to Jesus," and other spirituals, many of which Marian Anderson sang.

Ethel Waters, as she tells in *His Eye Is On the Sparrow,* was born in Chester in 1900. She was a chambermaid and laundress in a Philadelphia hotel and at seventeen became a singer. She starred in *Cabin in the Sky, As Thousands Cheer,* and other shows. Pearl Bailey was born in 1918 in Newport News, Virginia, but had her schooling in Philadelphia. She never had a formal music lesson, but for $15 a week sang night clubs in Philadelphia, Wilkes-Barre, Scranton, and Pottsville. She starred in *Carmen Jones, House of Flowers,* and *Hello Dolly.* Her father was a minister and her brother is the Bill Bailey of "Won't You Come Home, Bill Bailey?"

Billy Eckstine was born in Pittsburgh in 1914, the son of a chauffeur. In 1949-1950 he was the nation's leading popular male singer. Bill Cosby grew up on Philadelphia's Twenty-first Street, was a football player at Temple University, and became one of television's most successful comics. Chubby Checkers, born Ernest Evans in Philadelphia, made $800,000 as a rock 'n roll star before he was twenty-one.

Among the Pennsylvania Negroes who were born or lived in Pennsylvania and made names for themselves in sports are Roy Campanella, Richie Allen, Reggie Jackson, Wilt Chamberlain, Wayne Hightower, Guy Rodgers, Emlen Tunnell, Deacon Dan Towler, Herb Atterley, Joe Frazier, and Harold Johnson. Barney Ewell of Lancaster set the state's high school 100-yard dash mark of 9.7 seconds, tied in 1969 by Jim Scott, a black speedster from Carlisle.

Marcia Davenport wrote "Music Will Out" about Marian Anderson for the December 3, 1939, issue of *Collier's* magazine. Miss Davenport, born in New York in 1903, is the daughter of Alma Gluck, the great lyric soprano, and the stepdaughter of Efrem Zimbalist Sr., the Russian-born violinist and director of the Curtis Institute in Philadelphia. Miss Davenport has lived in both Philadelphia and Pittsburgh, and she married the late Russell Davenport, a Philadelphian and editor of *Fortune* and *Life*. In 1943 Charles Scribner's Sons published her best-selling, 790-page saga of three generations of Pittsburgh life, *The Valley of Decision*. Miss Davenport's autobiography, *Too Strong for Fantasy*, was a best-seller in 1967.

Music Will Out

by Marcia Davenport

In the drab kitchen of a Negro home in South Philadelphia, a little girl sat facing a bench, playing on it with her fingers as if it were a piano and singing while she accompanied herself. Her parents had no piano, nor much of anything else beyond the meagerest necessary possessions. Life was lived on the perilous brink of material insecurity. But in the heart of Anna Anderson, as she watched her wide-eyed child throbbing with music, there was a steadfast belief that for any worthy end, a way will come. It was the one form of security they knew.

The crowded alleys and raucous streets of South Philadelphia are inhabited by Negroes who earn the scantiest share of life by performing the city's hardest and most menial labor. They scrub its steps and pavements and buildings; they tend its furnaces and remove its trash; they cook its food and clean its houses and wash its clothes. By work of the latter sort, after her husband's early death, the widowed mother of three little girls kept up their poor and deeply religious home. One of those girls, the middle one, who "played the piano" as a baby in her mother's kitchen, has become one of the few great singers in the world today. Between South Philadelphia and the pinnacle of serious accomplishment lies Marian Anderson's story.

No impression of Marian Anderson's character could depict her better than her own face. It is a grave, broad face of solid modeling, serious in repose, passionate in music, and radiantly gay in the play of conversation. It is a dramatic face, a profoundly human face, and supremely a singer's face.

Marian as a small child was possessed by music. If she did not try, or succeed, in making it one way, she made it in another. A piano did find its way into the home, finally, but before that Marian, perhaps six years old, was begging for a violin. Her father was still alive at the time, and the slow accumulation of the $3 needed was one of the first dramas of its sort in her life. At last the money was saved, and she made the trip with her father to the pawnshop where he was going to buy the violin. She says her anxiety that it be a good violin, the very finest, was one of the earliest and keenest emotions she remembers. "You're sure it's a good violin?" she begged the pawnshop proprietor. "A really good one?"

She played it, she says, until her musical energy completely outgrew the limitations of the instrument, and she had to have a bigger field in which to exercise. That was when the piano appeared. Between it and the growing compulsion to sing, she felt more satisfied. By the time she was eight she had already revealed the rudiments of the contralto notes that amaze her hearers, on first introduction, to the point of gaping. She was already singing in the choir at the Union Baptist Church, and her neighbors had already discovered that the child possessed something so remarkable that one could charge money for the opportunity to hear it. Thus she retains a distorted memory of the first humble billing she ever received, the handbill announcing some little community concert at which "Marian Anderson, the 10-Year-Old Contralto" was to sing. And she remembers wondering about the untruth of the statement, because she was only eight years old at the time.

All through her school days she earned money, in infinitesimal a-mounts, by singing in choirs every Sunday and many times during the week, in her own church and often elsewhere, when other Negro churches in Philadelphia would engage her as soloist. The fees ranged from 50 cents to $2 or $3, and carfare. This groundwork of choir singing is responsible in part for her sound musicianship, and in part for that astounding range of voice—the "two voices" that set her apart from other singers altogether. "It came from learning all four parts of every anthem," she says. "Soprano, contralto, tenor, and even bass. If the bass hadn't come to choir practice, for instance, the leader would say, 'Marian, will you sing the bass today?' and I'd sing the part, of course an octave higher." This early and constant use of the voice, which might so easily have ruined her mature resources, seems not to have harmed Marian Anderson at all, and that is unusual enough to serve as a warning, rather than an example, to young girls.

In her own community she was loved and regarded with devoted pride. Her presence on the program of any concert or other money-raising communal activity was taken for granted. But she knew, and her mother knew, that she was destined for a far wider field; and for that she must have teaching and many other advantages that would perforce carry her over into that other world from which this country, to which they never asked to come, has done so much to shut her people out. Hungry for guidance and education in the great music to which, by every instinct, she belonged, she went in her early teens alone to a certain music conservatory to apply for instruction. She waited a long time in a bleak anteroom and finally an ill-bred young woman emerged from an office and stared at her. "Oh, you waiting here?" she said carelessly, "well, we don't take colored."

One wise and helpful friend was a remarkable woman who headed the South Philadelphia High School for Girls, where Marian was educated— Dr. Lucie L. W. Wilson. It was she who realized the immediate need for good teaching, and who undoubtedly foresaw the career that has followed. She paid the fee for Marian to have an audition with David Bispham. He advised Giuseppe Boghetti as a teacher, an Italian well known in teaching circles in New York and Philadelphia.

One hundred and twenty-five dollars was needed for the lessons. This was for the Andersons an enormous sum, but it was raised through the efforts of Marian's church, which organized a concert at which she sang.

She was in her early twenties when her teacher began to prepare her— without telling her about it, lest he make her nervous—for a singing competition the winner of which was to have an engagement to sing with the Philadelphia Orchestra at the Lewisohn Stadium in New York.

It was at this time that a new problem entered her life. One of the deplorable truths about music, Voltaire's Temple of Harmony, is that this temple is inhabited by various creditable and discreditable elements. Among the latter are certain managers whose tactics have an ominous resemblance to chicanery or even to exploitation.

The manager who sought out Marian Anderson, the unknown winner of the stadium contest, and put her under contract ought to have sensed something more in her than a gambling possibility.

For nearly three years, still desperately poor, still studying, yet presumably launched on a career, Marian Anderson struggled with the bafflement of getting nowhere. Of all the enormous discouragements of her life, that period was probably the most disheartening. And yet it turned out to be the lever by which she propelled herself from the obscurity of the young Philadelphia singer to the eminence of a world-famous and seasoned international artist.

The day she realized that she must go to Germany, to immerse herself in its language and its supreme classic tradition of song, was the day Marian Anderson came into her own. The pattern had been followed before her by such potent artists as Fremstad and Farrar; it was for opera that they went, but she went for *Lieder,* the backbone of the concert singer's repertoire and the cornerstone of her peculiar art. So Marian Anderson sailed for Europe. When she returned to sing again in New York in 1936, she came as a world celebrity and with one song swept her audience off its feet. In the interim, she had invested the full power of her fine intelligence and the wealth of her amazing voice in profound study of the German medium.

Until she began her study of German songs, her voice and the use she made of it had been the salient features of Marian Anderson as a singer. But the mere possession of a fine—even a magnificent or phenomenal—voice has never been enough to carry its owner to the heights. She must have at least two other rock-solid inherent powers: the will to work, and the resources of exceptionally fine perceptive and projective emotion. A great career in music comes only through the severest, unremitting, relentless toil, which polishes the natural equipment of the artist to exacting technical standards. Such an equipment, though, is useless without a heart. Marian Anderson was born with such a heart, and with the brains to make the most of it, just as her will to work has made the most of her natural voice. And through the medium of the world's greatest music, she has become one of those rare ministers to the hunger for poetry and lyric beauty shared by all.

Paris, as would be expected, went literally wild. London eagerly capitulated. Central Europe, in whose music she has reached towering expression, went mad about her. In the summer of 1935 I first heard her, in a small salon at Salzburg, before an audience hand-picked from the greatest musicians in the world. Some of them were too dumbfounded to say anything at all, others wonderingly shook their heads and declared hers a voice in a century, and her interpretations of classic music phenomenal. Calmly she went on her way. In Berlin a Scandinavian manager who was arranging concerts in Sweden and Denmark came to her with Kosti Vehanen, who was to become her permanent accompanist. Between pianist and singer there has grown up an intellectual and personal artistic sympathy of unusual quality. Mr. Vehanen is a Finn, and the day came when he went with her to Finland and introduced her to its greatest man, Sibelius. He too was captivated, and he has written songs especially for her. With Mr. Vehanen the northern world opened up magically. She adores Sweden, has learned the language and sings in it, as well as in Finnish. French and Italian music she had explored. Her singing in English is a delight to the ear, beyond the music, for her diction is crystalline.

She is, then, a true concert singer. The world being differently constituted, she might have been an opera singer, but it is a marvelous thing that she is not. Her repertoire is full of great operatic arias, especially the noblest classic ones to which she brings an inspiring breadth of style. But the singer who travels the whole world over, bringing music in its most natural form to people of every class and sort and doing this without the externally glamorous accouterments of the theater, is the singer whose grip on a public, once attained, is steel.

A contralto with a range of three full octaves, she has what might best
be described as a pair of voices. The upper half is brilliant and flexible
and heady, a soprano for all technical and interpretive purposes. The
lower half is that hair-raising deep voice the like of which I have never
heard, and which I suspect never has been heard before. In such songs as
Der Erlkoenig or *Der Tod und das Maedchen,* which consist of conver-
sations between two voices, a high one and a low, she is amazing. She
moves from one to the other not only with effortless ease but in doing so
holds her entire range firm in remarkable technical control. Her pianis-
simo is a marvel of muscular power absolutely round and velvety and
solid as her biggest tones. She is constantly "feeding" her voice, expanding her medium every year to include new types of music and language,
which enrich not only her repertoire but her vocal resources.

The whole world knows her now. She has sung in every capital of
Europe, has had all the proverbial and many novel forms of adulation,
has sent audiences wild with enthusiasm throughout Russia and South
America, and has won her own native land to universal vociferous acclaim. What is more, she is that certain powerful sort of musical attrac-
tion that people mean when they speak of "the good old days." Like the
"old-time religion," the old-time concert is waning: today there is nothing in it, as a rule, vital enough to compel the loyalty of millions. Of all
concert artists before the American public, exactly six are certain, auto-
matic box-office sellouts. Marian Anderson is one of these. In the next
two years, she has not room for one additional concert engagement. She
is booked solidly through. She is young, on the upcurve of her vocal
prime, and noble to look upon. When she stands on a platform, exquis-
itely dressed by Paris in white or a gleaming brocade, her strong, slen-
der figure and poised bearing proclaiming in every detail the ripened
mistress of a great art, she is one of the proudest ornaments of this country. And when, at the close of each concert, she sings a group of Negro
spirituals, and sings them with devoted sincerity and tender reverence
and a loving warmth of beautiful tone, the faith of Anna Anderson ani-
mates each thrilling note. Her simple shining belief, directed through the
character and will and genius of her daughter, has stood by her. A way
did come.

Concert at Lincoln Memorial
The New York Times

WASHINGTON, April 9—An enthusiastic crowd estimated at 75,000,
including many government officials, stood at the foot of Lincoln Memorial today and heard Marian Anderson, Negro contralto, give a concert and tendered her an unusual ovation. Permission to sing in Consti-

tution Hall had been refused Miss Anderson by the Daughters of the American Revolution.

The audience, about half composed of Negroes, was gathered in a semi-circle at the foot of the great marble monument to the man who emancipated the Negroes. It stretched half-way around the long reflecting pool. Miss Anderson was applauded heartily after each of her numbers and was forced to give an encore.

When the concert was finished the crowd, in attempting to congratulate Miss Anderson, threatened to mob her and police had to rush her back inside the Memorial where the heroic statue of Lincoln towers. Even there, well-wishers threatened to overwhelm her, and the prompt action of Walter White of the American Association for the Advancement of Colored People, who stepped to a microphone and appealed to the crowd, probably averted a serious incident.

Secretary Harold Ickes, who granted Miss Anderson permission to sing at this site, sat on her right on the monument's plaza, just above the specially arranged platform from which Miss Anderson sang into six microphones that carried the sound of her voice for blocks and over radio channels to millions throughout the country.

Next to Secretary Ickes was Secretary Henry Morgenthau and on Miss Anderson's left sat Rep. Caroline O'Day of New York. Among the others on the plaza were Senators Wagner and Mead of New York, Justice Hugo Black of the Supreme Court, Sen. Alben W. Barkley, majority leader of the chamber, and Senators Clark, Guffey and Capper. Rep. Mitchell of Illinois, a Negro, was among members of the House present.

Miss Anderson wore a tan fur coat with a bright orange and yellow scarf about her throat. She was bareheaded. Her mother was present.

In introducing Miss Anderson, Mr. Ickes referred to the Washington Monument at one end of the reflecting pool and to the Lincoln Memorial and in an implied rebuke to the D.A.R. remarked that "in our own time too many pay mere lip service to these twin planets in our democratic heaven."

"In this great auditorium under the sky all of us are free," the Secretary asserted. "When God gave us this wonderful outdoors and the sun, the moon and the stars, He made no distinction of race, or creed or color."

In a few brief remarks at the end of her concert, Miss Anderson said: "I am so overwhelmed, I just can't talk. I can't tell you what you have done for me today. I thank you from the bottom of my heart again and again."

The singer was conducted to the platform by Mrs. O'Day, who was born in Georgia, and Oscar Chapman, assistant Secretary of the Interior, who is a Virginian.

There has long been a rule that no photographs of the Lincoln statue can be taken from within the sanctum where the statue stands. This was broken during the confusion following the concert. Photographers took pictures of Miss Anderson making an appealing gesture to the figure of Lincoln.

After beginning with "America," Miss Anderson sang the aria "Mio Fernando" from "La Favorita" by Donizetti, Schubert's "Ave Maria," "Gospel Train" by Burleigh, "Trampin'" by Boatner, and Florence Price's "My Soul Is Anchored in the Lord." She was accompanied on the piano by Kosti Vehanen.

The Coatesville Lynching

The John Jay Chapman 1912 speech at the site of the Coatesville Lynching has been called the second most famous speech in modern Pennsylvania history, second only to the Gettysburg Address by President Lincoln.

On August 12, 1911, some citizens of Coatesville dragged Zacharia Walker, a black, from a prison cell, tied him to his cot, and burned him alive. Walker had been arrested on the charge of killing a steel company official. Though lynching then was not uncommon in the South, that it should have happened in a small northern community not known for intolerance astounded many Americans.

The following year on August 16, John Jay Chapman, a New York lawyer and journalist, came to Coatesville to give a commemorative address. Though only two persons heard Chapman's 1,200-word message, it has endured as one of the most pertinent statements of the American civil rights movement.

The lynching was "one of the most dreadful crimes in history," Chapman said. It occurred, not because of religious or political fanaticism, but because of the "cold dislike" in Pennsylvania of Americans who "stood like blighted things, like ghosts about Acheron, waiting for someone or something to determine their destiny for them."

The lynching, said Chapman, should give Americans "a glimpse into the unconscious soul of this country." The soul of America, however, will not be improved by "schemes of education." Raising his voice to a then unheeding Pennsylvania, Chapman exclaimed: "I say that our need is new life, and that books and resolutions will not save us, but only such disposition in our hearts and souls as will enable us the new life, love, force, hope, virtue, which surround us always, to enter into us."

Earlier in the year of the Walker Lynching, the first black man took a seat in the Pennsylvania Legislature, Harry W. Bass, a Republican from Philadelphia. Bass introduced a bill for the Commonwealth to celebrate and appropriate monies for the fiftieth anniversary of the Emancipation Proclamation in 1913. The celebration was held, and it was noted that in a half-century Pennsylvania's black population had grown from 60,000 to 200,000. Former Governor Samuel W. Pennypacker, of the elite of Philadelphia, was the honored speaker for the 1913 occasion. Pennypacker, a man of 70 who had served at the Battle of Gettysburg, created a national stir at the celebration by publicly resigning from the American Bar Association in protest against its refusal to admit Negroes to membership.

The words of John Jay Chapman and the action of Governor Pennypacker are small, but important, footnotes to the American blacks' struggle for justice which took almost a half-century more to develop.

meet
Sanford R. Starobin's
K. Leroy Irvis

Pennsylvania has been a state solidly against slavery but not solidly for the full citizenship rights of its black citizens. In 1969, however, K. Leroy Irvis was the first black man in the nation to become majority leader of a state house of representatives.

As a student of history, K. Leroy Irvis perhaps was aware in 1969 when he became Majority Leader of the Pennsylvania House of Representatives that he was not only the first black man to achieve such legislative authority in the nation, but also that he was occupying the post held 133 years before by Thaddeus Stevens.

The irascible Thad Stevens seldom cheered about anything in his own life, but he would have been pleased to know that civil rights had advanced far enough in his commonwealth that a black could have his old job. Stevens would have never doubted that a Negro could be worthy of such responsibilities. That the first such black would have the intelligence, grace, and leadership abilities of Irvis would have pleased Stevens. If old Thad could have changed anything, he would have made Irvis a Republican. That is all.

Irvis was elected to the Legislature in 1958, four years after Rep. Herbert Fineman of Philadelphia, who in 1969 became the first House Speaker of the Jewish faith in Pennsylvania. The two combined their experience and skill to make the House an effective legislative body and their bloc of Democrats a formidable opponent against the Shafer Republican Administration.

Both men come from the hard school of Pennsylvania politics. Fineman is an intellectual, a manipulator, and a combat commander. Irvis excels not only as a spokesman for his party but for all his fellow Pennsylvania blacks, especially the youth. In impromptu situations, he is doubly impressive. On July 26, 1967, when he was whip, or assistant floor leader to Fineman, he addressed the House on the subject of the racial crisis and urban riots, and his is one of the finest speeches in the legislative annals. His wit is not as cutting as Thad Stevens's was, but no contemporary can be as trenchant when there's a need to be. In 1967 in an attack on budgetary difficulties, for example, Irvis said offhandedly: "If I had been Governor of the state—and I think you may rest assured that I probably never shall be, although do not take that as a promise; you see, I still have some hope for you...."

Pennsylvania black history is complicated because this has been a state solidly against slavery but not solidly for the full rights of equal citizenship.

There were blacks living in Pennsylvania a half-century before Willian Penn established his commonwealth. In 1780 this was the first slave state to outlaw slavery. In 1790 it gave the Negro the right to vote, but took it back from 1838 to 1870 in one of its periodic repressive moods. The 1813 Legislature came close to trying to ban blacks from entering Pennsylvania, even though in the War of 1812 a fourth of the men serving on Commodore Perry's ships in the Battle of Lake Erie were Negroes. From 1854 to 1881 Pennsylvania had legal school segregation, and even today, because of housing patterns, it sadly lacks school integration. In 1867 it banned streetcar segregation, but Philadelphia did not employ Negro drivers and conductors until 1944. Fair employment in Pennsylvania didn't begin really until the 1960s.

Politically it was not Irvis' Democrats but the Republicans who initially sought to further the cause of the blacks. The great David Wilmot of Towanda in 1857, the GOP's first gubernatorial candidate, argued the unpopular truth that Negroes were God's children and "have been endowed with sacred rights we cannot disregard with impunity." Wilmot lost. Though 8,600 Pennsylvania blacks served in the Civil War, the Democratic Party Platform of 1866 read: "The white race alone is entitled to the control of the government of the Republic, and we are unwilling to grant to Negroes the right to vote." Philadelphia's outstanding black educator, Octavius V. Catto, replied: "The black man knows on which side of the line to vote." Catto was assassinated in 1871. The Negro remained on the Republican side until the Roosevelt era of the 1930s.

Pennsylvania didn't get its first Negro state legislator until 1911, Harry W. Bass of Philadelphia. Governor Leader in 1955 appointed the first Negro cabinet officer, Budget Secretary Andrew W. Bradley of Allegheny County. Four Philadelphia Negroes hold other firsts: Robert N. C. Nix Jr. to Congress in 1958; Mrs. Juanita Kidd Stout, county court judge in 1959; Theodore O. Spaulding, State Superior Court judge in 1966, and Herbert Arlene, state senator in 1967. Bass and Judge Spaulding were Republicans. The Alexander family, well known in the cultural life of Philadelphia, holds a number of "firsts." Judge Raymond Pace Alexander in 1959 became the first Pennsylvania Negro to go on the Common Pleas Court bench. His wife, Sadie, in 1926 was the nation's first Negro woman Ph.D., and in 1927 she became Pennsylvania's first Negro woman lawyer.

There are factual oddities that reveal the confused Pennsylvania attitude toward black people. Bud Fowler in New Castle in 1872 was the first Negro in America to sign with a white baseball team, but in 1947 ballplayer Jackie Robinson couldn't get a hotel room in Philadelphia. Jonathan Jasper Wright studied law in Montrose, was the first Negro admitted to the Pennsylvania Bar in 1866 and later was a South Carolina Supreme Court justice, but by 1969 Pennsylvania still had never had a Negro candidate for the U.S. Senate, governor, lieutenant governor, its Supreme Court, or for any of its mayorships. Lincoln University, the oldest college in the nation for Negroes, was founded in 1854 at Oxford, but in 1969 the federal government termed thirteen of Pennsylvania's public colleges as segregated, because they had only 362 black students, or less than 1 percent of their enrollment. Penn State came under fire because it had but 300 Negroes among 25,000 students at its publicly supported university campus.

The article on Majority Leader K. Leroy Irvis appeared in the *Philadelphia Inquirer,* February 2, 1969. Sanford R. Starobin, born in 1942 in Newark, New Jersey, graduated from New York University and joined the *Inquirer* in 1967. In the summer of 1969 he became the Harrisburg bureau chief of the Westinghouse Broadcasting System.

K. Leroy Irvis

by Sanford R. Starobin

When he was a child he was a black boy in a white world and he accepted it because it seemed natural. When he was a young man he was a black man in a white world and he hated it because it was ugly. Now, at forty-nine, K. Leroy Irvis is a black man who has become a leader in a white world, and while he realizes it isn't perfect, he believes it good enough to deserve improving.

When Irvis took his seat in the House of Representatives as majority leader of the Democrats, he became the first Negro ever to reach such rank in any state in the nation. The office has power, and Irvis has shown himself willing to embrace that power and expand it, to use it to accomplish what he thinks right.

In his nine years as a legislator, the short, barrel-chested Irvis has earned a reputation of putting the state first, his party second. When he speaks, both Democrats and Republicans listen. His admirers sit on both sides of the aisle.

It's a long way from the fields of New York's delightful Hudson Valley region to the ornate rotunda of the Pennsylvania capitol. It's a long way from the present system of state government to the ideal Irvis envisions. He made one trip. He's planning the second.

Born to a family that traces its lineage to free black men who came to this country in 1690 with the Dutch, Irvis spent his childhood around Kingston, N.Y. His paternal grandfather was white but his parents were black. His father was a chauffeur, a bakery truck driver and a maintenance man. His mother never worked because "my father was pretty old fashioned about that idea. He would take care of his own family."

Though he and his sisters were often the only black children in class and knew very few others, they were spared the vision of racial hatred that years later would come to grip the nation. Tolerance began at home.

"In our home," Irvis recalls, "no one mentioned color, no one. You didn't refer to a person as a colored man or a Negro or a white man and you did not refer to him as a Jew or anything else. You were caught up short by my dad if you started that. He would say, 'If you can't describe him any more accurately than that, then just keep quiet.' So you soon learned in our household that people were people. This has helped me a great deal, all along the road. It's let me look at people as people, even when they had violently disagreed with me, whether they happened to be white or black."

Although neither his father nor mother had finished high school, they kept books in their house and encouraged their children to read. Irvis did well in class and at fourteen entered what is now the State University of New York, graduating at eighteen.

After college, he tried to teach, was rebuffed because of his age, took his master's degree in English and then went to Baltimore, "frankly because Albany wouldn't hire any black teachers." Baltimore was startling to the youth from Upstate New York. "That was my first contact with a large aggregation of Negroes," he said. "I was shocked. I had never seen Negroes together in more than a number of, I guess, fifty in Albany." It was then he realized the importance of teaching Negro history in schools, of giving black children a long view of themselves and their culture, of giving them perspective.

He taught English in a segregated junior high school and during the summer at the all-Negro Morgan State College. When the Second World War began, he taught aircraft riveting and assembly to Negroes as a civilian in Baltimore. He had always liked flying and still retains an interest in designing and flying model planes. As a youth, he would slip out to a small airfield near his home and take plane rides with friendly pilots. He once thought of becoming an aircraft engineer, but says at that time the profession was closed to blacks.

By the time the war ended, he had spent five years in Baltimore. There had been a change in Leroy Irvis, but he didn't know what. It wasn't until a white friend in Albany said he seemed different that he realized what was the matter. Suddenly, he recalls, he disliked his friend, even though as boys they had played together and had been close. He disliked his friend because he was white. "I had become infected by that time with racism, having spent five years in Baltimore, having been rejected," he said. He was denied membership in a model airplane club because he was black and had taught only in segregated schools and lived only in segregated houses. "I'd had it," he said. He returned to Albany "for refuge."

He married "a marvelous girl" in 1945, and 1947 saw them living in

Pittsburgh and organizing that city's first picket lines around the major
department stores in an effort to smash discriminatory hiring practices.
He was working for the Urban League then as "a halfway social worker
and general trouble maker."

It was the picketing that first brought him to the attention of David L.
Lawrence, then Pittsburgh mayor and later Pennsylvania governor. He
recalls getting a telephone call at home one Sunday morning from
Lawrence, asking him to bring his people to the Mayor's Office the next
morning to meet with department store representatives. After the meeting, Negroes were hired in Pittsburgh department stores.

He was fired from the Urban League in 1948 because his activism was
about fifteen years premature and not yet popular. After convincing the
group to take him back, he quit.

He started a small toy factory "because I've always loved woodwork.
That failed, or rather I failed that." He took a job in the steel mills and
his wife opened a hot dog stand. "We got out of that before it had a
chance to fail."

After spending a year in the mills, his wife said he should stop talking
about law school and enroll. With $10 in his pocket he registered at the
University of Pittsburgh. "They said $9.50 please, and we had 50 cents
left for the weekend," Irvis recalls. He got two fellowships, took part-
time work and his wife held "some of the most miserable jobs," but
finally he graduated from law school.

"I came out with honors and no job," he said. Then, a "very singular
thing" happened. The dean of the law school sent him to a prestigious
law firm, all white, that needed a law clerk. "The senior partner interviewed me, called his secretary in and told her to get my Social Security
number, that I was employed. I would be able to work there for them,
use their library, file papers the way any law clerk, of course, has to,
but be given plenty of time to study. I got home and I was hilarious with
joy because sometimes my wife and I didn't eat. Sometimes we wouldn't
have eaten if friends hadn't fed us. This meant we could eat and I was
worried about her. She was never as strong as she might have been.
While we were hugging each other and dancing around the apartment
with joy the phone rang—the senior partner on the line, apologetically.
He was sorry. He hadn't known when they agreed to hire me that a
junior partner had already recruited a young man from Harvard. He
apologized over and over again, and I told him it wasn't necessary. I
knew what had happened. They just weren't hiring any Negro law
clerks."

So, with "no job and no offers of a job," Irvis worked as a newscaster
until his law school called again and said there was a law clerk's job
available with Common Pleas Court Judge Anne X. Alpern, who later
became the state's first woman attorney general and is still remembered

on Capitol Hill for her caustic description before the Public Utility Commission when an electric company was petitioning for a rate hike: "The Overcharge of the Light Brigade."

He worked as her clerk for two years, until 1957, and liked the job "because it gave me an opportunity to do the sort of careful, precise, scholarly research that I've always secretly enjoyed doing, although I do like the battle of the courtroom."

Then David Lawrence offered Irvis his first political job in the Pittsburgh District Attorney's Office. "I didn't particularly like the idea of being a prosecutor because I'm not a prosecutor by nature," Irvis said. "But the salary was better and it gave me an opportunity to develop my own law practice."

A day less than two years later, Irvis got a call from Democratic headquarters asking him to run for the House from Pittsburgh's all-black Hill District. "I was hit cold by the request," Irvis said, but after talking it over with his wife they agreed to give it a try.

The big fight was in the primary and he was bucking an incumbent whom the Democratic organization thought lacking and wanted to replace. "We battled for weeks and weeks and weeks for that primary and we won the primary," Irvis said. "And then having won the primary, winning the general election was no problem."

He served in the House as a regular member until he became a part of the Democratic leadership in 1963, "quite by accident, not by any brilliant achievement on my part at all." A fellow Democrat who was looking to be party leader was denied that job and refused to accept the caucus chairmanship, from which he felt he had graduated. Another member nominated Irvis.

"I have to confess," Irvis said, "that I was slumped down in my seat in the caucus, bored by the proceedings, convinced that the ticket had already been decided on. I was nothing but a second termer beginning my third term. So I had no idea that lightning would strike. And neither did David Lawrence or Bill Green Sr., the Philadelphia Democratic leader, because I looked into their faces and their mouths popped open."

A friend sitting next to him said, "'You s.o.b., why didn't you tell me? I second the nomination.' He thought that I was in on a plan. It took me a week to convince him I was not. Someone else jumped up in the startled silence and moved that the nominations be closed, and I was elected unanimously before anyone could do anything about it."

He rose through the leadership ranks and in 1967-1968, when the Democrats were in the minority, he was Democratic house whip. When the Democrats won control of the House and Herbert Fineman, of Philadelphia, moved from the minority leader's seat to the House Speaker's podium, Irvis became party leader.

As a leader, Irvis has worked persistently toward his goal of what he thinks state government should be in the late twentieth century. Besides civil rights, he has championed governmental reform and health legislation, taking pride in getting a law passed requiring babies to have PKU tests, which have saved hundreds of children from mental retardation.

He calls himself "a good government boy—and I don't say that in any distaste. I have a very deeply committed belief that our country offers man the damn best opportunity that he's ever had in his history to develop freedom—notice I said develop, we don't have it yet, black or white. No place on this earth ever before have ordinary men decided that they would govern themselves without a king until this country did it, and I think we are well on the way to eliminating the law of the pack, the idea of the pack being led by the leader who is strongest or the most cunning. That's the reason I think the legislative process is so important. We operate as a counter-balance to the king. We say by our presence that we are not a pack of wolves led by the wiliest and the strongest wolf."

He sees a need for drastic changes in governmental philosophy and operation.

"Education has to be absolutely free to everyone and absolutely public in all its ramifications, from pre-school right straight through graduate school. It must be, if we're going to survive, and I work in that direction, not hoping in my lifetime ever to see it, but hoping to see, and having seen, some improvements along the line. I think we have to move in the areas of transportation away from the idea of 'I own a railroad,' 'I own an airline.' Some people say, well, this is a socialist idea. I don't care what the label is. There was a time when you could not drive your mule train over a highway because I owned that highway or I owned the ferry or I owned the ford."

Irvis feels a fair salary will attract bright young people to government service, people who will want to give as much as get. He cites the Peace Corps and Vista as examples of young people willing to serve and says, "I'm very hopeful about the younger people in the country from that point of view."

Irvis is devoted to the House, has turned down a judgeship and a chance at a Senate seat for it, thinks the House takes a bad rap from its persistent critics but insists the critics shouldn't be silenced. Speaking only of the House and not the Senate, he said, "I don't know any out-and-out bums in the Pennsylvania Legislature. Now, I knew a few when I first came here. The Pennsylvania Legislature differs in capabilities, in competency, about as much, though not quite as much, as any village of 203 people would be apt to. Not quite as much because most of these people have had to be leaders in their own localities to even get here. Now, some of them are at a lower level of competency than the others. That's obviously going to be true in any group. But, out-and-out dishonesty, out-and-out lack of sincerity, I simply don't know about it if it exists."

Roy Irvis lives alone. His wife died in 1959 and they had no children. He has a "raggle-taggle" law practice ("I get my clients angry at me most of the time because I miss their court cases and can't see them when they want to be seen") and spends much of his time in Harrisburg. He still sculptures in wood and builds model planes, but for the most part he works at being a legislator.

He sees the immediate trend in this country as conservative, but is sure that taken in the context of history the country is moving toward liberalism. He is sure that man will not desert his fellow man and says improved communications insure that.

"We're going to get rid of the ghettos because people are aware that the ghettos exist. It's now only a matter of time before they're eliminated. We're going to equalize opportunities because now people realize opportunities are not equal. This is basically a belief in the decency of human beings. I don't mean that we're saints. I don't think any of us are. But neither are we devils. And once human beings recognize that their help is needed, generally the help is forthcoming."

Instant Legislation

Rep. H. Jack Seltzer introduced a proposal in the General Assembly in 1966 for "instant resolutions." Seltzer, of Palmyra, had served ten years in the legislature and had grown weary of approving noncontroversial puff resolutions on the House floor. "Too much time is lost on trivialities," he complained.

Seltzer suggested there be form-made resolutions of congratulations for: birthdays of House members and Pennsylvanians with friends in the legislature, the birth of children of House members and Pennsylvanians with legislative connections, marriages of legislators and nonlegislators of influence, and for coaches, teams, public figures, and beauty queens who achieve distinction on the athletic field and off.

Just seconds before the House voted on Seltzer's proposed instant legislation, it approved a resolution congratulating Knoch High School in Saxonburg, Butler County, for winning a basketball tournament.

introducing
Pennsylvania's 400

Here is the answer to Theodore Dreiser's carping query about the Commonwealth, "Why hasn't it produced anything in particular?"

There are two contrary opinions about the talent that has come out of Pennsylvania: that there has been a lot of it, and that there has been disgracefully little of it.

Theodore Dreiser, who worked in both Philadelphia and Pittsburgh and knew Pennsylvania quite well, said he couldn't think of a famous poet, writer, or painter from the Commonwealth. "Why hasn't it produced anything in particular?" he asked in 1915.

The question of Pennsylvania talent was asked Beaver Falls' native-born hero, football star Joe Namath, in 1969. Namath wasn't the least bit puzzled. He rattled off the names of twelve nationally known personalities, plus his own. "They got great soil for growing stars in my state," he said.

Few would argue that in politics Pennsylvania has but a handful of bright names. It lacks even a tradition, since the Founding Fathers days, for having men who put public service above self-interest. John F. Kennedy in *Profiles of Courage* used Pennsylvania's Boies Penrose as an example of what a U.S. senator should not be, and Penrose served from 1897 to 1921, longer than any other Pennsylvanian in the Senate. Great political talent just has not come out of Pennsylvania. This state has contributed but one President, one Vice President, and since 1950 only one Cabinet member, Eisenhower's Secretary of Defense, Thomas S. Gates Jr.

The record in other fields of endeavor, however, glitters with famous names. Religion, law, the military, business, the fine arts—the Pennsylvania product is known world-wide. In sports, which Pennsylvania has long over-emphasized (62,000 high school footballers on 885 teams, at last count), the record is exceptional. If any other state could field a better all-star foot-ball or baseball team, Pennsylvanians would have to be shown.

"Pennsylvania's 400" is a list of the notables and the notorious, some-times the state's best and often just its most illustrious. It's a game anyone can play. There's no guarantee that a name left off is less worthy of atten-tion than a personality included.

The list is actually Benjamin Franklin plus 399 others. Franklin's renown and his accomplishments make most other Pennsylvanians sink into oblivion. Old Ben's name appears in four categories, and it wouldn't be stretching matters to include him in a few more. He was, as his biographer Carl Van Doren once wrote, "a harmonious human multitude."

Pennsylvania's 400

Business

Max Hess, Allentown. Sebastian S. Kresge, Bald Mount. Charles M. Schwab, Braddock. John Roach, Chester. L. B. Sheppard, Hanover. Milton S. Hershey, Hershey. William Piper, Lock Haven. Asa Packer, Mauch Chunk. S. H. Kress, Nanticoke.

Mathias Baldwin, Dr. Albert C. Barnes, Nicholas Biddle, Jay Cooke, Ellis Gimbel, Stephen Girard, Simon Gratz, Atwater Kent, Joseph N. Pew, John B. Stetson, John Wanamaker, and Peter A. B. Widener, all Philadelphia.

Coffee salesman John Arbuckle, Andrew Carnegie, Henry Clay Frick, Henry J. Heinz, Edgar J. Kaufmann, and the Mellon family, all Pittsburgh.

William T. Grant, Stevensville. John J. Newberry, Sunbury. Allen Price Kirby, Wilkes-Barre.

Entertainment

Henry Mancini, Aliquippa. Perry Como, Cannonsburg. Jimmy Stewart, Indiana. Tommy Dorsey, Lansford.

Pearl Bailey; Ethel, Lionel, and John Barrymore; Bill Cosby; John Drew; W. C. Fields; Eddie Fisher; Edwin Forrest; Charles Goren; Joe Jefferson II; Grace Kelly; Fanny Kremble; Mario Lanza; Jeanette MacDonald; Arthur Penn, and Ed Wynn, all Philadelphia.

Errol Garner, Gene Kelly, Oscar Levant, Adolphe Menjou, and Lillian Russell, all Pittsburgh.

Evelyn Nesbit, Tarentum. Fred Waring, Tyrone. Anna Moffo, Wayne.

Baseball

Pitchers: Chief Bender, Carlisle Indian School; Stanley Covelski, Shamokin; Sam McDowell, Pittsburgh; Christy Mathewson, Factoryville; Herb Pennock, Kennett Square; Eddie Plank, Gettysburg; Robin Roberts, Flourtown; Bobby Shantz, Pottstown; Rube Waddell, Bradford; Big Ed Walsh, Plains, and Bucky Walters, Philadelphia.

Catchers: Roy Campanella, Philadelphia; Ray Mueller, Steelton, and Steve O'Neill, Minooka. First Base: Richie Allen, Wampum; Rip Collins, Altoona, and Mickey Vernon, Marcus Hook. Second Base: Max Bishop, Waynesboro; Nellie Fox, St. Thomas, and Eddie Stankey, Philadelphia. Third Base: Billy Cox, Newport; Jimmy Dykes, Philadelphia, and Whitey Kurowski, Reading.

Shortstops: Charlie Gelbert, Scranton; Dick Groat, Swissdale; Hughie Jennings, Pittston, and Honus Wagner, Carnegie. Outfield: Rocky Colavito, Temple; Carl Furillo, Stony Creek Mills; One-arm Pete Gray, Nanticoke; Reggie Jackson, Wyncote; Stan Musial, Donora, and Hack Wilson, Ellwood City.

Football

Quarterbacks: Terry Hanratty, Butler; Johnny Lujack, Connellsville; Joe Namath, Beaver Falls; Babe Parilli, Rochester, and John Unitas, Bloomfield. Backs: Herb Atterley, Philadelphia; Red Grange, Forksville; Mike Holovak, Lansford; Lenny Moore, Reading; Jim Thorpe, Carlisle Indian School; Charley Trippi, Pittston; Emlen Tunnell, Garrett Hill, and Tom Woodeshick, Wilkes-Barre.

Kicker: Lou Michaels, Swoyersville. Ends: Fred Biletnikoff, Erie; Gary Collins, Williamstown; Mike Ditka, Aliquippa; Leon Hart, Turtle Creek; Larry Kelley, Williamsport; Ted Kwalick, McKees Rocks; Joe Muggsy Skladany, Larksville, and Joe Walton, Beaver Falls.

Center: Chuck Bednarik, Bethlehem. Linemen: Stan Jones, Lemoyne; Bucko Kilroy, Philadelphia; Walt Michaels, Swoyersville; Dick Modzelewski, Natrona Heights; Dennis Onkotz, Northampton; John Paluck, Swoyersville; Myron Pottios, Brownsville; Mike Reid, Altoona; Glenn Ressler, Dornsife; Joe Schmidt, Pittsburgh, and Chuck Walker, Allison Park.

Miscellaneous Sports

Auto Racing: Mario Andretti, Nazareth; Mark Donahue, Media; Bill Holland, Reading, and Eddie Sachs, Allentown. Basketball: Wilt Chamberlain, Overbrook; Bob Davies, Harrisburg, and Tom Gola, Philadelphia. Billiards: Ralph Greenleaf and Willie Mosconi, both Philadelphia, and Stanley Stonik, Plymouth.

Boxing: Terrible Terry McGovern, Johnstown; Joe Frazier, Benny Leonard, Tommy Loughran, and Philadelphia Jack O'Brien, all Philadelphia; Billy Conn, Harry Greb, and Fritzie Zivic, all Pittsburgh. Golf: Arnold Palmer, Latrobe; Mike Souchak, Berwick, and Art Wall Jr., Poconos. Gymnastics: Steve Cohen, Philadelphia.

Horse Racing: Bill Hartack, Black Lick. Rowing: Jack Kelly Jr., Philadelphia. Tennis: Vic Seixas and Bill Tilden, both Philadelphia. Track: Horace Ashenfelter, Collegeville, and Barney Ewell, Lancaster. Weightlifting: Bob Hoffman, York. Wrestling: Bill Blacksmith, Lemoyne; Sammy Corson, Forty Fort; Gus D'Augustino, Grove City, and Ed and Hugh Perry, Shaler Township.

The Fine Arts

George Grey Barnard, Bellefonte. Edward Hicks, Bucks County. Andrew Wyeth, Chadds Ford. Henry Burleigh, Erie. Charles Demuth, Lancaster. John Sloan, Lock Haven. Andy Warhol, McKeesport. Peter Frederick Rothermel, Nescopek.

Marian Anderson, Marc Blitzstein, Alexander Calder I, Thomas Eakins, architect Louis Kahn, Eugene Ormandy, Charles Willson Peale, John Singer Sargent, Leopold Stokowski, architect William Strickland, Thomas Sully, Henry O. Tanner, and Benjamin West, all Philadelphia.

Mary Cassatt, Stephen Collins Foster, Martha Graham, John Kane, and William Steinberg, all Pittsburgh.

Samuel Barber and Horace Pippin, both West Chester. George Catlin and Franz Kline, both Wilkes-Barre. George Luks, Williamsport.

Literature

Robinson Jeffers and Gertrude Stein, both Allegheny City. Maxwell Anderson, Atlantic. Malcolm Cowley, Belsano. Stephen Vincent Benét, Bethlehem. Marianne Moore, Carlisle. Zane Grey, Lackawaxen. Marc Connelly, McKeesport. Pearl Buck, Perkasie.

Catherine Drinker Bowen, Richard Harding Davis, Benjamin Franklin, James Gibbons Huneker, Weir Mitchell, Christopher Morley, Clifford Odets, Ezra Pound, Jacqueline Susann, and Owen Wister, all Philadelphia.

Conrad Richter, Pine Grove. James Michener, Pipersville. George S. Kaufman, Pittsburgh. John O'Hara, Pottsville. Wallace Stevens, Reading. Jean Collins Kerr and Charles MacArthur, both Scranton. Mary Roberts Rinehart, Sewickley. John Updike, Shillington. Rolfe Humphries, Towanda. William Snodgrass, Wilkinsburg.

Law

U.S. Justice James Wilson, Carlisle. U.S. Atty. Gen. Wayne Mac-Veigh, Chester County. James Scarlet, Danville. State Chief Justice John Bannister Gibson, Perry County.

Judge Raymond Pace Alexander, State Justice Curtis Bok, John Dickinson, Andrew Hamilton, State Atty. Gen. Jared Ingersoll, John G. Johnson, William Draper Lewis, State Atty. Gen. Thomas D. McBride, State Chief Justice and Governor Thomas McKean, Chippy Paterson, U.S. Sen. George Wharton Pepper, U.S. Justice Owen J. Roberts, State Atty. Gen. William A. Schnader, John R. K. Scott, American Bar President Bernard Segal, John Sergeant, State Welfare Secretary Harry Shapiro, State Chief Justice Robert von Moschzisker, and Morris Wolf, all Philadelphia.

State Atty. Gen. Anne X. Alpern and U.S. Justice Robert C. Grier, both Pittsburgh. State Atty. Gen. Charles J. Margiotti, Punxsutawney. State Justice Michael A. Musmanno, Stowe Township. U.S. Justice Robert H. Jackson, Warren County. State Chief Justice George W. Woodward, Wilkes-Barre. U.S. Atty. Gen. Jeremiah S. Black, York.

National Politics

U.S. Sen. Matt Quay, Beaver. U.S. House Speaker Frederick A. Muhlenberg, Berks County. U.S. Sen. Charles R. Buckalew, Bloomsburg. U.S. Secretary of Labor William B. Wilson, Blossburg. Financier Joseph R. Grundy, Bristol. Presidential candidate James G. Blaine, Brownsville. Cong. Francis "Tad" Walter, Easton. Cong. Thomas E. Morgan, Fredericktown. Secretary of War Simon Cameron and U.S. Sen. William Maclay, both Harrisburg. President James Buchanan and Cong. Thaddeus Stevens, both Lancaster.

Ambassador William C. Bullitt, U.S. Sen. Joseph S. Clark Jr., Vice President George M. Dallas, Benjamin Franklin, financier Matt McCluskey, pamphleteer Tom Paine, U.S. Sen. Boies Penrose, U.S. House Speaker Samuel J. Randall, U.S. Sen. Hugh Scott and Presidential candidate Harold Stassen, all Philadelphia.

U.S. Sen. Joseph F. Guffey, Secretary of State Philander C. Knox, and Secretary of War Edwin M. Stanton, all Pittsburgh.

Socialist Darlington Hoopes, Reading. U.S. Treasurer Albert Gallatin, Somerset County. U.S. Atty. Gen. A. Mitchell Palmer, Stroudsburg. U.S. House Speaker Galusha A. Grow, Susquehanna County. Cong. David Wilmot, Towanda.

State Politics

Gov. Andrew Gregg Curtin, Bellefonte. GOP leader George I. Bloom, Burgettstown. Sen. George N. Wade, Camp Hill. Sen. Charles B. Penrose, Carlisle. Gov. James H. Duff, Carnegie. Col. Alexander K. McClure, Chambersburg. State Treasurer William H. Berry, Chester. John McClure, Delaware County boss. Gov. George H. Earle III, Devon. Gov. George Wolf, Easton. Sen. M. Harvey Taylor, Harrisburg. Gov. Raymond P. Shafer, Meadville. Gov. Gifford Pinchot, Milford.

Publisher Walter H. Annenberg, Mayor Richardson Dilworth, House Speaker Herbert Fineman, Benjamin Franklin, Gov. Thomas Mifflin, Gov. Robert E. Pattison, Milton J. Shapp, and Cong. William Vare, all Philadelphia.

Secretary of Internal Affairs Genevieve Blatt and Gov. David L. Lawrence, both Pittsburgh. Mayor Terence V. Powderly, Mrs. Marion Margery Warren Scranton, and Gov. William W. Scranton, all Scranton. Gov. Simon Snyder, Selinsgrove. Gov. Edward Martin, Ten Mile. Sen. G. Mason Owlett, Wellsboro. Gov. George M. Leader and Lt. Gov. Sam Lewis, both York.

The Military

Daniel Boone, Baumstown. Gen. Carl Spaatz, Boyertown. Rear Adm. William H. Behrens Jr., Camp Hill. Mad Anthony Wayne, Chester County. Gen. Peyton C. March, Easton. Gen. Joseph T. McNarney, Emporium. Gen. Hap Arnold, Gladwyne. Capt. Simon Girty the renegade, Halifax. Gen. Lyman L. Lemnitzer, Honesdale. Adm. William S. Sims, Huntingdon County. Maj. Gen. John F. Reynolds and Lt. Gen. Dan Strickler, both Lancaster County. Gen. Tasker H. Bliss, Lewisburg.

Gen. Arthur St. Clair, Ligonier. Lt. Gen. James M. Gavin, Mount Carmel. Maj. Gen. and Governor John White Geary, New Cumberland. Maj. Gen. Winfield Scott Hancock, Norristown. Col. Francis S. Gabreski, World War II ace, Oil City.

Commodore John Barry, Adm. John Dahlgren, Gen. George G. Meade, Gen. Peter Muhlenberg, and Marine Sgt. Al Schmid, blinded World War II hero, all Philadelphia. Pvt. Thomas F. Enright, the first American killed in World War I, and Gen. Matthew B. Ridgway, both Pittsburgh.

Gen. George C. Marshall, Uniontown. Astronaut Charles "Pete" Conrad Jr., Wayne. Marine Maj. Gen. Smedley Darlington Butler, West Chester. Adm. Harold R. Stark, Wilkes-Barre. Gen. Jacob Devers, York.

Religion

Rev. Charles Taze Russell, founder of Jehovah's Witnesses, Allegheny. Rev. James M. McKim, Presbyterian abolitionist, Carlisle. Evangelist Ira D. Sankey, Edinburg. Conrad Beissel, Ephrata. Bishop John Mark Gannon, Erie. Johann Georg Rapp, mystic, Harmony.

Rabbi Philip David Bookstaber; the Rev. Silas Comfort Swallow, Presidential Prohibition candidate; and the Rev. John Winebrenner, founder of the Church of God, all Harrisburg. Rufus Jones, Quaker, Haverford. Gov. Martin G. Brumbaugh, ordained minister, Huntingdon.

Michael Novak, lay writer, Johnstown. Jacob Albright, founder of Evangelical Church, Kleinfeltersville. Martin Boehm, founder of United Brethren Church, Lancaster.

Bishop Richard Allen, founder of African Methodist Episcopal Church; Bishop Fred Pierce Corson; Dennis Cardinal Dougherty; John Cardinal Krol; Lucretia Coffin Mott, Quaker reformer; Blessed John Neumann; John Cardinal O'Hara; the Rev. Daniel A. Poling; the Rev. Leon Sullivan; and Bishop William White, Continental Congress chaplain, all Philadelphia.

Father James R. Cox and John Cardinal Wright, both Pittsburgh. Francis Cardinal Brennan, Shenandoah. Bishop Tikhon, later Patriarch of Russia, South Canaan. Rev. Henry Melchior Muhlenberg, Trappe. Father Joseph Murgas, inventor, Wilkes-Barre.

Science and Scholarship

Historian Lawrence H. Gipson, Bethlehem. Nobel Prize winner Dr. Haldan K. Hartline, Bloomsburg. Educator Albert Bushnell Hart, Clarksville. Explorer Robert E. Perry, Cresson. Christopher L. Sholes, typewriter inventor, Danville. Inventor Daniel Drawbaugh, Eberly's Mill. Ida Tarbell, Erie County. Educator Clark Kerr, Johnstown. Inventor Robert Fulton, Lancaster.

John Bartram; economist Henry Carey; Dr. Nathaniel Chapman, first president of the AMA; educator Russell Conwell; W. E. B. DuBois; anthropologist Loren Eiseley; historian Louis Fischer; Benjamin Franklin; economist Henry George; anthropologist Margaret Mead; historian Roy F. Nichols; historian Robert Proud; David Rittenhouse, and Dr. Benjamin Rush, all Philadelphia.

Historian Henry Steele Commager, inventor Charles Hall, Dr. Jonas Salk, and George Westinghouse, all Pittsburgh.

Bridge-builder John A. Roebling, Saxonburg. Rachel Carson, Springdale. Historian Philip S. Klein, State College. Behaviorist B. F. Skinner, Susquehanna County.